Encyclopedia of 300 Crochet Patterns, Stitches and Designs

by Phyllis Mayfield
and The Editors of FC&A Craft Publishing

"He has filled them with skill to do all manner of work . . . — those who do every work and those who design artistic works."

Ex. 35:35

The heavens declare the glory of God; And the firmament shows His handiwork.

Ps. 19:1

Trust in the Lord with all your heart, and lean not to your own understanding; In all your ways acknowledge Him, And He shall direct your paths.

Prov. 3:5,6

FC&A Craft Publishing
103 Clover Green
Peachtree City, GA 30269 USA

We have made every effort to ensure the accuracy and completeness of these instructions, photos and drawings. We cannot, however, be responsible for human error, typographical mistakes, or variations in individual work.

Table of Contents

Introduction 7

Chapter 1

    Basic Crochet Stitches 9

    Understanding Crochet Terms 12

    Design Your Own Patterns By Mastering Multiples 13

    Flowered Geometric Afghan...........................13

    International Crochet Symbols 14

    Abbreviations 14

Chapter 2

    Chain, Picot and Single Crochet 15

    Textured Afgan 20

    Queen Anne's Lace Table Topper 21

    Ponytail Twist 22

Chapter 3

    Chain, Picot, Single and Half-Double Crochet..............................23

    Ribbed Sweater Vest....................................25

    Gingerbread Shelf Edging 26

Chapter 4

    Double Crochet 27

    Parlor Lampshade Cover 39

    Fuzzy Wuzzy Bear 40

Chapter 5

    Treble Crochet 41

    Flowered Trellis Sweater 48

    Decorative Mantel Trim 49

    Evening Clutch Bag 50

    Child's Corner Cuddler.................................50

Chapter 6

    V-Stitch and Shell..51

    Christening Gown Set 65

    Tailored Trellis Placemat 67

Chapter 7

    Relief Stitch 69

    Lacy Winter Scarf..72

    Lacy Winter Hat 72

Chapter 8

    Puff Stitch..73
    Boudoir Bolster Pillow 78

Chapter 9

    Popcorn Stitch 79
    Victorian Accent Afghan 84
    Popcorn Trivet 84

Chapter 10

    Cluster Stitch 85
    Classic Crop Top 92
    Baby Bunting Blanket...92

Chapter 11

    Dropped Stitch 93
    Open Diamond Dresser Scarf 97
    Pocket Embellishment 97

Chapter 12

    X-Stitch...99
    T-Shirt Trim...103
    Ladies Jazzy Pearl Tie 104

Chapter 13

    Wraparound Stitch 105
    Ruffled Eyelet Curtain Valance 108
    Crocheted Rug 108

Chapter 14

    Y-Stitch...109
    Sachet Bag...110
    Summer Rose Hat 110

Chapter 15

    Motifs 111
    Quick Easy Tote Bag 136
    Boutique Sweater...137
    Sunflower Bouquet Vest...139

Chapter 16

    Edgings and Trims 141
    Ruffles And Bows Infant Set...165
    Scalloped Collar 166

Introduction

Are you one of those rare people who give unique, beautiful crocheted gifts and have special touches like lace doilies and homemade afghans around your home? Or are you a rare person who has the skill and patience to learn the fine art of crochet?

Whether you are a beginner or an advanced crochet connoisseur, this book is for you. It has clear, easy-to-follow guidelines for the crochet novice and intricate designs to intrigue the expert.

Our goal in putting together the *Encyclopedia of 300 Crochet Patterns, Stitches and Designs* was to give you a source of fabulous designs that are as simple as possible to create. We want to help you keep alive an ancient art that has been passed from grandmother to grandchild, but is in danger of dying out.

These days, machines crochet items as small as doilies and as large as sweaters and afghans. All crochet pieces are beautiful, but machine crochet items just don't have the special splendor or the special meaning that a piece crocheted by hand does.

Crocheting items for yourself and for others is a rewarding experience. A gift that you've crocheted yourself is a gift from the heart. Your work may even become an heirloom that will be handed down from generation to generation. Crocheting gifts takes time and effort, but it's always appreciated and kind to your budget.

A gift of lace to an old friend or a newly married couple is always elegant and appreciated. A pillowcase trimmed in lace is beautiful and makes a wonderful gift. A plain tablecloth or napkins look elegant with a bit of lace around the edge.

Can't think what to get for your teenage granddaughter? Find an old jacket of her dad's and use a crochet design from this book to add lasting style to it. That look is "in" and always will be. You can also trim sweaters and vests.

You don't have to buy a new chair to spruce up your bedroom, either. That old rocking chair would look charming with a colorful afghan draped across the back. An afghan would come in handy on those cold winter nights, too. Crocheted items in a house say "home"!

Encyclopedia of 300 Crochet Patterns, Stitches and Designs gives you all the instructions, diagrams and basic information you need to create beautiful crocheted items. Every pattern is different in size and appearance, so you should be able to find a project that suits your style and fits your time frame. We also provide the old-fashioned know-how you need to create your own unique designs.

The only tools you need to crochet are a crochet hook and thread or yarn, but you have many choices to make when you buy these tools. You can completely change the appearance of any pattern by substituting yarn weights or changing the size of your hook. Our designs give you the freedom to experiment with these tools and complete a one-of-a-kind project.

You'll notice that the diagrams in this book are based on the International Crochet symbols. This old European code, still widely used today, has been handed down from the oldest written crochet instructions in existence.

These instructions were found in France — the country that is credited with keeping alive the ancient art of crochet — the art that was known simply as "nun's work" in the Middle Ages. The word "crochet" is the French word for "hook."

Once you learn the International Crochet symbols, you'll be able to follow patterns easily and quickly. People who have mastered the symbols can create whole pieces by using only the diagrams.

You certainly don't have to attempt this mastery, though. You'll probably enjoy yourself more if you use the clearly written instructions. Most people need the combination of photos, instructions and symbols to accomplish the more difficult patterns.

Some of the chapters provide instructions for specific crocheted items, but other chapters will let you use your creative flair. By using one or more of the motifs in chapter XV, for example, you can create original bedspreads, tablecloths, dresser scarves, dressy collars and afghans. The motifs include the Granny-Square

Wheel, Old American Square, Geometric Circle, Wreath and Shamrock.

The chapter on trims and edgings will show you how to give your work a neatly finished, decorative edge. Lace and trim can add a special look to many plain items — pillowcases, tablecloths, napkins, collars, blankets and bows.

Once you get started, you'll think of endless possibilities. You'll have fun exploring what you can do with a little hook and thread.

If you are a beginner, don't feel overwhelmed when you look at the directions. Just take one step at a time, following each instruction precisely.

Punctuation is very important! As you complete a step, you may want to check it off at the punctuation mark.

If you practice regularly, you'll master this type of needlework before you know it. Most importantly, enjoy yourself as you keep alive the old, elegant art of crochet.

Chapter 1

Basic Crochet Stitches, Abbreviations and Symbols

Slip Knot

Make a loop, put hook in loop, pull yarn through loop, (1) pull yarn end gently to secure to hook. (2)

Chain Stitch (ch)

Slip knot onto hook. Put hook in your right hand, hold the end of yarn extending from the loop in your left hand, weave yarn over the ring and forefinger of your left hand to allow even tension. Place yarn over hook and pull yarn through to make the first chain. (1) Repeat to make chain as long as desired. (2) Stitches have been numbered to assist with hook placement. For other crochet stitches, refer to diagram as needed.

Slip Stitch (sl st)

Make chain. Put hook in chain and place yarn over hook. (1) Pull yarn through the chain and loop on hook. (2)

Single Crochet (sc)

Make chain. Put hook into the 2nd chain from hook. Place yarn over hook and pull yarn through the chain. (1) Place yarn over hook and pull yarn through 2 loops (2) leaving 1 loop on hook. (3)

Half Double Crochet (hdc)

Make chain. Place yarn over hook. Put hook into 3rd chain from hook. (1) Place yarn over hook and pull yarn through the chain. Place yarn over hook and pull through all 3 loops (2) leaving 1 loop on hook. (3)

Double Crochet (dc)

Make chain. Place yarn over hook. Put hook into 4th chain from hook. (1) Place yarn over hook and pull yarn through the chain. Place yarn over hook and pull through first 2 loops on hook, (2) leaving 2 loops on hook. (3) Place yarn over hook and pull through last 2 loops leaving 1 loop on hook. (4)

Treble Crochet (tr)

Make chain. Place yarn over hook twice. Put hook into 5th chain from hook. (1) Place yarn over hook and pull yarn through the chain. Place yarn over hook and pull through first 2 loops. (2) Place yarn over hook and pull through next 2 loops. (3) Place yarn over hook and pull through last 2 loops, (4) leaving 1 loop on hook. (5)

Popcorn Stitch (pc st)

Make chain. Crochet 3 or more double crochet in same chain. (1) Remove hook from loop and place in top of first double crochet. Place hook in unworked loop. (2) Pull yarn through all 3 loops on hook. (3) Can use 2 to 6 double crochet.

Puff Stitch

Make chain. Put hook into 3rd chain from hook. Place yarn over hook and pull yarn through the chain. (1) Place yarn over hook and insert hook into same chain. Place yarn over hook and pull through the chain. Place yarn over hook, pull through as many times as you desire. Place yarn over hook and pull through all loops, (2) leaving 1 loop on hook. Place yarn over hook and pull through last loop on hook. (3) Can use 2 to 6 loops.

Picot Stitch

Make a single crochet. Ch 3, insert hook through top of single crochet. (1) Place yarn over hook and pull through all loops on hook. (2) Picot stitch can be made with all crochet stitches and as many chains as desired. (3)

Cluster Stitch (cl st)

Make chain. Place yarn over hook. Put hook in chain. Place yarn over hook and pull yarn through the chain. Place yarn over hook and pull through 2 loops. Place yarn over hook and into same chain stitch. Place yarn over hook and pull yarn through the chain. Place yarn over hook and pull through 2 loops, leaving 3 loops on hook. (1) Place yarn over hook and pull yarn through all loops, leaving 1 loop on hook. (2) Can use 2 to 6 loops.

X Stitch

Make a double crochet. Place yarn over hook and insert in stitch behind double crochet just worked. (1) Place yarn over hook and pull through. (2) Complete stitch following double crochet directions. (3) Skip next chain, repeat instructions. (4)

Double X-Stitch

Make chain. Place yarn over hook twice. Make a treble crochet, leaving 3 loops on hook. (1) Skip 1 chain, make a treble crochet in next chain, (2) (yarn over and pull yarn through 2 loops) 4 times. (3) Chain 2, make 1 double crochet in the middle of the 2nd treble crochet post. (4) Repeat instructions. (5)

Y-Stitch

Make chain. Place yarn over hook twice. Make a treble crochet. Chain 3, (1) make 1 double crochet in the middle of the treble crochet post. (2)

Inverted V or Shell Stitch

Make chain. Start double crochet in 4th chain from hook. Place yarn over hook and pull through 2 loops, (1) leaving 1 loop on hook. Make as many double crochets as you like, following these directions. (2) Place yarn over hook and pull yarn through all loops, (3) leaving one loop on hook. (4)

Relief Double Crochet

Follow directions for double crochet, except insert hook around post of the previous crochet stitch. You can circle the post from the front, right to left, (1) or from the back, right to left. (2)

Working in Rounds

Make number of chains required for pattern. Insert hook in first chain made. (1) Place yarn over hook and pull through all loops on hook. (2) Follow pattern directions working around chain loop just made.

Understanding Crochet Terms (and Other Helpful Information)

Turning Chain (tch)

Used to bring yarn to required height for the first stitch of next row. Most patterns unless noted otherwise count the turning chain as one stitch. Standard turning chains for stitches are: Sc-ch 1; hdc-ch 2; dc-ch 3; tr-ch 4; dtr-ch 5.

Increasing Crochet Stitches

Increasing involves making 2 stitches in the same space. This is done by making an extra stitch of your pattern in the same space as your last stitch. It is best to increase in the beginning or at the end of crochet row.

Decreasing Crochet Stitches

Decreasing involves the working off of 2 stitches as 1, thus losing 1 stitch. This is done by working a stitch until 2 loops remain on hook, work the same stitch in next space until 3 loops remain on hook. Place yarn over hook and pull through all 3 loops. It is best to decrease in the beginning or at the end of the crochet row.

Gauge

To ensure the proper finished size, a gauge swatch must be made to compare with the pattern's stated gauge. A 6" square laid on a hard flat surface is sufficient to determine if an adjustment in hook size is needed. Check your gauge as work progresses so your finished item is the required size.

Punctuation

All crochet patterns have punctuation to allow you to work in steps. Many find it helpful to read the directions through and then go back and mark the punctuation as each step is completed. It is very important that directions separated by a comma, parentheses, or brackets be worked as one step.

Example: Sc in next 3 ch, sk next sc and 3 ch, sc in next 5 ch, ch 3, turn. The comma before and after sk next sc and 3 ch means this is one step: sk both 1 sc and a ch-3 space: not sk 1 sc and make ch 3.

Parentheses or brackets allow a step to be repeated and are usually followed by a number indicating the amount of repetitions to be made. Parentheses can also separate a group of stitches to be made in an indicated space or to explain a step just completed. Read the directions out loud if you experience difficulty, taking care to pause at each punctuation mark.

Stitch Diagrams

Stitch diagrams are included for each pattern using the international crochet symbols found on page 14. They show at a glance the design of a pattern and can be followed without written instructions when they become familiar. Diagram stitches are sometimes enhanced to convey the continuity of the pattern in your crocheted work and are not an exact representation of finished stitch size. Use our stitch diagrams to guide you for ease and accuracy.

Finishing Techniques

Smooth Seams — Sew pieces together with an overcast stitch.

Overcast Stitch — Lay pieces to be joined together, right side up. With a blunt sewing needle and the same thread used to crochet piece, sew the pieces together by passing the needle from left to right through the crochet stitches on the outer edge.

Smooth Decorative Seam — Use a blunt needle and the same yarn or thread used in the crocheted item. Join with an overcast or whip stitch in back loop or both strands of stitches, whichever pleases you best. Don't pull yarn or thread too tightly as you sew. The seam should have about the same amount of "give" as the crocheted item.

Ridge on Underside — Use a hook one size larger than the crocheted item. Align work; slip stitch in every crochet stitch under both strands of two pieces being joined, or only in the back loops. This will form a ridge on the underside. Work with right sides facing.

Ridge on Right Side — To obtain a seam that can be observed easily, align both pieces of crochet with wrong sides facing and work single crochet stitches in back loops of both pieces. You will have a ridge on the right side between both pieces being joined.

Whip Stitch — To join crochet pieces together — Use a blunt sewing needle and the same thread used to crochet. Sew right sides of the crochet pieces together, using the back loops only.

Finished Ends — To prevent unraveling or unsightly knots in your work, take time to weave in loose ends. Best results are obtained using a yarn needle and the back side of completed work. Weave yarn through as many stitches as desired taking care not to draw work too tight. Clip any remaining length close to work.

Blocking — Sometimes even the most vigilant effort on checking gauge does not produce a symmetrical crochet piece. To obtain smooth edges or enhance the final shaping, blocking may be desirable. "Set" your work using rust proof pins to desired shape. Mist with water and leave to dry. A steam iron may be used if care is given not to place iron directly on the crocheted item.

Design Your Own Patterns By Mastering Multiples

Mastering "Multiples" is the basic first step in designing your own patterns, using the stitches and designs included in this book.

"Multiples of" refers to the number of chains needed to complete the pattern shown. This allows you to repeat the pattern and obtain the size you require. For example: multiples of 14; to make a square tablecloth you might make a beginning ch of 140 or 14 x 10. When a multiple 14 plus 7 is required simply multiply 14 x 10 and add 7 more chs = 147 chs. For our pattern, the added 7 chs are needed to begin the first dc (dc in 4th ch from hk), and add 4 dc to pattern edge.

The pattern below is for a standard size afghan. Using the given multiple of 14 plus 7, a foundation ch of 21 (14 x 1 + 7) was made. The pattern was completed through Row 6 with a finished size of 6 1/2" x 3 1/2".

The 4 dc added to the pattern (plus 7), are not included in determining the number of pattern repeats needed. Measure only the gauge of your multiple stitches (14 st = 5"), to determine the number of pattern repeats. To make an afghan approximately 80" wide, divide your desired width by multiple gauge (80" ÷ 5") to determine that 16 pattern repeats are needed. The foundation row would begin with 231 ch (14 x 16 + 7).

Once you determine the gauge of your multiple, any stitch design in our book can be created according to your size requirements. **Note:** When more exact final measurements are required, such as for clothing items, take into account the added width of any plus number stitches when determining the number of multiple repeats needed.

Some multiple designs, when worked in one repeat only, will have more stitch instructions than your beginning foundation chain allows. This is due to the need for continuation of a pattern worked with more repeats. If necessary, refer to the diagram and the "ending row with" instructions when working with one multiple repeat.

Flowered Geometric Afghan
(See Chapter 8, #4)
Materials needed: *Approximately 64 ounces worsted weight white yarn; size J crochet hook.*
Finished size: *81" x 87 1/2"*
Gauge: *14 st = 5"*
          6 rows dc = 3 1/2"
Ch 231.
Row 1: Dc in 4th ch from hk, dc in next 3 ch, * (ch 1, sk next ch, dc in next ch) 5 times, dc in next 4 ch, rep from *, ending row with dc in last 4 ch, ch 3, turn.
Row 2: Sk 1st dc, dc in next 4 dc, *(ch 1, sk next ch, dc in next dc) 5 times, dc in next 4 dc, rep from *, ending row with dc in last 3 dc, dc in tch, ch 3, turn.
Row 3: Sk 1st dc, *dc in next 4 dc, (ch 1, sk next ch, dc in next dc) 2 times, 4-lp puff st in next ch-1 sp, dc in next dc, (ch 1, sk next ch, dc in next dc) 2 times, rep from *, ending row with dc in last 3 dc, dc in tch, ch 3, turn.
Row 4: Sk 1st dc, dc in next 4 dc, *ch 1, dc in next dc, 4-lp puff st in next ch-1 sp, dc in next dc, ch 1, dc in next dc, 4-lp puff st in next ch-1 sp, dc in next dc, ch 1, dc in next 5 dc, rep from *, ending row with dc in last 4 dc, dc in tch, ch 3, turn.
Row 5: Sk 1st dc, dc in next 4 dc, *(ch 1, dc in next

dc) 2 times, 4-lp puff st in next ch-1 sp, dc in next dc, (ch 1, dc in next dc) 2 times, dc in next 4 dc, rep from *, ending row with dc in last 3 dc, dc in tch, ch 3, turn.
Row 6: Sk 1st dc, dc in next 4 dc, * (ch 1, dc in next dc) 5 times, dc in next 4 dc, rep from *, ending row with dc in last 3 dc, dc in tch, ch 3, turn.
Rows 7-151: Rep Rows 2-6.
Row 152: Rep Row 2, **F.O.**

International Crochet Symbols

Stitch	
Chain Stitch	⬯
Slip Stitch	⬤
Single Crochet	✕
Half Double Crochet	⊤
Double Crochet	⟊
Treble Crochet	⟊
Picot	⋒
Popcorn	⬮
Puff Stitch	⬚
Cluster Stitch	⬚
X-Stitch	⋎
V-Stitch	⋎
Shell	⟱
Inverted V-Stitch	⋏
Y-Stitch	⅄
Solomon's Knot	⌒
Relief Stitch (front)	⌇
Relief Stitch (back)	⌇
Dropped Stitch	↓
Wraparound Stitch	⌣

Back or Front Loop Only — **Bold Type**

Abbreviations

beg . . . . .begin / beginning
bl . . . . .block
ch . . . . .chain
cl . . . . .cluster
dc . . . . .double crochet
dec . . . . .decrease
dtr . . . . .double treble crochet
F.O. . . . . .fasten off
fol . . . . .following
grp . . . . .group
hdc . . . . .half double crochet
inc . . . . .increase
lp(s) . . . . .loops
pat . . . . .pattern
pc . . . . .popcorn
prev . . . . .previous
rem . . . . .remaining
rep . . . . .repeat
rnd(s) . . . . .rounds
sc . . . . .single crochet
sk . . . . .skip
sl st . . . . .slip stitch
sm . . . . .same
sp . . . . .space
st(s) . . . . .stitch(es)
rep . . . . .repeat
rf . . . . .relief stitch front
rb . . . . .relief stitch back
rnd . . . . .round
tch . . . . .turning chain
thro . . . . .through
tog . . . . .together
tr . . . . .treble crochet
yo . . . . .wrap yarn over hook
* . . . . .repeat from * as indicated
( ) . . . . .repeat between ( ) as indicated
[ ] . . . . .repeat between [ ] as indicated

Chapter 2

Chain, Picot and Single Crochet

1. Multiples of any number plus 1.

Row 1: Sc in 2nd ch from hk and in each ch across row, ch 1, turn.
Row 2: Sc in each sc across row, ch 1, turn.
Rep Row 2 for pattern.

2. Multiples of 8 plus 3.

Row 1: Sc in 2nd ch from hk and in each ch across row, ch 1, turn.
Row 2: Sc in each sc across row, ch 1, turn.
Row 3: Sc in 1st 2 sc, * 4-ch picot, sc in next 8 sc, rep from *, across row.

3. Multiples of 8 plus 4.

Row 1: Sc in 2nd ch from hk and in next 2 ch, * ch 7, sk 5 ch, sc in next 3 ch, rep from *, ending row with sc in last 3 ch, ch 1, turn.
Row 2: Sc in 1st 2 sc, * ch 4, sc in center of ch-7 arch, make 4-ch picot, ch 4, sk next sc, sc in next sc, rep from *, ending row with sc in last 2 sc.

4. Multiples of 3 plus 2.

Row 1: Sc in 2nd ch from hk, * ch 5, sk 2 ch, sc in next ch, rep from *, ending row with sc in last ch, ch 5, turn.
Row 2: Sc in center of next ch-5 arch, * ch 2, make 3-ch picot, ch 2, sc in center of next ch-5 arch, rep from *, ending row with ch 5, sl st in last sc.

○ *Chain*　⋒ *Picot*　✕ *Single Crochet*

5. Multiples of 2 plus 2.

Row 1: 2 sc in 4th ch from hk,* sk 1 ch, 2 sc in next ch, rep from *, ending row with 2 sc in last ch, ch 1, turn.
Row 2: Sk 1st sc, * 2 sc in next sc, sk next sc, rep from *, ending row with 2 sc in last sc, ch 1, turn.
Rep Row 2 for pattern.

6. Multiples of 5 plus 2.

Row 1: Sc in 2nd ch from hk and in each ch across row, ch 1, turn.
Row 2: Sc in 1st sc, * ch 2, make 3-ch picot, ch 2, sk 4 sc, sc in next sc, rep from *, ending row with sc in last sc, ch 1, turn.
Row 3: Sc in 1st sc, * ch 3, make 3-ch picot, ch 3, sc in next sc, rep from *, ending row with sc in last sc.

7. Multiples of 4 plus 2.

Row 1: Sc in 2nd ch from hk, * ch 5, sk 3 ch, sc in next ch, rep from *, ending row with sc in last ch, ch 5, turn.
Row 2: * Sc in center of next ch-5 arch, ch 5, rep from *, ending row with sc in last ch-5 arch, ch 2, dc in last sc, ch 1, turn.
Row 3: Sc in dc, * ch 5, sc in center of next ch-5 arch, rep from *, ending row with sc in 3rd ch of last ch-5 arch, ch 5, turn.
Row 4: * Sc in center of next ch-5 arch, ch 5, rep from *, ending row with ch 2, dc in last sc, ch 1, turn.
Row 5: Sc in dc, * ch 5, sc in center of next ch-5 arch, rep from *, ending row with sc in 3rd ch of last ch-5 arch, ch 3, turn.
Row 6: * Make 3-ch picot, ch 3, sc in center of next ch-5 arch, ch 3, rep from *, ending row with sl st in last sc.

8. Multiples of 6 plus 2.

Row 1: Sc in 2nd ch from hk, * ch 5, sk 5 ch, sc in next ch, rep from *, ending row with sc in last ch, ch 1, turn.
Row 2: * Sc in next sc, ch 5, rep from *, ending row with sc in last sc, ch 1, turn.
Row 3: * Sc in next sc, ch 7, rep from *, ending row with sc in last sc, ch 1, turn.
Row 4: * Sc in next sc, ch 8, rep from *, ending row with sc in last sc, ch 1, turn.
Row 5: * Sc in next sc, ch 9, rep from *, ending row with sc in last sc, ch 1, turn.
Row 6: * Sc in next sc, 5 sc around 1st half of ch-9 arch, make 3-ch picot, 5 sc around 2nd half of ch-9 arch, rep from *, ending row with sc in last sc.

9. Multiples of 8 plus 4.

Row 1: Sc in 2nd ch from hk and in each ch across row, ch 1, turn.
Row 2: Sc in 1st 3 sc, * ch 8, sk next 5 sc, sc in next 3 sc, rep from *, ending row with sc in last 3 sc, ch 1, turn.
Row 3: Sc in 1st 2 sc, * 3 sc around beg of next ch-8 arch, 3-ch picot, (3 sc around same ch-8 arch, 3-ch picot) 2 times, 3 sc around same ch-8 arch, sk 1 sc, sc in next sc, rep from *, ending row with sc in last 2 sc.

10. Multiples of 3 plus 2.

Row 1: Sc in 2nd ch from hk, * ch 5, sk 2 ch, sc in next ch, rep from *, ending row with sc in last ch, ch 4, turn.
Row 2: Sc in center of next ch-5 arch, * ch 2, sc in center of next ch-5 arch, rep from *, ending row with ch 1, dc in last sc, ch 1, turn.
Row 3: Sc in dc, sc in ch-1 sp, * ch 2, sc in next ch-2 sp, rep from *, ending row with ch 2, sc in 2nd ch of tch, ch 5, turn.
Row 4: * Sc in next ch-2 sp, ch 5, rep from *, ending row with ch 2, dc in last sc, ch 1, turn.
Row 5: Sc in dc, * ch 2, sc in center of next ch-5 arch, rep from *, ending row with ch 2, sc in 3rd ch of tch, ch 1, turn.
Row 6: Sc in 1st sc, ch 1, * sc in next ch-2 sp, ch 2, rep from *, ending row with sc in last sc, ch 5, turn.
Rep Rows 4-6 for pattern.

◯ *Chain* ♈ *Picot* ✕ *Single Crochet*

11. Multiples of 4 plus 1 (Solomon's Knot).

Row 1: * Draw 1/4" lp on hk, yo, pull through lp, sc in single back lp (Solomon's Knot completed), sk 3 ch, sc in next ch, rep from *, ending row with sc in last ch, ch 3, turn.

Row 2: * Solomon's Knot, sc around center of next Solomon's Knot, rep from *, ending row with dc in 1st ch of foundation, ch 3, turn.

Row 3: * Solomon's Knot, sc around center of next Solomon's Knot, rep from *, ending row with dc in tch, ch 3, turn.

Rep Row 3 for pattern.

12. Multiples of 2 plus 1.

Row 1: Sc in 2nd ch from hk, * dc in next ch, sc in next ch, rep from *, ending row with dc in last ch, ch 1, turn.

Row 2: * Sc in next dc, dc in next sc, rep from *, ending row with dc in last sc, ch 1, turn.

Rep Row 2 for pattern.

13. Multiples of 2 plus 2.

Row 1: 2 sc in 4th ch from hk, * sk 1 ch, 2 sc in next ch, rep from * across row, ch 2, turn.

Row 2: * Sk next 2 sc, 2 sc in sp before next sc, rep from *, ending row with 2 sc in tch, ch 2, turn.

Rep Row 2 for pattern.

14. Multiples of 2 plus 1.

Row 1: Sc in 2nd ch from hk, * hdc in next ch, sc in next ch, rep from *, ending row with hdc in last ch, ch 1, turn.

Row 2: * Sc in next hdc, hdc in next sc, rep from *, ending row with hdc in last sc, ch 1, turn.

Rep Row 2 for pattern.

15. Multiples of 4.

Row 1: (Sc, ch 3, sc) in 4th ch from hk (picot made), * ch 5, sk 3 ch, picot in next ch, rep from * across row, ch 5, turn.
Row 2: * Picot in center of next ch-5 arch, ch 5, rep from *, ending row with sc in tch of prev row, ch 5, turn.
Row 3: * Picot in center of next ch-5 arch, ch 5, rep from *, ending row with picot in 3rd ch of tch, ch 5, turn.
Rep Row 3 for pattern.

16. Multiples of 9.

Row 1: Sc in 2nd ch from hk, sc in next 2 ch, * ch 7, sk 2 ch, sc in next 7 ch, rep from *, ending row with sc in last 3 ch, ch 1, turn.
Row 2: Sc in 1st 2 sc,* ch 3, sk 3 ch, sc in next ch, ch 3, sk 3 ch and next sc, sc in next 5 sc, rep from *, ending row with sc in last 2 sc, ch 1, turn.
Row 3: Sc in 1st sc, * ch 3, sk 2 ch, sc in next ch, sc in next sc, sc in next ch, ch 3, sk 2 ch and next sc, sc in next 3 sc, rep from *, ending row with sc in last sc, ch 1, turn.
Row 4: Sc in 1st sc, * ch 3, sk next 2 ch, sc in next ch, sc in next 3 sc, sc in next ch, ch 3, sk 2 ch and next sc, sc in next sc, rep from *, ending row with sc in last sc, ch 1, turn.
Row 5: Sc in 1st sc, ch 3, * sk 2 ch, sc in next ch, sc in next 5 sc, sc in next ch, ch 7, sk 2 ch and next sc, rep from *, ending row with ch 3, sc in last sc, ch 1, turn.
Row 6: Sc in 1st sc, ch 3, sk 3 ch and next sc, * sc in next 5 sc, ch 3, sk 1 sc and next 3 ch, sc in next ch, ch 3, sk 3 ch and next sc, rep from *, ending row with ch 3, sc in last sc, ch 1, turn.
Row 7: Sc in 1st sc, ch 3, sk 3 ch and next sc, * sc in next 3 sc, ch 3, sk 1 sc and next 2 ch, sc in next ch, sc in next sc, sc in next ch, ch 3, sk 2 ch and next sc, rep from *, ending row with ch 3, sk 1 sc and next 3 ch, sc in last sc, ch 1, turn.
Row 8: Sc in 1st sc, * sc in next ch, ch 3, sk 2 ch and next sc, sc in next sc, ch 3, sk 1 sc and next 2 ch, sc in next ch, sc in next 3 sc, rep from *, ending row with ch 3, sc in last ch, sc in last sc, ch 1, turn.
Row 9: Sc in 1st 2 sc, sc in next ch, * ch 7, sk (ch 2, sc, ch 2), sc in next ch, sc in next 5 sc, sc in next ch, rep from *, ending row with ch 7, sc in last ch, sc in last 2 sc, ch 1, turn.
Repeat Rows 2-9 for pattern.

Patterns Using Chain, Picot and Single Crochet

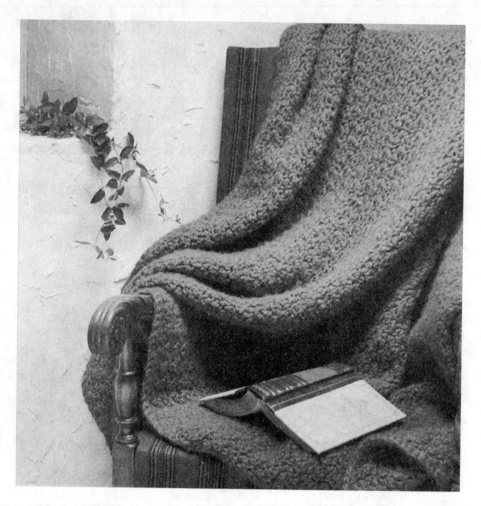

Textured Afgan

Materials needed: *Approximately 93 ounces of dark red acrylic worsted weight yarn; size G crochet hook.*
Finished size: *60" x 72"*
Gauge: *4 dc = 1"*
2 rows of dc = 1"

Note: To create the textured feel of our afgan without buying specialty yarn, we have a simple alternative. Before beginning our pattern instructions, take the skeins of yarn and work 1 long row of chains. You may choose to do all at once or each skein as needed. Wrap each skein's chain into balls for easier handling. Specialty effect without the high price.

Ch 15.
Row 1: SC in 4th ch from hk, * dc in next ch, sc in next ch, rep from * across row, ch 3, turn.
Row 2: Sk 1st sc, * sc in next dc, dc in next sc, rep from *, ending row with sc in top of tch, ch 3, turn. Rep row 2 until work measures 72", **F.O.**

Edging

Join with sl st to any corner, sc evenly around, work 3 sc in each corner sp, join with sl st to beg sc, **F.O.**

Queen Anne's Lace Table Topper

Materials Needed: *Approximately 450 yards of #30 white cotton thread; #10 steel crochet hook.*
Finished Size: *33" diameter*
Gauge: *Ch 10 = 1-1/2"*

Ch 6, join with sl st to form a ring.
Rnd 1: Ch 1, 16 sc in ring, join with sl st to beg sc.
Rnd 2: * Ch 10, sl st in next sc, ch 5, sl st in next sc, rep from * around. (8 ch-10 lp — 8 ch-5 lp)
Rnd 3: Sl st to top of 1st ch-10 lp of Rnd 2, * (ch 5, sl st in sm sp) 3 times (ch-5 group made), ch 3, sl st in top of next ch-5 lp, ch 3, sl st in top of next ch-10 lp, rep from * around, join with sl st in top of beg ch-10 lp. (8 ch-5 groups made)
Rnd 4: Sl st over to top of center ch-5 lp of 1st ch-5 group, * ch 10, sc in top of next center ch-5 group, rep from * around, join with sl st to top of beg center ch-5 group. (8 ch-10 lp made)
Rnd 5: * Ch 6, sk 2 ch, sl st in next ch, rep from * around, join with sl st to bottom of beg ch 6. (24 ch-6 lp made)
Rnd 6: Sl st to top of 1st ch-6 lp, * ch 6, sc in top of next ch-6 lp, rep from * around, join with sl st to bottom of beg ch 6.
Rnd 7: Sl st to top of 1st ch-6 lp, * ch 8, sc in top of next ch-6 lp, rep from * around, join with sl st to bottom of beg ch-8 lp.
Rnd 8: Sl st to top of 1st ch-8 lp, * ch 10, sc in top of next ch-8 lp, rep from * around, join with sl st to bottom of beg ch-10 lp.
Rnd 9: Sl st to top of 1st ch-10 lp, * ch 12, sc in top of next ch-10 lp, rep from * around, join with sl st to bottom of beg ch-12 lp.
Rnd 10: Sl st to top of 1st ch-12 lp, * (ch 5, sl st in sm sp) 3 times, ch 10, sc in top of next ch-12 lp, rep from * around, join with sl st to bottom of beg ch 5.
Rnd 11: Sl st to top of center ch-5 lp in 1st ch-5 group, * ch 12, sc in top of next center ch-5 lp, rep from * around, join with sl st to bottom of beg ch 12.
Rnd 12: * Ch 5, sk next 2 ch, sc in next ch, rep from * around, join with sl st to bottom of beg ch 5.
Rnd 13: Sl st to top of 1st ch-5 lp, * ch 6, sc in top of next ch-5 lp, rep from * around, join with sl st to bottom of beg ch 6.
Rnd 14: Sl st to top of 1st ch-6 lp, * ch 8, sc in top of next ch-6 lp, rep from * around, join with sl st to bottom of beg ch 8.
Rnd 15: Sl st to top of 1st ch-8 lp, * (ch 3, sl st in sm sp) (picot made), ch 8, sc in top of next ch-8 lp, rep from * around, join with sl st to bottom of beg ch 3, F.O.
Rnd 16: Turn work over, join with sl st to center of any ch-5 group in Rnd 10, * ch 20, sc in center of next ch-5 group, rep from * around, join with sl st to bottom of beg ch 20.
Rnd 17: Sl st to top of 1st ch-20 lp, * ch 20, sc in top of next ch-20 lp, rep from * around, join with sl st to bottom of beg ch 20.
Rnd 18: Sl st to top of 1st ch-20 lp, * (ch 5, sl st in sm sp) 3 times, ch 13, sc in top of next ch-20 lp, rep from * around, join with sl st to bottom of beg ch 5.
Rnd 19: Sl st to top of center ch-5 lp, * ch 20, sc in top of next center ch-5 lp, rep from * around, join with sl st to bottom of beg ch 20.
Rnd 20: Sl st to top of 1st ch-20 lp, * ch 22, sc in top

of next ch-20 lp, rep from * around, join with sl st to bottom of beg ch 22.

Rnd 21: Rep Rnd 20 except work in ch-22 lp.

Rnd 22: Sl st to top of 1st ch-22 lp, * (ch 5, sl st in sm sp) 3 times, ch 18, sc in top of next ch-22 lp, rep from * around, join with sl st to bottom of beg ch 5.

Rnd 23: Sl st to top of center ch-5 lp, * ch 24, sc in top of next center ch-5 lp, rep from * around, join with sl st to bottom of beg ch 24.

Rnd 24: Sl st to top of 1st ch-24 lp, * ch 26, sc in top of next ch-24 lp, rep from * around, join with sl st to bottom of beg ch 26.

Rnd 25: * Ch 10, sk next 6 ch of 1st ch-26 lp, sc in next ch, (ch 10, sk next 5 ch, sc in next ch) 2 times, ch 10, sk next 6 ch, sc in last ch of ch-26 lp, rep from * in each ch-26 lp around, join with sl st to bottom of beg ch 10.

Rnd 26: Sl st to top of 1st ch-10 lp, * ch 10, sc in top of next ch-10 lp, rep from * around, join with sl st to bottom of beg ch 10.

Rnd 27: Sl st to top of 1st ch-10 lp, * ch 12, sc in top of next ch-10 lp, rep from * around, join with sl st to bottom of beg ch 12.

Rnd 28: Sl st to top of 1st ch-12 lp, * ch 12, sc in top of next ch-12 lp, (ch 4, sl st in sm sp) picot made, rep from * around, join with sl st to bottom of beg ch 12, F.O.

Rnd 29: Turn work over, join with sl st to center of any ch-26 lp in Rnd 24, * ch 20, sc in center of next ch-26 lp, rep from * around, join with sl st to bottom of beg ch 20.

Rnd 30: Sl st to top of 1st ch-20 lp, * ch 20, sc in top of next ch-20 lp, rep from * around, join with sl st to bottom of beg ch 20.

Rnd 31: Rep Rnd 18.

Rnd 32: Rep Rnd 19.

Rnd 33: Rep Rnd 20.

Rnd 34: Rep Rnd 21.

Rnd 35: Rep Rnd 22.

Rnd 36: Sl st to top of center ch-5 lp, * ch 10, sc in center of next 18-ch lp, (ch 5, sl st in sm sp) 3 times, rep from * around, join with sl st to bottom of beg ch 5, **F.O.**

Stiffen if desired.

Ponytail Twist

Materials Needed: *Approximately 150 yards of #20 variegated rayon thread; size E crochet hook; 6" length of elastic cord; sewing needle; white sewing thread.*

Finished Size: *One size fits all*

Gauge: *10 sc = 1-1/2"*

8 rows of sc = 1"

Ch 161.

Row 1: Sc in 2nd ch from hk, * hdc in next ch, sc in next ch, rep from *, ending row with hdc in last ch, ch 1, turn.

Row 2: * Sc in next hdc, hdc in next sc, rep from *, ending row with hdc in last sc, ch 1, turn.

Rep Row 2 until work measures 4".

Finishing: Fold work in half lengthwise, sc first and last rows tog (tube formed). Thread elastic cord through tube, sew elastic ends tog with sewing needle and thread, sew tube edges tog.

Chapter 3

Chain, Picot, Single and Half-Double Crochet

1. Multiples of any number plus 2.

Row 1: Hdc in 3rd ch from hk and in each ch across row, ch 2, turn.
Row 2: Hdc in each hdc across row, ch 2, turn.
Rep Row 2 for pattern.

2. Multiples of 2 plus 1.

Row 1: Hdc in 5th ch from hk, * ch 1, sk 1 ch, hdc in next ch, rep from * across row, ch 3, turn.
Row 2: * Sk 1 hdc, hdc in next ch-1 sp, ch 1, rep from *, ending row with hdc in top of tch, ch 3, turn.
Rep Row 2 for pattern.

3. Multiples of 15 plus 5.

Row 1: Hdc in 5th ch from hk and in each ch across row, ch 3, turn.
Row 2: Sk 1st hdc, dc in next hdc, * ch 3, sk 3 hdc, tr in next hdc, (ch 1, sk 1 hdc, tr in next hdc) 3 times, ch 3, sk 3 hdc, dc in next 2 hdc, rep from *, ending row with dc in last hdc and tch, ch 3, turn.
Row 3: Sk 1st dc, dc in next dc, * ch 5, dc in next 4 tr, ch 5, dc in next 2 dc, rep from *, ending row with dc in last dc and tch, ch 3, turn.
Row 4: Sk 1st dc, dc in next dc, * ch 5, sc in next 4 dc, ch 5, dc in next 2 dc, rep from *, ending row with dc in last dc and tch, ch 3, turn.
Row 5: Sk 1st dc, dc in next dc, * ch 5, sc in next 4 sc, ch 5, dc in next 2 dc, rep from *, ending row with dc in last dc and tch, ch 3, turn.

Row 6: Sk 1st dc, dc in next dc, * ch 3, dc in next sc, (ch 1, dc in next sc) 3 times, ch 3, dc in next 2 dc, rep from *, ending row with dc in last dc and tch, ch 3, turn.

Row 7: Sk 1st dc, dc in next dc, * ch 3, tr in next dc, (ch 1, tr in next dc) 3 times, ch 3, dc in next 2 dc, rep from *, ending row with dc in last dc and tch, ch 3, turn.

Row 8: Hdc in each st and ch across, ending row with hdc in tch, ch 3, turn.

Rep Rows 2-8 for pattern.

4. Multiples of 2.

Row 1: Sc in 2nd ch from hk and in each ch across row, ch 1, turn.

Row 2: Sc in each sc across row, ch 1, turn.

Row 3: Sc in each sc across row, ch 3, turn.

Row 4: Sk 1st 2 sc, hdc in next sc, * ch 1, sk 1 sc, hdc in next sc, rep from * across row, ch 1, turn.

Row 5: Sc in each hdc and ch-1 sp across, ending row with hdc in 1st and 2nd ch of tch, ch 1, turn.

Rep Rows 2-5 for pattern.

5. Multiples of 2.

Row 1: 2 hdc in 4th ch from hk, * sk 1 ch, 2 hdc in next ch, rep from *, ending row with 2 hdc in last ch, ch 2, turn.

Row 2: Sk 1st 2 hdc, * 2 hdc in sp before next hdc, sk 2 hdc, rep from *, ending row with hdc in tch, ch 2, turn.

Row 3: Hdc in 1st hdc, * sk 2 hdc, 2 hdc in sp before next hdc, rep from *, ending row with hdc in last hdc and tch, ch 2, turn.

Rep Rows 2-3 for pattern.

6. Multiples of 10 plus 4. (Add 6 for foundation chain)

Row 1: Dc in 4th ch from hk and in each ch across row, ch 2, turn.

Row 2: Sk 1st dc, hdc in next 3 dc, * ch 6, hdc in next 10 dc, rep from *, ending row with ch 6, hdc in last 3 dc and tch, ch 6, turn.

Row 3: * (Sc, hdc, dc, 2 tr, dc, hdc, sc) in next ch-6 arch, ch 8, rep from *, ending row after last ch-6 arch with ch 3, dc in tch, ch 1, turn.

Row 4: Sc in 1st dc, * ch 3, sk next 4 st in ch-6 arch, dc in sp before next tr, 3-ch picot, (ch 1, dc in sm sp, 3-ch picot) 2 times, ch 3, sk next 4 st and 3 ch, sc in next ch, ch 3, sc in next ch, rep from *, ending row with ch 3, sc in 4th ch of tch.

7. Multiples of 2 plus 1.

Row 1: Sc in 2nd ch from hk and in each ch across row, ch 1, turn.
Row 2: Hdc in 1st sc, * sk next sc, hdc in next sc, hdc in skipped sc, rep from *, ending row with hdc in last sc, ch 1, turn.
Row 3: Working in front lp only, sc in each hdc across row, ch 1, turn.
Rep Rows 2-3 for pattern.

8. Multiples of 8 plus 6.

Row 1: Sc in 2nd ch from hk and in each ch across row, ch 2, turn.
Row 2: Sk 1st sc, hdc in next 4 sc, * ch 1, sk 1 sc, hdc in next sc, ch 1, sk 1 sc, hdc in next 5 sc, rep from * across row, ch 1, turn.
Row 3: Sc in each hdc and ch-1 sp across, ending row with sc in tch, ch 4, turn.
Row 4: Sk 1st 2 sc, hdc in next sc, * ch 1, sk 1 sc, hdc in next 5 sc, ch 1, sk 1 sc, hdc in next sc, rep from *, ending row with ch 1, sk 1 sc, hdc in last sc, ch 1, turn.
Row 5: Sc in each hdc and ch-1 sp across, ending row with sc in 1st and 2nd ch of tch, ch 2, turn.
Rep Rows 2-5 for pattern.

Patterns Using Chain, Picot, Single and Half Double Crochet

Ribbed Sweater Vest

Materials Needed: Approximately 15 ounces worsted weight light blue yarn; size J crochet hook; 5 yards dark blue ribbon.
Finished Size: Women's Medium (To increase or decrease size, use larger or smaller hook for desired gauge.)
Gauge: 2 rows of 4 hdc = 1"
Ch 201.
Row 1: Hdc in 2nd ch from hk, hdc in next 34 ch, dc in next 130 ch, hdc in last 35 ch, ch 1, turn.
Row 2: Hdc in next 35 hdc, dc in next 130 dc, hdc in next 35 hdc, ch 1, turn.
Rows 3-21: Rep Row 2.
Row 22: Hdc in next 35 hdc, dc in next 35 dc, ch 50, sk next 50 dc, dc in next 45 dc (neck opening formed), hdc in rem 35 hdc, ch 1, turn.
Row 23: Hdc in next 35 hdc, dc in next 45 dc, dc in next 50 ch, dc in next 35 dc, hdc in rem 35 hdc, ch 1, turn.
Rows 24-43: Rep Row 2.

Finishing: Fold work in half lengthwise. Pin sides tog leaving desired size opening for armhole. Sew vest tog using whip st.
Edging for armholes, neck opening and bottom of vest:
Join yarn to bottom of vest with sl st, * ch 3, sc in last st of next row, rep from * around, **F. O.**

Join yarn into armhole opening with a sl st, * ch 3, sc in next st, rep from * around, **F.O.**
Rep for 2nd armhole and neck opening. Weave ribbon over and under st around neck opening and armhole edging. Block if desired.

Gingerbread Shelf Edging

Refer to # 6 on page 24 for a drawing of this pattern. Using this pattern to make an easy edging shows how simple it is to create your own designs with this book. There are many patterns useful in creating trims and edgings. If this is not your favorite pattern, choose another and improvise!

Materials Needed: Approximately 500 yards of # 20 white cotton thread; size E crochet hook.
Finished Size: 48" length
Gauge: *1 pattern repeat = 2 1/2"*
Ch 250.
Row 1: Dc in 4th ch from hk and in each ch across row, ch 2, turn.
Row 2: Sk 1st dc, hdc in next 3 dc, * ch 6, hdc in next 10 dc, rep from *, ending row with ch 6, hdc in last 3 dc and tch, ch 6, turn.
Row 3: * (Sc, hdc, dc, 2 tr, dc, hdc, sc) in next ch-6 arch, ch 8, rep from *, ending row after last ch-6 arch with ch 3, dc in tch, ch 1, turn.
Row 4: Sc in 1st dc, * ch 3, sk next 4 st in ch-6 arch, dc in sp before next tr, 3-ch picot, (ch 1, dc in sm sp, 3-ch picot) 2 times, ch 3, sk next 4 st and 3 ch, sc in next ch, ch 3, sc in next ch, rep from *, ending row with ch 3, sc in 4th ch of tch.
Finishing: Stiffen if desired.

Chapter 4

Double Crochet

1. Multiples of any number plus 2.

Row 1: Dc in 4th ch from hk and in each ch across row, ch 3, turn.
Row 2: Sk 1st dc, dc in each dc across, dc in tch, ch 3, turn.
Rep Row 2 for pattern.

2. Multiples of 2 plus 6.

Row 1: Dc in 6th ch from hk, * ch 1, sk 1 ch, dc in next ch, rep from *, ending row with dc in last ch, ch 4, turn.
Row 2: Sk 1st dc, * dc in next dc, ch 1, rep from *, ending row with dc in 2nd ch of tch, ch 4, turn.
Rep Row 2 for pattern, (Can use in filet crochet.)

3. Multiples of 4 plus 5.

Row 1: Dc in 4th ch from hk and in each ch across row, ch 4, turn.
Row 2: Sk 1st 2 dc, dc in next dc, * ch 1, sk 1 dc, dc in next dc, rep from *, ending row with ch 1, dc in tch,

ch 3, turn.
Row 3: Sk 1st dc, dc in each ch and dc across, dc in 1st and 2nd ch of tch, ch 3, turn.
Row 4: Sk 1st dc, dc in next 2 dc, * ch 1, sk 1 dc, dc in next 3 dc, rep from *, ending row with dc in last 2 dc, dc in tch, ch 3, turn.
Row 5: Sk 1st dc, dc in each dc and ch across, dc in tch, ch 4, turn.
Rep Rows 2-5 for pattern.

4. Multiples of 6 plus 4.

Row 1: Dc in 4th ch from hk, dc in next 2 ch, * ch 3, sk 3 ch, dc in next 3 ch, rep from *, ending row with ch 3, dc in last ch, ch 3, turn.
Row 2: 3 dc in 1st ch-3 sp, * ch 3, 3 dc in next ch-3 sp, rep from *, ending row with ch 3, dc in tch, ch 3, turn.
Rep Row 2 for pattern.

5. Multiples of 6 plus 2.

Row 1: Dc in 8th ch from hk, dc in next 3 ch, * ch 2, sk 2 ch, dc in next 4 ch, rep from *, ending row with ch 2, sk 2 ch, dc in last ch, ch 3, turn.
Row 2: 2 dc in ch-2 sp, dc in next dc, * ch 2, sk 2 dc, dc in next dc, 2 dc in next ch-2 sp, dc in next dc, rep from *, ending row with dc in tch, ch 5, turn.
Row 3: Sk 1st 3 dc, * dc in next dc, 2 dc in next ch-2 sp, dc in next dc, ch 2, sk 2 dc, rep from *, ending row with dc in tch, ch 3, turn.
Rep Rows 2-3 for pattern.

6. Multiples of 3.

Row 1: Dc in 4th ch from hk and in each ch across row, ch 5, turn.
Row 2: Sk 1st 3 dc, dc in next dc, * ch 2, sk 2 dc, dc in next dc, rep from *, ending row with dc in tch, ch 3, turn.
Row 3: Sk 1st dc, dc in each ch and dc across, dc in 1st, 2nd and 3rd ch of tch, ch 5, turn.
Rep Rows 2-3 for pattern.

7. Multiples of 9 plus 3.

Row 1: Dc in 4th ch from hk, dc in next ch, * ch 2, sk 2 ch, dc in next 7 ch, rep from *, ending row with dc in last 5 ch, ch 3, turn.

Row 2: Sk 1st dc, dc in next 4 dc, * 2 dc in next ch-2 sp, ch 2, sk 2 dc, dc in next 5 dc, rep from *, ending row with ch 2, dc in tch, ch 3, turn.

Row 3: * 2 dc in next ch-2 sp, dc in next 4 dc, ch 2, sk 2 dc, dc in next dc, rep from *, ending row with dc in tch, ch 3, turn.

Row 4: * 2 dc in next ch-2 sp, ch 2, sk 2 dc, dc in next 5 dc, rep from *, ending row with dc in last 4 dc, dc in tch, ch 3, turn.

Rep Rows 2-4 for pattern.

8. Multiples of 3 plus 1.

Row 1: (Dc, ch 3, dc) in 4th ch from hk, * sk 2 ch, (dc, ch 3, dc) in next ch, rep from * across row, ch 3, turn.

Row 2: * (Dc, ch 3, dc) in next ch-3 sp, rep from *, ending row with dc in tch, ch 3, turn.

Rep Row 2 for pattern.

9. Multiples of 19 plus 17.

Row 1: Dc in 4th ch from hk, dc in next 8 ch, * (ch 4, sk 4 ch, dc in next ch) 2 times, dc in next 9 ch, rep from *, ending row with ch 4, dc in last ch, ch 1, turn.

Row 2: Sc in next dc, ch 4, * sk 4 ch, dc in next 4 dc, ch 2, sk 2 dc, dc in next 4 dc, ch 4, sk 4 ch, sc in next dc, ch 4, rep from *, ending row with dc in last 3 dc, dc in tch, ch 3, turn.

Row 3: Sk 1st dc, dc in next dc, ch 2, sk 2 dc, 2 dc in next ch-2 sp, ch 2, sk 2 dc, dc in next 2 dc, * ch 4, sk

3 ch, sc in next ch, ch 1, sk next sc, sc in next ch, ch 4, dc in next 2 dc, ch 2, sk 2 dc, 2 dc in next ch-2 sp, ch 2, sk 2 dc, dc in next 2 dc, rep from *, ending row with ch 4, sc in last sc, ch 1, turn.

Row 4: Sc in sc, ch 4, * dc in next 2 dc, 2 dc in next ch-2 sp, ch 2, 2 dc in next ch-2 sp, dc in next 2 dc, ch 4, sc in ch-1 sp, ch 4, rep from *, ending row with dc in last dc, dc in tch, ch 3, turn.

Row 5: Sk 1st dc, dc in next 3 dc, * 2 dc in next ch-2 sp, dc in next 4 dc, ch 4, dc in sc, ch 4, dc in next 4 dc, rep from *, ending row with ch 4, dc in last sc, ch 3, turn.

Row 6: 5 dc around 1st ch-4 sp, * ch 4, sk 4 dc, dc in next dc, ch 4, sk 5 dc, (5 dc around next ch-4 sp) 2 times, rep from *, ending row with ch 4, sk 4 dc, dc in tch, ch 7, turn.

Row 7: Sk 1st dc and 4 ch,* sc in next dc, ch 4, dc in next 4 dc, ch 2, sk 2 dc, dc in next 4 dc, ch 4, sk 4 ch, rep from *, ending row with dc in last 5 dc and tch, ch 3, turn.

Row 8: Sk 1st dc, dc in next 5 dc, * ch 4, sk 3 ch, sc in next ch, ch 1, sk next sc, sc in next ch, ch 4, sk 3 ch, dc in next 2 dc, ch 2, sk 2 dc, 2 dc in next ch-2 sp, ch 2, sk 2 dc, dc in next 2 dc, rep from *, ending row with ch 4, dc in 5th ch of tch, ch 7, turn.

Row 9: Sk 4 ch, sc in ch-1 sp, ch 4, * dc in next 2 dc, 2 dc in next ch-2 sp, ch 2, sk 2 dc, 2 dc in next ch-2 sp, dc in next 2 dc, ch 4, sc in ch-1 sp, ch 4, rep from *, ending row with dc in next 4 dc, ch 1, sk last dc, dc in tch, ch 3, turn.

Row 10: Dc in ch-1 sp, dc in next 4 dc, * ch 4, sk 4 ch, dc in next sc, ch 4, sk 4 ch, dc in next 4 dc, 2 dc in next ch-2 sp, dc in next 4 dc, rep from *, ending row with ch 4, dc in 5th ch of tch, ch 3, turn.

Row 11: 4 dc around 1st ch-4 sp, 5 dc around next ch-4 sp, * ch 4, sk 5 dc, dc in next dc, ch 4, sk 4 dc, (5 dc around next ch-4 sp) 2 times, rep from *, ending row with ch 4, sk 5 dc, dc in tch, ch 1, turn.
Rep Rows 2-11 for pattern.

10. Multiples of 12 plus 8.

Row 1: Sc in 2nd ch from hk, * ch 5, sk 5 ch, sc in next ch, rep from *, ending row with sc in last ch, ch 3, turn.

Row 2: * 5 dc in next ch-5 sp, ch 3, sc in center of next ch-5 sp, ch 3, rep from *, ending row with 5 dc in last ch-5 sp, dc in last sc, ch 3, turn.

Row 3: Sk 1st dc, * dc in next 5 dc, ch 3, sc in next sc, ch 3, rep from *, ending row with dc in last 5 dc, dc in tch, ch 3, turn.

Row 4: Sk 1st dc, * dc in next 5 dc, ch 3, sc in next sc, 3-ch picot, ch 3, rep from *, ending row with dc in last 5 dc, dc in tch.

11. Multiples of 5 plus 3.

Row 1: Dc in 4th ch from hk, dc in next 3 ch, * ch 1, sk 1 ch, dc in next 4 ch, rep from *, ending row with dc in last ch, ch 1, turn.

Row 2: Sc in 1st dc, * ch 4, sc in next ch-1 sp, rep from *, ending row with ch 4, sk last 4 dc, sc in tch, ch 3, turn.

Row 3: * 4 dc in next ch-4 sp, ch 1, rep from *, ending row with dc in last sc, ch 1, turn.
Rep Rows 2-3 for pattern.

12. Multiples of 10 plus 7.

Row 1: Dc in 11th ch from hk, * dc in next 2 ch, (ch 3, sk 3 ch, dc in next ch) 2 times, rep from *, ending row with ch 3, sk 3 ch, dc in last ch, ch 5, turn.
Row 2: Sk 1st dc and 2 ch, * dc in next ch, dc in next 3 dc, dc in next ch, ch 5, sk (ch 2, dc, ch 2), rep from *, ending row with ch 2, sk 2 ch, dc in next ch, ch 6, turn.
Row 3: Sk 1st dc, * sk 2 ch and dc, dc in next 3 dc, ch 3, sk dc and 2 ch, dc in next ch, ch 3, rep from *, ending row with ch 3, sk next dc and 2 ch, dc in next ch, ch 3, turn.
Row 4: Sk 1st dc, dc in next ch, * ch 3, sk 2 ch and dc, dc in next dc, ch 3, sk dc and 2 ch, dc in next ch, dc in dc, dc in next ch, rep from *, ending row with ch 3, sk dc and 2 ch, dc in next 2 ch, ch 3, turn.
Row 5: Sk 1st dc, dc in next dc, dc in next ch, * ch 5, sk (ch 2, dc, ch 2), dc in next ch, dc in next 3 dc, dc in next ch, rep from *, ending row with ch 5, sk (ch 2, dc, ch 2), dc in next ch, dc in dc, dc in tch, ch 3, turn.
Row 6: Sk 1st dc, dc in next dc, * ch 3, sk dc and 2 ch, dc in next ch, ch 3, sk 2 ch and dc, dc in next 3 dc, rep from *, ending row with ch 3, dc in last dc, dc in tch, ch 6, turn.
Row 7: Sk next 2 dc and 2 ch, * dc in next ch, dc in next dc, dc in next ch, ch 3, sk next 2 ch and dc, dc in next dc, ch 3, sk next dc and 2 ch, rep from *, ending row with ch 3, dc in tch, ch 5, turn.
Rep Rows 2-7 for pattern.

13. Multiples of 9 plus 7.

Row 1: Dc in 8th ch from hk, dc in next 5 ch, * ch 5, sk 3 ch, dc in next 6 ch, rep from *, ending row with ch 2, sk 2 ch, dc in last ch, ch 1, turn.
Row 2: Sc in 1st dc, * ch 3, sk 2 ch, dc in next dc, ch 1, sk 4 dc, dc in next dc, ch 3, sk 2 ch, sc in next ch, rep from *, ending row with ch 3, sc in 3rd ch of tch, ch 5, turn.
Row 3: Sk 1st sc and 2 ch, * dc in next ch, dc in dc, 2 dc in ch-1 sp, dc in next dc, dc in next ch, ch 5, sk (ch 2, sc, ch 2), rep from *, ending row with ch 2, dc in last sc, ch 1, turn.
Rep Rows 2-3 for pattern.

14. Multiples of 8 plus 9.

Row 1: Dc in 7th ch from hk, * ch 1, sk 1 ch, dc in next ch, rep from * across row, ch 4, turn.
Row 2: Sk 1st dc, dc in next dc, ch 1, * (dc in next dc, dc in next ch-1 sp) 2 times, (dc in next dc, ch 1) 2 times, rep from *, ending row with dc in 2nd ch of tch, ch 4, turn.
Row 3: Sk 1st dc, dc in next dc, ch 1, * dc in next 5 dc, ch 1, dc in next dc, ch 1, rep from *, ending row with dc in 2nd ch of tch, ch 4, turn.
Row 4: Sk 1st dc, * dc in next dc, ch 1, sk next st, rep from *, ending row with dc in 2nd ch of tch, ch 4, turn.
Rep Rows 2-4 for pattern.

15. Multiples of 34 plus 2.

Row 1: Dc in 4th ch from hk, * ch 5, sk 5 ch, sc in next 3 ch, ch 5, sk 5 ch, dc in next 4 ch, rep from *, ending row with dc in last 2 ch, ch 3, turn.
Row 2: Sk 1st dc, * dc in next dc, 3 dc in next ch, ch 4, sk 4 ch and 1 sc, sc in next sc, ch 4, sk 1 sc and 4 ch, 3 dc in next ch, dc in next dc, ch 3, sk 2 dc, rep from *, ending row with 3 dc in last ch, dc in last dc, dc in tch, ch 1, turn.
Row 3: Sc in 1st dc, * ch 4, sk 3 dc, dc in next dc, 3 dc in next ch, ch 2, sk (ch 3, sc, ch 3), 3 dc in next ch, dc in next dc, ch 4, sk 3 dc, sc in center of ch-3 sp, rep from *, ending row with ch 4, sc in tch, ch 8, turn.
Row 4: Sk 4 ch and 4 dc, * 4 dc in ch-2 sp, ch 5, sk 4 dc and 3 ch, sc in next ch, sc in next sc, sc in next ch, ch 5, sk 3 ch and 4 dc, rep from *, ending row with ch 5, dc in last sc, ch 1, turn.
Row 5: Sc in 1st dc, * ch 4, sk 4 ch, 3 dc in next ch, dc in next dc, ch 3, sk 2 dc, dc in next dc, 3 dc in next ch, ch 4, sk 4 ch and 1 sc, sc in next sc, rep from *, ending row with ch 4, sc in 6th ch of tch, ch 5, turn.
Row 6: Sk 1st sc and 3 ch, * 3 dc in next ch, dc in next dc, ch 4, sk 3 dc, sc in center of ch-3 sp, ch 4, sk 3 dc, dc in next dc, 3 dc in next ch, ch 2, sk (ch 3, sc, ch 3), rep from *, ending row with ch 2, dc in last sc, ch 3, turn.
Row 7: Dc in 1st dc, ch 5, sk (ch 2, 4 dc, ch 3), * sc in next ch, sc in sc, sc in next ch, ch 5, sk 3 ch and 3 dc, dc in next dc, 2 dc in ch-2 sp, dc in next dc, ch 5, sk 3 dc and 3 ch, rep from *, ending row with ch 5, 2 dc in 3rd ch of tch, ch 3, turn.
Rep Rows 2-7 for pattern.

16. Multiples of 26 plus 3.

Row 1: Dc in 5th ch from hk, * ch 1, sk 1 ch, dc in next ch, rep from *, ending row with dc in last ch, ch 4, turn.

Row 2: Sk 1st dc and ch-1 sp, * dc in next dc, (ch 1, dc in next dc) 5 times, dc in next ch-1 sp, dc in next dc, (ch 1, dc in next dc) 6 times, ch 1, rep from *, ending row with dc in 2nd ch of tch, ch 4, turn.

Row 3: Sk 1st dc and ch-1 sp, * dc in next dc, (ch 1, dc in next dc) 4 times, dc in ch-1 sp, dc in next 3 dc, dc in next ch-1 sp and dc, (ch 1, dc in next dc) 5 times, ch 1, rep from *, ending row with dc in 2nd ch of tch, ch 4, turn.

Row 4: Sk 1st dc and ch-1 sp, * dc in next dc, (ch 1, dc in next dc) 3 times, dc in ch-1 sp, dc in next 3 dc, ch 1, sk 1 dc, dc in next 3 dc, dc in ch-1 sp, dc in next dc, (ch 1, dc in next dc) 4 times, ch 1, rep from *, ending row with dc in 2nd ch of tch, ch 4, turn.

Row 5: Sk 1st dc and ch-1 sp, * dc in next dc, (ch 1, dc in next dc) 2 times, dc in next ch-1 sp, dc in next 3 dc, ch 1, sk 1 dc, dc in next dc, ch 1, sk next ch-1 sp, dc in next dc, ch 1, sk next dc, dc in next (3 dc, ch-1 sp, dc), (ch 1, dc in next dc) 3 times, ch 1, rep from *, ending row with dc in 2nd ch of tch, ch 4, turn.

Row 6: Sk 1st dc and ch-1 sp, * dc in next dc, ch 1, dc in next dc, dc in ch-1 sp, dc in next 3 dc, ch 1, sk next dc, dc in next dc, (ch 1, dc in next dc) 3 times, ch 1, sk next dc, dc in next (3 dc, ch-1 sp, dc), (ch 1, dc in next dc) 2 times, ch 1, rep from *, ending row with dc in 2nd ch of tch, ch 4, turn.

Row 7: Sk 1st dc and ch-1 sp, * dc in next dc, ch 1, dc in next dc, ch 1, sk next dc, dc in next (3 dc, ch-1 sp, dc), (ch 1, dc in next dc) 3 times, dc in next ch-1 sp and 3 dc, ch 1, sk 1 dc, dc in next dc, (ch 1, dc in next dc) 2 times, ch 1, rep from *, ending row with dc in 2nd ch of tch, ch 4, turn.

Row 8: Sk 1st dc and ch-1 sp, * dc in next dc, (ch 1, dc in next dc) 2 times, ch 1, sk 1 dc, dc in next (3 dc, ch-1 sp and dc), ch 1, dc in next (dc, ch-1 sp, 3 dc), ch 1, sk next dc, dc in next dc, (ch 1, dc in next dc) 3 times, ch 1, rep from *, ending row with dc in 2nd ch of tch, ch 4, turn.

Row 9: Sk 1st dc and ch-1 sp, * dc in next dc, (ch 1, dc in next dc) 3 times, ch 1, sk next dc, dc in next (3 dc, ch-1 sp, 3 dc), ch 1, sk next dc, dc in next dc, (ch 1, dc in next dc) 4 times, ch 1, rep from *, ending row with dc in 2nd ch of tch, ch 4, turn.

Row 10: Sk 1st dc and ch-1 sp, * dc in next dc, (ch 1, dc in next dc) 4 times, ch 1, sk next dc, dc in next 3 dc, ch 1, sk 1 dc, dc in next dc, (ch 1, dc in next dc) 5 times, ch 1, rep from *, ending row with dc in 2nd ch of tch, ch 4, turn.

Row 11: Sk 1st dc and ch-1 sp, * dc in next dc, (ch 1, dc in next dc) 5 times, ch 1, sk next dc, dc in next dc, (ch 1, dc in next dc) 6 times, ch 1, rep from *, ending row with dc in 2nd ch of tch, ch 4, turn.

Rep Rows 2-11 for pattern.

17. Multiples of 3 plus 6.

Row 1: Sl st in 3rd ch from hk, ch 5, sk 5 ch, dc in next ch, * 3-ch picot, ch 5, sk 2 ch, dc in next ch, rep from *, ending row with dc in last ch, 3-ch picot, ch 6, turn.
Row 2: * Dc in center of next ch-5 arch, 3-ch picot, ch 5, rep from *, ending row with ch 3, dc in 4th ch of tch, ch 3, turn.
Row 3: Make * 3-ch picot, ch 5, dc in center of next ch-5 arch, rep from *, ending row with dc in 4th ch of tch, 3-ch picot, ch 6, turn.
Rep Row 2-3 for pattern.

18. Multiples 4 plus 2.

Row 1: Sc in 2nd ch from hk and in each ch across row, ch 4, turn.
Row 2: Sk 1st 2 sc, *dc in next sc, ch 1, sk next sc, rep from *, ending row with dc in last sc, ch 1, turn.
Row 3: Sc in dc, * ch 5, sk (ch 1, dc, ch 1), dc in next dc, rep from *, ending row with sc in 2nd ch of tch, ch 5, turn.
Row 4: * Sc in 3rd ch of next 5-ch arch, ch 5, rep from *, ending row with ch 2, dc in last sc, ch 1, turn.
Row 5: Sc in dc, * ch 5, sc in 3rd ch of next ch-5 arch, rep from *, ending row with ch 5, sc in 3rd ch of tch, ch 1, turn.
Row 6: Sc in sc, * (hdc, 3 dc, hdc) in next ch-5 arch, rep from *, ending row with sc in last sc.

19. Multiples of 30 plus 4.

Row 1: Dc in 6th ch from hk, * (ch 1, sk next ch, dc in next ch) 6 times, dc in next 2 ch, (ch 1, sk next ch, dc

in next ch) 7 times, ch 1, sk next ch, dc in next ch, rep from *, ending row with dc in last ch, ch 4, turn.

Row 2: Sk 1st dc and ch-1 sp, dc in next dc, * (ch 1, dc in next dc) 5 times, dc in next ch-1 sp and dc, ch 3, sk next dc, dc in next (dc, ch-1 sp, dc), (ch 1, dc in next dc) 6 times, ch 1, dc in next dc, rep from *, ending row with dc in 2nd ch of tch, ch 4, turn.

Row 3: Sk 1st dc and ch-1 sp, dc in next dc, * (ch 1, dc in next dc) 4 times, dc in next ch-1 sp and dc, ch 3, sk next 2 dc, sc in 2nd ch of ch-3 sp, ch 3, sk 2 dc, dc in next (dc, ch-1 sp, dc), (ch 1, dc in next dc) 5 times, ch 1, dc in next dc, rep from *, ending row with dc in 2nd ch of tch, ch 4, turn.

Row 4: Sk 1st dc and ch-1 sp, dc in next dc, * (ch 1, dc in next dc) 3 times, dc in next ch-1 sp and dc, ch 3, sk next 2 dc and 2 ch, sc in next (ch 1, sc, ch 1), ch 3, sk next 2 ch and 2 dc, dc in next (dc, ch-1 sp, dc), (ch 1, dc in next dc) 4 times, ch 1, dc in next dc, rep from *, ending row with dc in 2nd ch of tch, ch 4, turn.

Row 5: Sk 1st dc and ch-1 sp, dc in next dc, * (ch 1, dc in next dc) 2 times, dc in next ch-1 sp and dc, ch 4, sk 2 dc and 2 ch, sc in next (ch 1, 3 sc, ch 1), ch 4, sk next 2 ch and 2 dc, dc in next (dc, ch-1 sp, dc), (ch 1, dc in next dc) 3 times, ch 1, dc in next dc, rep from *, ending row with dc in 2nd ch of tch, ch 4, turn.

Row 6: Sk 1st dc and ch-1 sp, dc in next dc, * (ch 1, dc in next dc) 2 times, ch 1, sk next dc, dc in next dc and next 2 ch, ch 4, sk 2 ch and next sc, sc in next 3 sc, ch 4, sk next sc and 2 ch, dc in next 2 ch, dc in next dc, ch 1, sk next dc, dc in next dc, (ch 1, dc in next dc) 3 times, ch 1, dc in next dc, rep from *, ending row with dc in 2nd ch of tch, ch 4, turn.

Row 7: Sk 1st dc and ch-1 sp, dc in next dc, * (ch 1, dc in next dc) 3 times, ch 1, sk next dc, dc in next dc and 2 ch, ch 3, sk next 2 ch and sc, sc in next sc, ch 3, sk next sc and 2 ch, dc in next 2 ch and dc, ch 1, sk next dc, dc in next dc, (ch 1, dc in next dc) 4 times, ch 1, dc in next dc, rep from *, ending row with dc in 2nd ch of tch, ch 4, turn.

Row 8: Sk 1st dc and ch-1 sp, dc in next dc, * (ch 1, dc in next dc) 4 times, ch 1, sk next dc, dc in next dc, dc in next 2 ch, ch 1, sk next (ch 1, sc, ch 1), dc in next 2 ch and dc, ch 1, sk next dc, dc in next dc, (ch 1, dc in next dc) 5 times, ch 1, dc in next dc, rep from *, ending row with dc in 2nd ch of tch, ch 4, turn.

Row 9: Sk 1st dc and ch-1 sp, dc in next dc, * (ch 1, dc in next dc) 5 times, ch 1, sk next dc, dc in next dc, dc in ch-1 sp, dc in next dc, ch 1, sk next dc, dc in next dc, (ch 1, dc in next dc) 6 times, ch 1, dc in next dc, rep from *, ending row with dc in 2nd ch of tch, ch 4, turn.

Rep Rows 2-9 for pattern.

20. Multiples of 18 plus 5.

Row 1: Dc in 8th ch from hk, (ch 2, sk 2 ch, dc in next ch) 2 times, * dc in next 9 ch, (ch 2, sk 2 ch, dc in next ch) 3 times, rep from *, ending row with 9 dc, ch 3, turn.

Row 2: Sk 1st dc, dc in next 3 dc, * ch 2, sk 2 dc, dc in next 4 dc, ch 2, sk 2 ch, dc in next dc, 2 dc in next ch-2 sp, dc in next dc, ch 2, sk 2 ch, dc in next 4 dc, rep from *, ending row with ch 2, sk 2 ch, dc in next ch of tch, ch 5, turn.

Row 3: Sk 1st dc and next 2 ch, * dc in next dc, ch 2, sk 2 dc, dc in next dc, ch 2, sk 2 ch, dc in next 4 dc, 2 dc in next ch-2 sp, dc in next 4 dc, ch 2, sk 2 ch, rep from *, ending row with dc in last 3 dc, dc in tch, ch 5, turn.

Row 4: Sk 1st 3 dc, dc in next dc, * (ch 2, sk 2 dc, dc in next dc) 2 times, (2 dc in next ch-2 sp, dc in next dc) 3 times, ch 2, sk 2 dc, dc in next dc, rep from *, ending row with dc in 3rd ch of tch, ch 3, turn.

Rep Rows 2-4 for pattern.

21. Multiples of 10 plus 2.

Row 1: Sc in 4th ch from hk (counts as 2 sc), sc in next 3 ch, * dc in next 5 ch, sc in next 5 ch, rep from *, ending row with 5 dc, ch 1, turn.

Row 2: * Sc in next 5 dc, dc in next 5 sc, rep from * across row, ch 1, turn.
Rep Row 2 for pattern.

22. Multiples of 6 plus 8.

Row 1: Sc in 2nd ch from hk, sc in next ch, * ch 3, sk 3 ch, sc in next 3 ch, rep from *, ending row with ch 3, sk 3 ch, sc in last 2 ch, ch 1, turn.

Row 2: Sc in next sc, sk next sc, ch 2, * 5 dc in next ch-3 sp, sc in 2nd sc of 3-sc group, rep from *, ending row with 5 dc, ch 2, sc in last sc, ch 1, turn.

Row 3: Sc in next sc, ch 2, * sc in 3 center dc of next 5-dc group, ch 3, rep from *, ending row with ch 2, sc in last sc, ch 3, turn.

Row 4: 2 dc in ch-2 sp, * sc in 2nd sc of 3-sc group, 5 dc in next ch-3 sp, rep from *, ending row with sc in 2nd sc of last 3-sc group, 2 dc in last ch-2 sp, dc in last sc, ch 1, turn.

Row 5: Sc in 1st 2 dc, * ch 3, sc in 3 center dc of 5-dc group, rep from *, ending row with ch 3, sc in last dc, sc in tch, ch 1, turn.
Rep Rows 2-5 for pattern.

23. Multiples of 4 plus 7.

Row 1: Dc in 4th ch from hk, dc in next ch, sk 1 ch, * (dc, ch 3, dc) in next ch, sk 1 ch, rep from *, ending row with dc in last 3 ch, ch 3, turn.

Row 2: * (3 dc, ch 3, sc) in next ch-3 sp, rep from *, ending row with dc in top of tch, ch 3, turn.
Rep Row 2 for pattern.

24. Multiples of 13.

Row 1: Dc in 4th ch from hk, dc in next 3 ch, 3 dc in next ch, dc in next 5 ch, * sk 2 ch, dc in next 5 ch, 3 dc in next ch, dc in next 5 ch, rep from * across row, ch 3, turn.
Row 2: Sk 1st dc, dc in next 5 dc, * 3 dc in next dc, dc in next 5 dc, sk 2 dc, dc in next 5 dc, rep from *, ending with dc in last 5 dc, ch 3, turn.
Rep Row 2 for pattern.

25. Multiples of 2 plus 2.

Row 1: Sk 2 ch, 3-lp puff st as follows (insert hk in ch, yo, pull through lp, insert hk in next ch, yo, pull through lp, yo and pull through all 3 lps), * 3-lp puff st (insert hk in last sp worked for prev puff st), complete puff st in next ch, rep from * across row, ch 2, turn.
Row 2: * 3-lp puff st in each st across, ending row with last puff st completed in top of tch, ch 2, turn.
Rep Row 2 for pattern.

26. Multiples of 4 plus 2.

Row 1: Sc in 2nd ch from hk and in each ch across row, ch 2, turn.
Row 2: * Sk next sc, dc in next 3 sc, insert hk in skipped sc, yo, pull through lp, yo, pull through 2 lps on hk, rep from *, ending row with dc in last sc, ch 1, turn.
Row 3: Sc in each st across row, ch 2, turn.
Rep Row 2-3 for pattern.

27. Multiples of 3 plus 2.

Row 1: Dc in 7th ch from hk, * ch 1, dc in ch behind dc just worked, sk 2 ch, dc in next ch, rep from *, ending row with dc in last ch, ch 4, turn.
Row 2: Sk 1 dc, dc in next dc, ch 1, dc in last skipped dc, * sk next dc, dc in next dc, ch 1, dc in skipped dc, rep from *, ending row with sk 1 ch, dc in next ch, ch 4, turn.
Rep Row 2 for pattern.

28. Multiples of 16 plus 16.

Row 1: 2 dc in 4th ch from hk, * ch 8, sk 11 ch, (2 dc, ch 2, 2 dc) in next ch, sk 3 ch, (2 dc, ch 2, 2 dc) in next ch, rep from *, ending row with 3 dc in last ch, ch 3, turn.

Row 2: 2 dc in 1st dc, * ch 4, sc around center of ch-8 sp, ch 4, (2 dc, ch 2, 2 dc in next ch-2 sp) 2 times, rep from *, ending row with ch 4, 3 dc in tch, ch 3, turn.

Row 3: 2 dc in 1st dc, * ch 5, sk 4 ch, sc in sc, ch 3, turn, 5 dc around ch-5 sp just made, ch 3, turn, sk 1 dc, dc in next 3 dc, sk next dc, dc in top of tch, (2 dc, ch 2, 2 dc in next ch-2 sp) 2 times, rep from *, ending row with 3 dc in top of tch, ch 3, turn.

Row 4: 2 dc in 1st dc, * ch 8, (2 dc, ch 2, 2 dc in next ch-2 sp) 2 times, rep from *, ending row with ch 8, 3 dc in tch, ch 3, turn.

Rep Rows 2-4 for pattern.

29. Multiples of 9 plus 5.

Row 1: Dc in 4th ch from hk, dc in next 2 ch, * ch 5, sk 4 ch, dc in next 5 ch, rep from *, ending row with dc in last 4 ch, ch 3, turn.

Row 2: Sk 1st dc, dc in next 2 dc, sk 1 dc, * ch 3, dc in center of ch-5 sp, ch 3, sk 1 dc, dc in next 3 dc, sk 1 dc, rep from *, ending row with ch 3, sk 1 dc, dc in last 2 dc, dc in tch, ch 3, turn.

Row 3: Sk 1st dc, dc in next dc, * ch 3, dc in ch-3 sp, dc in dc, dc in ch-3 sp, ch 3, sk 1 dc, dc in next dc, sk 1 dc, rep from *, ending row with ch 3, sk 1 dc, dc in last dc, dc in tch, ch 6, turn.

Row 4: Sk 1st 2 dc, dc in ch-3 sp, * dc in next 3 dc, dc in next ch-3 sp, ch 5, sk next dc, dc in next ch-3 sp, rep from *, ending row with ch 3, dc in tch, ch 3, turn.

Row 5: Dc in 1st dc, * ch 3, sk next dc, dc in next 3 dc, ch 3, dc in ch-5 sp, rep from *, ending row with ch 3, 2 dc in tch, ch 3, turn.

Row 6: Dc in 1st 2 dc, * ch 3, dc in center dc of next 3-dc group, ch 3, dc in ch-3 sp, dc in next dc, dc in ch-3 sp, rep from *, ending row with ch 3, 2 dc in last dc, dc in tch, ch 3, turn.

Row 7: Dc in 1st 3 dc, * ch 5, sk next dc, dc in ch-3 sp, dc in next 3 dc, dc in ch-3 sp, rep from *, ending row with ch 5, dc in last 2 dc, 2 dc in tch, ch 3, turn.

Rep Rows 2-7 for pattern.

30. Multiples of 18 plus 4.

Row 1: Dc in 4th ch from hk, dc in next ch, * sk 2 ch, (dc, ch 3, dc) in next ch, sk 2 ch, dc in next 4 ch, rep from *, ending row with dc in last 3 ch, ch 3, turn.

Row 2: Sk 1st 2 dc, dc in next dc, * ch 2, 5 dc around ch-3 sp, ch 2, beg dc in 1st dc of 4-dc group (leave 2 lps on hk), beg next dc in 4th dc of same 4-dc group (leave 3 lps on hk), yo hk, pull through all lps (inverted V-st made), rep from *, ending row with ch 2, dc in next dc (leave 2 lps on hk), dc in tch (3 lps on hk), yo hk, pull through all lps, ch 4, turn.

Row 3: Dc in top of 1st inverted V-st, * dc in next 5 dc, dc in top of next inverted V-st, ch 3, dc in top of same V-st, rep from *, ending row with (dc, ch 1, dc) in 3rd ch of tch, ch 3, turn.

Row 4: Dc in ch-1 sp, * ch 2, inverted V-st over 1st and 5th dc of next 5-dc group, ch 2, 5 dc in next ch-3 sp, rep from *, ending row with ch 2, 2 dc in tch, ch 3, turn.

Row 5: Dc in 1st 2 dc, * (dc, ch 3, dc) in top of next inverted V-st, dc in next 5 dc, rep from *, ending row with 2 dc in last dc, dc in tch, ch 3, turn.

Row 6: Sk 1st 2 dc, dc in next dc, * ch 2, 5 dc around ch-3 sp, ch 2, inverted V-st over 1st and 5th dc of next 5-dc group, rep from *, ending row with ch 2, dc in next dc (leave 2 lps on hk), dc in tch (3 lps on hk) yo hk, pull through all lps, ch 4, turn.

Rep Rows 3-6 for pattern.

Patterns Using Double Crochet

Parlor Lampshade Cover

This lampshade is made from a simple rectangular shape, gathered to create the illusion of an old-fashioned parlor shade.

Materials Needed: *Approximately 300 yards of # 20 white cotton thread; #12 steel crochet hook; two 12" lengths of white cord elastic; tapestry needle; lampshade frame with 12" top diameter and 24" bottom diameter.*

Finished Size: *34" x 12" (before gathered with elastic cord).*

Gauge: *6 ch-3 sp = 3"*
         1 row of dc = 1/4"

Note: Throughout pattern turning ch 5 counts as (dc, ch 2), turning ch 6 counts as (dc, ch 3).

Ch 437.

Row 1: Dc in 9th ch from hk, * ch 3, sk next 3 ch, dc in next ch, rep from * across, ch 5, turn. (108 ch-3 sp)

Row 2: * Sc in center of next ch-3 sp, ch 2, dc in next dc, ch 2, rep from * across, end with dc, ch 6, turn. (216 ch-2 sp)

Row 3: * Dc in next dc, ch 3, rep from * across, end with dc, ch 5, turn.

Rows 4-37: Rep Rows 2 and 3 alternately, turn work at end of Row 37.

Scalloped Edging

Row 1: Sl st in next 3 ch, sl st in next dc, ch 5, sc in center of next ch-3 sp, ch 2, dc in next dc, (ch 2, sc in center of next ch-3 sp, ch 2, dc in next dc) 4 times, ch 6, turn. (10 ch-2 sp)

Row 2: Dc in next dc, (ch 3, dc in next dc) 4 times, ch 5, turn. (5 ch-3 sp)

Row 3: Rep Row 1 except work ( ) 2 times. (3 ch-3 sp)

Row 4: Rep Row 2 except work ( ) 2 times. (3 ch-3 sp)

Row 5: Rep Row 1 until reaching ( ), ch 6, turn. (2 ch-2 sp)

Row 6: Dc in next dc, **F.O.** (1 ch-3 sp)
Rep Rows 1-6 for remaining scallops.

Optional Scalloped Trim

* Ch 5, sl st to beg edge of scallop, rep from * evenly spacing ch-5 lp around entire scallop, in ch-3 sp bet each scallop work (ch 2, sc in center of ch-3 sp, ch 2), sl st to beg edge of next scallop, **F.O.** at end of work.

Finishing: Thread elastic cord through tapestry needle, weave over and under dc posts of Row 5, rep with rem cord in Row 9, pull tog to gather, secure ends. Place cover on lampshade frame.

Fuzzy Wuzzy Bear

Materials Needed: 24 ounces of mohair-look yarn; size H hook; tapestry needle; 26mm plastic eyes; 30mm nose; fiberfil for stuffing.

Gauge: 3 lp st = 1" wide

Finished Size: 24 inches tall

Instructions for Loop Stitch: Insert hook into st, wrap yarn around finger 2 times clockwise, insert hook from left to right through all loops on finger, pull loops through stitch. Drop loops from finger. Yarn over. Pull through all loops on hook, yarn over. Pull remaining 2 loops on hook.

Legs (make two)

Ch 4, join with sl st to form ring.

Rnd 1: Ch 3, (counts as 1 dc), make 11 dc in ring, join with sl st to top of beg ch 3 (12 dc).

Rnd 2: Ch 3, dc in sm sp (counts as 2 dc), 2 dc in each dc around, join with sl st to top of beg ch 3. (24 dc).

Rnd 3: Ch 3, dc in sm sp (counts as 2 dc), 2 dc in each of next 11 dc, dc in each of next 12 dc, join as above. (36 dc)

Rnd 4: Ch 3, dc in each dc around, join as above. (36 dc)

Rnd 5: Ch 3, dec in next 11 dc, dc in each of next 12 dc, dec in next 12 dc, join as above. (24 dc)

Rnd 6: Ch 3, (working in bk lp only) dc in each dc around, join. (24 dc)

Rnd 7: Ch 2, (working in bk lp only) lp st in each dc around, join with sl st to top of ch 2. (24 lp st)

Rnds 8-24: Rep Rnd 8. F.O. at end of Rnd 24.

Arms (make 2)

Ch 4, join with sl st to form a ring.

Rnds 1-2: Rep leg Rnds 1-2.

Rnds 3-4: Rep leg Rnd 6.

Rnds 5-19: Rep leg Rnd 7, F.O. at end of Rnd 19. Lightly stuff legs and arms.

Body and Head

Ch 71, join with sl st to form large ring.

Rnd 1: Ch 2, lp st in each ch around, join with sl st to top of beg ch-2. (70 lp st)

Rnd 2: Ch 2, lp st in each lp st around, join as above.

Rnds 3-6: Rep Rnd 2.

Rnds 7-8: Rep Rnd 2 except work in bk lp only.

Rnd 9: Ch 2, * lp in st in next 4 lp st, sk next lp st (dec every 5th lp st made), rep from * around, join as above. (56 lp st)

Rnd 10: Ch 2, * lp st in next 3 lp st, sk next lp st, (dec every 4 lp st made), rep from * around, join as above. (42 lp st)

Rnds 11-22: Rep Rnd 2. (42 lp st)

Using same thread and tapestry needle, sew legs to beg rnd by placing legs against each side. There will be a small gap in center between legs. Sew this gap closed.

Optional: Picking one side to be the back; pinch 2 inches of work along the center inside thru Rnd 9 and sew tog for a better defined "bottom." Continue to work as follows, lightly stuff body and head as you go.

Rnd 23: Ch 2, * lp st in next two lp st, sk next lp st, rep from * around, join as above. (28 lp st)

Rnds 24-27: Rep Rnd 2. (28 lp-st)

Rnd 28: Ch 2, * lp st in each of next two lp st, 2 lp st in next lp st, rep from * around, join as above. (42 lp st)

Rnds 29-42: Rep Rnd 2. (42 lp st)

Rnd 43: Ch 2, * lp st in each of next 3 lp st, sk next lp st, rep from * around, join as above. (32 lp st)

Rnd 44-50: Rep Rnd 2. (32 lp st)

Rnd 51: Ch 2, * lp st in each of next 3 lp st, sk next lp st, rep from * around, join as above. (24 lp st)

Rnd 52: Rep Rnd 2. (24 lp st)

Rnd 53: Ch 2, * lp st in each of next 3 lp st, skip next lp st, rep from * around, join as above. (18 lp st)

Rnd 54: Rep Rnd 2. (18 lp st)

Rnd 55: Ch 2, * lp st in next 2 lp st, sk next lp st, rep from * around, join as above. (12 lp st)

Rnds 56-57: Rep Rnd 2. (12 lp st)

Rnd 58: Ch 2, * lp st in each of next 2 lp st, sk next lp st, rep from * around, join as above. (8 lp st)

Rnd 59: Rep Rnd 59. (6 lp st)

Sew top of head closed, sew arms to sides of body.

Ears (make two).

Ch 4, join with sl st to form ring.

Rnd 1: Ch 3, 9 dc in ring, join with sl st to top of beg ch 3. (10 dc)

Rnd 2: Ch 2, lp st in each dc around, join with sl st to top of beg ch 2. (10 lp st)

Rnds 3-4: Ch 2, lp st in each lp st around, join as above.

Rnds 5-6: Ch 2, (working in bk lp only) 2 lp st in each lp st around, join. (20 lp st)

Rnd 7: Ch 2, 2 lp st in each lp st around, join. (40 lp st) F.O. leaving 12" for sewing to head. Sew ears to head. Shape face with hands to form muzzle. Glue or sew on eyes and nose.

Caution: For very small children, do not glue on eyes. Securely sew eyes and nose to head using same thread and tapestry needle. Periodically check to see that sewing is still secure.

Chapter 5

Treble Crochet

1. Multiples of any number.

Row 1: Tr in 5th ch from hk and in each ch across row, ch 4, turn.
Row 2: Sk 1st tr, tr in each tr across row, tr in top of tch, ch 4, turn.
Rep Row 2 for pattern.

2. Multiples of 2 plus 7.

Row 1: Tr in 7th ch from hk, * ch 1, sk 1 ch, tr in next ch, rep from *, ch 5, turn.
Row 2: Sk 1st tr and ch-1 sp, * tr in next tr, ch 1, sk next ch-1 sp, rep from *, ending row with tr in 2nd ch of tch, ch 5, turn.
Rep Row 2 for pattern.

3. Multiples of 3 plus 4.

Row 1: Tr in 5th ch from hk, * ch 1, tr in next ch, sk next ch, tr in next ch, rep from *, ending row with tr in last ch, ch 4, turn.
Row 2: * (Tr, ch 1, tr) in next ch-1 sp, rep from *, ending row with tr in top of tch, ch 4, turn.
Rep Row 2 for pattern.

4. Multiples of 2 plus 1.

Row 1: Sc in 2nd ch from hk and in each ch across row, ch 1, turn.
Row 2: Sc in each sc across row, ch 1, turn.
Row 3: Sc in each sc across row, ch 5, turn.
Row 4: Sk 1st sc, * tr in next sc, ch 1, sk next sc, rep from *, ending row with tr in last sc, ch 1, turn.
Row 5: Sk 1st tr, * 2 sc in next ch-1 sp, rep from *, ending row with 2 sc in tch, ch 1, turn.
Rep Rows 2-5 for pattern.

5. Multiples 4 plus 7.

Row 1: Dc in 5th ch from hk, dc in next ch, * tr in next 2 ch, dc in next 2 ch, rep from *, ending row with tr in last ch, ch 6, turn.
Row 2: * Sk next 2 dc, dc in next 2 tr, ch 2, rep from *, ending row with tr in tch, ch 4, turn.
Row 3: * 2 dc in next ch-2 sp, tr in next 2 dc, rep from *, ending row with 2 dc in last ch-2 sp, tr in tch, ch 6, turn.
Rep Rows 2-3 for pattern, end with Row 3.

6. Multiples of 4 plus 3.

Row 1: Sk 5 ch, * (2 tr, ch 3, 2 tr) in next ch, sk 3 ch, rep from *, ending row with tr in last ch, ch 4, turn.
Row 2: * (2 tr, ch 3, 2 tr) in next ch-3 sp, rep from *, ending row with tr in top of tch, ch 4, turn.
Rep Row 2 for pattern.

7. Multiples of 6 plus 5.

Row 1: Tr in 5th ch from hk, tr in next 2 ch, * ch 3, tr in next ch, sk 2 ch, tr in next 3 ch, rep from *, ending row with ch 3, tr in next ch, sk 2 ch, tr in last ch, ch 4, turn.
Row 2: * 3 tr in next ch-3 sp, ch 3, tr in same ch-3 sp, rep from *, ending row with tr in tch, ch 4, turn.
Rep Row 2 for pattern.

8. Multiples of 12 plus 10.

Row 1: Tr in 5th ch from hk, tr in next 5 ch, * ch 5, sk 5 ch, tr in next 7 ch, rep from * across row, ch 4, turn.
Row 2: Sk 1st tr, tr in next 6 tr, * ch 5, tr in next 7 tr, rep from *, ending row with tr in last 6 tr, tr in tch, ch 4, turn.
Row 3: Sk 1st tr, tr in next 5 tr, * ch 5, tr around center of next ch-5 sp, ch 5, sk next tr, tr in next 5 tr, rep from *, ending row with tr in tch, ch 5, turn.
Row 4: Sk 1st 2 tr, tr in next 3 tr, * ch 6, sk next tr and 5 ch, (tr, ch 2, tr) in next tr, ch 6, sk next 5 ch and tr, tr in next 3 tr, rep from *, ending row with ch 1, sk last tr, tr in tch, ch 6, turn.
Row 5: Sk 1st tr, * sc in center tr of next 3-tr group, ch 5, (1 tr, 3-ch picot in next ch-2 sp) 5 times, ch 5, rep from *, ending row with sc in center tr of next 3-tr group, ch 3, dc in tch.

9. Multiples of 9 plus 12.

Row 1: Tr in 5th ch from hk, * ch 4 , sk 1 ch, dc in next 3 ch, ch 4, sk 1 ch, tr in next 4 ch, rep from *, ending row with tr in last 2 ch, ch 1, turn.

Row 2: Sc in 1st 2 tr, * ch 4, sk 4 ch, dc in next 3 dc, ch 4, sk 4 ch, sc in next 4 tr, rep from *, ending row with sc in last tr, sc in tch, ch 1, turn.

Row 3: Sc in 1st 2 sc, * ch 4, sk 4 ch, dc in next 3 dc, ch 4, sk 4 ch, sc in next 4 sc, rep from *, ending row with ch 4, sc in last 2 sc, ch 1, turn.

Row 4: Rep Row 3 except ch 4, turn.

Row 5: Sk 1st sc, tr in next sc, * ch 1, sk 4 ch, dc in next 3 dc, sk 4 ch, (ch 1, tr in next sc) 4 times, rep from *, ending row with ch 1, tr in last 2 sc, ch 3, turn.

Row 6: Sk 1st tr, dc in next tr, * dc in next ch-1 sp, dc in next 3 dc, (dc in next ch-1 sp, dc in next tr) 4 times, rep from *, ending row with dc in last ch-1 sp, dc in last tr, dc in tch, ch 4, turn.

Row 7: Sk 1st dc, tr in next dc, * ch 4, sk next dc, dc in next 3 dc, ch 4, (sk next dc, tr in next dc) 4 times, rep from *, ending row with ch 4, sk next dc, tr in last dc, tr in tch, ch 1, turn.

Rep Rows 2-7 for pattern.

10. Multiples of 18 plus 3.

Row 1: Dc in 5th ch from hk, * ch 2, sk 2 ch, dc in next ch, rep from *, ending row with dc in last ch, ch 3, turn.

Row 2: Sk 1st dc, dc in next dc, * (ch 2, dc in next dc) 2 times, 2 dc in next ch-2 sp, dc in next dc, (ch 2, dc in next dc) 3 times, rep from *, ending row with dc in tch, ch 3, turn.

Row 3: Sk 1st dc, dc in next dc, * ch 2, dc in next dc, 2 dc in next ch-2 sp, dc in next dc, ch 2, sk 2 dc, dc in next dc, 2 dc in next ch-2 sp, dc in next dc, (ch 2, dc in next dc) 2 times, rep from *, ending row with dc in tch, ch 3, turn.

Row 4: Sk 1st dc, * dc in next dc, 2 dc in next ch-2 sp, dc in next dc, ch 5, sk 3 dc, tr in center of next ch-2 sp, ch 5, sk 3 dc, dc in next dc, 2 dc in next ch-2 sp, dc in next dc, ch 2 , rep from *, ending row with dc in tch, ch 3, turn.

Row 5: Sk 1st dc, dc in next dc, * ch 5, sk 3 dc and 4 ch, sc in next ch, dc in tr, sc in next ch, ch 5, sk 4 ch and 3 dc, dc in next dc, 2 dc in next ch-2 sp, dc in next dc, rep from *, ending row with dc in last dc, dc in tch, ch 3, turn.

Row 6: Sk 1st dc, * dc in next dc, dc in next 3 ch, ch 5, sc in next (sc, dc, sc), ch 5, sk 2 ch, dc in next 3 ch, dc in next dc, ch 2, sk 2 dc, rep from *, ending row with dc in last dc, dc in tch, ch 3, turn.

Row 7: Sk 1st dc, dc in next dc, * ch 2, sk 2 dc, dc in next dc, ch 5, tr in center sc of 3-sc group, ch 5, dc in next dc, ch 2, sk 2 dc, dc in next dc, ch 2, dc in next dc, rep from *, ending row with dc in tch, ch 3, turn.

Row 8: Sk 1st dc, dc in next dc, * ch 2, dc in next dc, dc in next 3 ch, ch 2, sk next (ch 2, tr, ch 2), dc in next 3 ch, dc in next dc, (ch 2, dc in next dc) 2 times, rep from *, ending row with dc in last dc, dc in tch, ch 3, turn.

Row 9: Sk 1st dc, dc in next dc, * ch 2, dc in next dc, ch 2, sk 2 dc, dc in next dc, 2 dc in next ch-2 sp, dc in next dc, ch 2, sk 2 dc, dc in next dc, (ch 2, dc in next dc) 2 times, rep from *, ending row with dc in last dc, dc in tch, ch 3, turn.

Row 10: Sk 1st dc, dc in next dc, (ch 2, dc in next dc) 2 times, * ch 2, sk 2 dc, dc in next dc, (ch 2, dc in next dc) 5 times, rep from *, ending row with dc in last dc, dc in tch, ch 3, turn.

Rep Rows 2-10 for pattern.

11. Multiples of 9 plus 15.

Row 1: Tr in 5th ch from hk, * ch 3, sk 3 ch, sc in next ch, ch 3, sc in next ch, ch 3, sk 3 ch, 4 tr in next ch, rep from *, ending row with ch 3, tr in last 2 ch, ch 1, turn.

Row 2: Sc in 1st tr, * ch 3, sk next (tr, ch-3 sp, sc), 4 tr in next ch-3 sp, ch 3, sk next (sc, ch-3 sp, tr), sc in next tr, ch 3, sc in next tr, rep from *, ending row with ch 3, sc in tch, ch 4, turn.

Row 3: Tr in sc, ch 3, sk next ch-3 sp and tr, * sc in next tr, ch 3, sc in next tr, ch 3, sk next (tr, ch-3 sp, sc), 4 dc in next ch-3 sp, ch 3, sk next (sc, ch-3 sp, tr), rep from *, ending row with ch 3, 2 tr in last sc, ch 1, turn.

Rep Rows 2-3 for pattern.

12. Multiples of 11 plus 6.

Row 1: Dc in 5th ch from hk and in each ch across row, ch 3, turn.
Row 2: Sk 1st dc, dc in next 2 dc, * ch 3, sk 2 dc, tr in next 4 dc, ch 3, sk 2 dc, dc in next 3 dc, rep from *, ending row with dc in last 2 dc, dc in tch, ch 3, turn.
Row 3: Sk 1st dc, dc in next 2 dc, * ch 3, sc in next 4 tr, ch 3, dc in next 3 dc, rep from *, ending row with dc in last 2 dc, dc in tch, ch 3, turn.
Row 4: Sk 1st dc, dc in next 2 dc, * ch 3, sc in next 4 sc, ch 3, dc in next 3 dc, rep from *, ending row with dc in last 2 dc, dc in tch, ch 3, turn.
Row 5: Sk 1st dc, dc in next 2 dc, * ch 3, sc in next 4 sc, ch 3, dc in next 3 dc, rep from *, ending row with dc in last 2 dc, dc in tch, ch 3, turn.
Row 6: Sk 1st dc, dc in next 2 dc, * ch 3, tr in next 4 sc, ch 3, dc in next 3 dc, rep from *, ending row with dc in last 2 dc, dc in tch, ch 3, turn.
Row 7: Sk 1st dc, dc in next 2 dc, * 2 dc in next ch-3 sp, dc in next 4 tr, 2 dc in next ch-3 sp, dc in next 3 dc, rep from *, ending row with dc in last 2 dc, dc in tch, ch 3, turn.
Rep Rows 2-7 for pattern.

13. Multiples 15 plus 10.

Row 1: 3 tr in 5th ch from hk, * sk 4 ch, 4 tr in next ch, ch 5, sk 4 ch, dc in next ch, ch 5, sk 4 ch, 4 tr in next ch, rep from * across row, ch 4, turn.
Row 2: 3 tr in 1st tr, * sk next 6 tr, 4 tr in next tr, ch 5, dc in next dc, ch 5, 4 tr in next tr, rep from *, ending row with sk next 6 tr, 4 dc in tch, ch 4, turn.

Row 3: 3 tr in 1st tr, * sk next 6 tr, 4 tr in next tr, ch 5, dc in next dc, ch 5, 4 tr in next tr, rep from *, ending row with sk next 6 tr, 4 tr in tch, ch 6, turn.

Row 4: * Dc in sp bet next 2 4-tr group, ch 5, sk 4 tr and 2 ch, 4 tr in next ch, sk (ch 2, dc, ch 2), 4 tr in next ch, ch 5, rep from *, ending row with dc in sp bet last 2 4-tr group, ch 3, dc in tch, ch 6, turn.

Row 5: Sk 1st dc, * dc in next dc, ch 5, 4 tr in next tr, sk 6 tr, 4 tr in next tr, ch 5, rep from *, ending row with dc in next dc, ch 3, dc in 4th ch of tch, ch 6, turn.

Row 6: Sk 1st dc, * dc in next dc, ch 5, 4 tr in next tr, sk 6 tr, 4 tr in next tr, ch 5, rep from *, ending row with dc in next dc, ch 3, dc in 4th ch of tch, ch 4, turn.

Row 7: 3 tr in 1st dc, sk (ch 3, dc, ch 2), 4 dc in next ch, * ch 5, dc in sp bet next 2 4-dc group, ch 5, sk 4 tr and 2 ch, 4 tr in next ch, sk (ch 2, dc, ch 2), 4 tr in next ch, rep from *, ending row with 4 tr in 3rd ch of tch, ch 4, turn.

Rep Rows 2-7 for pattern.

14. Multiples of 3 plus 7.

Row 1: Dc in 7th ch from hk, * ch 2, sk 2 ch, dc in next ch, rep from * across row, ch 4, turn.

Row 2: Tr in 1st dc, * 3 tr in next dc, rep from *, ending row with 2 tr in 3rd ch of tch, ch 5, turn.

Row 3: * Sk 1st 3 tr, dc in next tr (center tr of 3-tr group), * ch 2, sk next 2 tr, dc in next tr, rep from *, ending row with ch 2, dc in tch, ch 4, turn.

Rep Rows 2-3 for pattern.

15. Multiples of 3 plus 4.

Row 1: Dc in 4th ch from hk and in each ch across row, ch 4, turn.

Row 2: Sk 1st dc, tr in next dc, * ch 1, sk next dc, tr in next 2 dc, rep from *, ending row with tr in last dc, tr in tch, ch 4, turn.

Row 3: 2 tr in 1st ch-1 sp, * ch 1, 2 tr in next ch-1 sp, rep from *, ending row with ch 1, tr in tch, ch 3, turn.

Row 4: Sk 1st tr, dc in each ch-1 sp and tr across row, dc in tch, ch 4, turn.

Rep Rows 2-4 for pattern.

Patterns Using Treble Crochet

Flowered Trellis Sweater

Materials Needed: *Approximately 30 ounces of sport weight, white cotton thread; size E crochet hook; 12 4mm pearl beads; 4-1/2" white buttons, sewing needle and thread; craft glue.*

Finished Size: *Chest = 36"*
Sleeve length = 17"

Note: To increase size, increase by multiples of 2, see stitch design #2 in this chapter.

Gauge: *6 tr = 1"*
2 rows of tr = 1"

Ch 287, sweater is worked in 1 piece until reaching armholes.

Row 1: Tr in 7th ch from hk, * ch 1, sk 1 ch, tr in next ch, rep from * , ch 5, turn.

Row 2: Sk 1st tr and ch-1 sp, *tr in next tr, ch 1, sk next ch-1 sp, rep from *, ending row with tr in 2nd ch of tch, ch 5, turn.

Rows 3-20: Rep Row 2.

Armhole Shaping

Row 21: Sk 1st tr and ch-1 sp, *tr in next tr, ch 1, sk next ch-1 sp, rep from *32 times, tr in next tr, ch 5, turn.

Rows 23-33: Rep Row 2.

Shoulder Shaping

Row 34: Rep Row 21 except rep from *21 times, tr in next tr, F.O. Rep Rows 21-34 to other front side, reversing shaping.

Sweater Back

Row 21: Sk 1 tr on Row 20, join with sl st to next tr, ch 5, * tr in next tr, ch 1, sk next ch-1 sp, rep from * across, leaving last tr before armhole shaping unworked.

Rows 23-31: Rep Row 2.

Back Sholder Shaping

Row 33: Rep row 21 except rep from *21 times, tr in next tr, ch 5, turn.

Row 34: Rep row 2, F.O. Rep to other side oof back, reversing shaping.

Sleeves (make 2)
Ch 67.

Rows 1-2: Rep Rows 1 and 2 of sweater.

Row 3: Tr in 1st tr (inc made), ch 1, *tr in next tr, ch 1, sk next ch-1 sp, rep from *ending row with (tr, ch 1, tr) in last tr (inc made).

Row 4: Sk 1st tr and ch-1 sp, * tr in next tr, ch 1, sk next ch-1 sp, rep from * ending row with tr in 2nd ch of tch, ch 5, turn.

Rows 5-30: Rep Rows 3-4 alternately, **F.O.** at end of Row 30. Sew sleeve tog, ease in armhole opening and sew in place, rep to other sleeve.

Sweater Edging

Row 1: Join with sl st to bottom edge of sweater, ch 4, tr evenly across, ch 4, turn.

Row 2: Sk 1st tr, tr in each tr across, tr in top of ch 4, **F.O.**

Rep above directions to sweater neckline, both sides of sweater front opening and sleeve edges.

Flower (make 12)

Ch 8, join with sl st to form a ring.

Rnd 1: Ch 1, 12 sc in ring, join with sl st to beg sc.

Rnd 2: Ch 1, sc in 1st sc, * ch 3, sk next sc, sc in next sc, rep from * around, join with sl st to beg sc.

Rnd 3: *In next ch-3 sp work (sc, ch 3, 3 dc, ch 3, sc), rep from * around, **F.O.** Sew 4 flowers evenly spaced on right front sweater edge, sew 4 buttons behind flowers on underneath side of same edging strip. To close front of sweater, slip buttons through tr posts of other front edging strip. Place remaining 8 flowers randomly on sweater fronts, sew securely.

Leaves (make 2)

Ch 8.

Row 1: Sc in 2nd ch from hk, hdc in next ch, dc in next 3 ch, hdc in next ch, sc in last ch, ch 2, turn and work in bottom of row just completed.

Row 2: Sc in sc, hdc in hdc, dc in next 3 dc, hdc in next hdc, sc in last sc, **F.O.** Sew as desired to flower edges.

Flower Vines

Make chs desired length and sew or glue to sweater between flowers. Sew pearl beads to flower centers.

Decorative Mantel Trim

Materials Needed: Approximately 450 yards of #20 white cotton thread; #10 steel crochet hook.

Finished size: 96" x 2"

Gauge: 7 tr = 1"

5 rows of tr = 2"

Ch 682.

Row 1: Tr in 5th ch from hk, tr in next 5 ch, * ch 5, sk 5 ch, tr in next 7 ch, rep from * across row, ch 4, turn.

Row 2: Sk 1st tr, tr in next 6 tr, * ch 5, tr in next 7 tr, rep from *, ending row with tr in last 6 tr, tr in tch, ch 4, turn.

Row 3: Sk 1st tr, tr in next 5 tr, * ch 5, tr around center of next ch-5 sp, ch 5, sk next tr, tr in next 5 tr, rep from *, ending row with tr in tch, ch 5, turn.

Row 4: Sk 1st 2 tr, tr in next 3 tr, * ch 6, sk next tr and 5 ch, (tr, ch 2, tr) in next tr, ch 6, sk next 5 ch and tr, tr in next 3 tr, rep from *, ending row with ch 1, sk last tr, tr in tch, ch 6, turn.

Row 5: Sk 1st tr, *sc in center tr of next 3-tr group, ch 5, (1 tr, 3-ch picot in next ch-2 sp) 5 times, ch 5, rep from *, ending row with sc in center tr of next 3-tr group, ch 3, dc in tch, **F.O.**

Note: To obtain the correct size for your mantle divide your mantle length by the multiple gauge (refer to design #8 in this chapter). Our mantle measured 96" (and after making a sample of the pattern, it

was determined that the multiple of 12 measured 1.7" (The length needed was divided by the multiple gauge (96 ÷ 1.7 = 56 rounded). To achieve the desired length, take the quotient of 56 and multiply by 12 and add 10. (56 x 12 = 672 + 10 = 682). This would be your number of beginning chains. Refer to Chapter 1: Mastering Multiples, for other information.

Evening Clutch Bag

Materials Needed: Approximately 250 yards of #20 metallic thread; #11 steel crochet hook; 32" length of 2" ribbon to match thread; two 7" lengths of plastic canvas; black sewing thread; sewing needle; black cloth; snap; yarn needle.

Finished Size: 8" x 7"

Gauge: 12 tr = 1"

4 rows of tr = 1"

Purse Side (Make 2)

Note: Tch counts as tr throughout pattern.

Ch 83.

Row 1: Tr in 5th ch from hk and in each ch across row, ch 4, turn. (80 tr)

Row 2: Sk 1st tr, tr in each tr across row, tr in top of tch, ch 4, turn.

Row 3: Tr in 1st tr (inc made), tr in each tr across row, 2 tr in tch, ch 4, turn. (82 tr)

Rows 4-16: Rep pattern of Row 3: Inc at beg and end of each row, you will have 108 tr at end of Row 16.

Row 17: * Tr in next 10 tr, 2 tr in next tr, rep from *, ending row with tr in last 8 tr, 2 tr in tch, ch 4, turn. (119 tr)

Row 18: Rep Row 17. (131 tr)

Row 19: * Tr in next 10 tr, 2 tr in next tr, rep from *, ending row with tr in last 9 tr, 2 tr in tch, **F.O.**

Joining: Using yarn needle and metallic thread, whip st 2 purse sides tog along side edges and bottom row. Weave thread over and under tr of last row for 1 purse side, pull gently to gather. Rep with rem purse side.

Finishing: Cut ribbon into 4 equal lengths, place 2 ribbon pieces tog (right sides out). Fold ends 1/4", sew ends tog with black thread and sewing needle. Sew bottom ribbon edges to top gathered row of purse side using a whip st, cut plastic canvas to fit and place between 2 ribbon pieces, sew top ribbon edges tog. Rep with rem 2 ribbon pieces and 2nd purse side. Sew snap to insides of ribbon band.

Child's Corner Cuddler

This popular item is usually used in a child's room to store toys. However, it could serve many useful purposes. This variation is easy to make and very durable.

Materials Needed: Approximately 260 yards of rug yarn (any color); size K crochet hook; three 2" rings.

Finished Size: 50 inches on each of three sides.

Note: You will be working from the center out, the instructions for Rnd 4 are for one side of a three sided triangle. Each time you turn your work you will be working one side of triangular shape.

Rnd 1: Ch 8, 1 tr in first ch made, forming a small triangle.

Rnd 2: Ch 8, 1 dc in the top of triangle, (same sp as 1st ch in Rnd 1), ch 3, 1 tr in same sp. (Pretzel shape formed.)

Rnd 3: Turning work to right, so that last tr made is horizontal, ch 8, 1 dc in middle of tr, ch 3, dc in next ch-8 lp, ch 3, tr in sm sp.

Rnd 4: Turning work as before, ch 8, dc in middle of tr, ch 3, dc in next lp, ch 3, (dc, ch 3, tr) in last lp.

Rnds 5-43: Rep Rnd 4 adding one (ch 3, dc, ch 3) for each rnd, do not **F.O.**

Finishing: Sl st around all three sides, attaching rings at each corner with a sl st, **F.O.**

Chapter 6

V-Stitch and Shell

1. Multiples of 2 plus 5.

Row 1: 2 dc in 5th ch from hk, * sk 1 ch, 2 dc in next ch, rep from *, ending row with sk 1 ch, dc in last ch, ch 3, turn.
Row 2: Sk 1st 2 dc, * 2 dc in sp before next dc, sk next 2 dc, rep from *, ending row with dc in tch, ch 3, turn.
Rep Row 2 for pattern.

2. Multiples of 2 plus 4.

Row 1: Sc in 2nd ch from hk and in each ch across row, ch 3, turn.
Row 2: Dc in 1st sc, * sk next sc, 2 dc in next sc, rep from *, ending row with dc in last sc, ch 1, turn.
Row 3: Sc in each dc across row, sc in tch, ch 3, turn.
Rep Rows 2-3 for pattern.

3. Multiples of 4 plus 6.

Row 1: 4 dc in 6th ch from hk, * sk 3 ch, 4 dc in next ch, rep from *, ending row with 3 dc in last ch, ch 1, turn.
Row 2: Sc in each dc across row, sc in tch, ch 3, turn.
Row 3: 2 dc in 1st sc, * sk 3 sc, 4 dc in next sc, rep from *, ending row with sk 2 sc, dc in last sc, ch 1, turn.
Rep Rows 2-3 for pattern.

4. Multiples of 3 plus 2.

Row 1: Sc in 2nd ch from hk, * ch 2, sk 2 ch, sc in next ch, rep from * across row, ch 3, turn.
Row 2: 3 dc in each ch-2 sp across, ending row with dc in last sc, ch 1, turn.
Row 3: Sc in 1st dc, * ch 2, sk 3 dc, sc in sp before next dc, rep from *, ending row with ch 2, sk last dc, sc in tch, ch 3, turn.
Rep Rows 2-3 for pattern.

5. Multiples of 3 plus 5.

Row 1: (Dc, ch 2, sc) in 4th ch from hk, * sk 2 ch, (2 dc, ch 2, sc) in next ch, rep from *, ending row with dc in last ch, ch 3, turn.
Row 2: * (2 dc, ch 2, sc) in next ch-2 sp, rep from *, ending row with sc in tch, ch 3, turn.
Rep Row 2 for pattern.

6. Multiples of 6 plus 4.

Row 1: Dc in 4th ch from hk, * ch 2, sk 1 ch, sc in next 2 ch, ch 2, sk 1 ch, dc in next 2 ch, rep from *, ending row with dc in last 2 ch, ch 1, turn.
Row 2: Sc in 1st 2 dc, * ch 2, sk ch-2 sp, dc in next 2 sc, ch 2, sk ch-2 sp, sc in next 2 dc, rep from *, ending row with sc in last dc, sc in tch, ch 3, turn.
Row 3: Sk 1st sc, dc in next sc, * ch 2, sk ch-2 sp, sc in next 2 dc, ch 2, sk ch-2 sp, dc in next 2 sc, rep from *, ending row with dc in last 2 sc, ch 1, turn.
Rep Rows 2-3 for pattern.

7. Multiples of 4 plus 3.

Row 1: (3 dc, ch 1, 3 dc) in 7th ch from hk, * sk 3 ch, (3 dc, ch 1, 3 dc) in next ch, rep from *, ending row

with sk 3 ch, dc in last ch, ch 3, turn.
Row 2: *(3 dc, ch 1, 3 dc) in next ch-1 sp, rep from *, ending row with dc in tch, ch 3, turn.
Rep Row 2 for pattern.

8. Multiples of 6 plus 1.

Row 1: (2 dc, ch 1, 2 dc) in 5th ch from hk, * sk 2 ch, (dc, ch 1, dc) in next ch, sk 2 ch, (2dc, ch 1, 2 dc) in next ch, rep from *, ending row with sk 1 ch, dc in last ch, ch 3, turn.
Row 2: * (2 dc, ch 1, 2 dc) in next ch-1 sp, (dc, ch 1, dc) in next ch-1 sp, rep from *, ending row with (2 dc, ch 1, 2 dc) in last ch-1 sp, dc in tch, ch 3, turn.
Rep Row 2 for pattern.

9. Multiples of 8 plus 6.

Row 1: Sc in 2nd ch from hk and in each ch across row, ch 1, turn.
Row 2: Sc in 1st sc, * ch 5, sk 3 sc, sc in next sc, rep from * across row, ch 1, turn.
Row 3: Sc in 1st sc, ch 3, sc in center of 1st ch-5 sp, * ch 3, 3 dc in next ch-5 sp, ch 3, sc in center of next ch-5 sp, rep from *, ending row with ch 3, sc in last sc, ch 1, turn.
Row 4: Sc in 1st sc, ch 5, sk 1st ch-3 sp, * sc in next ch-3 sp, ch 5, rep from *, ending row with ch 5, sk last ch-3 sp, sc in last sc, ch 1, turn.
Row 5: Sc in 1st sc, ch 3, 3 dc in 1st ch-5 sp, * ch 3, sc in center of ch-5 sp, ch 3, 3 dc in next ch-5 sp, rep from *, ending row with ch 3, sc in last sc, ch 1, turn.
Row 6: Sc in 1st sc, ch 5, sc in 2nd ch-3 sp, * ch 5, sc in next ch-3 sp, rep from *, ending row with ch 5, sk last ch-3 sp, sc in last sc, ch 1, turn.
Rep Rows 3-6 for pattern.

10. Multiples of 6 plus 1.

Row 1: 3 dc in 4th ch from hk, * sk 2 ch, sc in next ch, sk 2 ch, 4 dc in next ch, rep from *, ending row with sc in last ch, ch 3, turn.

∇ *V-Stitch* ∇ *Shell*

Row 2: 3 dc in 1st sc, * sc bet 2nd and 3rd dc of next 4-dc group, 4 dc in next sc, rep from *, ending row with sc in tch, ch 3, turn.
Rep Row 2 for pattern.

11. Multiples of 10 plus 4.

Row 1: (Dc, ch 3, dc) in 4th ch from hk, * ch 3, sk 3 ch, sc in next 3 ch, ch 3, sk 3 ch, (dc, ch 3, dc) in next ch, rep from * across row, ch 3, turn.
Row 2: * 7 dc in next ch-3 sp, ch 3, sc in 2nd sc of 3-sc group, ch 3, sk next ch-3 sp, rep from *, ending row with 7 dc, dc in tch, ch 1, turn.
Row 3: * Sc in each dc of next 7-dc group, ch 5, rep from *, ending row with 7 sc, ch 6, turn.
Row 4: * Sk 2 sc, sc in next 3 sc, ch 3, (dc, ch 3, dc) in 3rd ch of next ch-5 sp, ch 3, rep from *, ending row with sc in next 3 sc, ch 3, dc in last sc, ch 6, turn.
Row 5: * Sc in 2nd sc of 3-sc group, ch 3, sk next ch-3 sp, 7 dc in next ch-3 sp, ch 3, rep from *, ending row with ch 3, sc in 2nd sc of last 3-sc group, ch 3, dc in 4th ch of tch, ch 1, turn.
Row 6: Sc in dc, ch 5, * sc in next 7 dc, ch 5, rep from *, ending row with sc in 4th ch of tch, ch 3, turn.
Row 7: * (Dc, ch 3, dc) in 3rd ch of next ch-5 sp, ch 3, sk 2 sc, sc in next 3 sc, ch 3, rep from *, ending row with (dc, ch 3, dc) in 3rd ch of last ch-5 sp, dc in last sc, ch 3, turn.
Rep Rows 2-7 for pattern.

12. Multiples of 13 plus 4.

Row 1: Dc in 4th ch from hk and in each ch across row, ch 3, turn.
Row 2: Sk 1st dc, dc in next 3 dc, * ch 3, sk 3 dc, sc in next dc, ch 3, sk 3 dc, dc in next 6 dc, rep from *, ending row with dc in last 3 dc, dc in tch, ch 3, turn.
Row 3: Sk 1st dc, dc in next 3 dc, *(ch 3, sc in next ch-3 sp) 2 times, ch 3, dc in next 6 dc, rep from *, ending row with dc in last 3 dc, dc in tch, ch 3, turn.
Row 4: Sk 1st dc, dc in next 3 dc, * sk next ch-3 sp, 7 dc in next ch-3 sp, dc in next 6 dc, rep from *, ending row with dc in last 3 dc, dc in tch, ch 3, turn.
Rep Rows 2-4 for pattern.

13. Multiples of 6 plus 4.

Row 1: 2 dc in 4th ch from hk, * sk 2 ch, sc in next ch, sk 2 ch, 4 dc in next ch, rep from *, ending row with 3 dc in last ch, ch 1, turn.
Row 2: Sc in 1st dc, * 4 dc in next sc, sc bet 2nd and 3rd dc of 4-dc group, rep from *, ending row with 4 dc in last sc, sc in tch, ch 3, turn.
Row 3: 2 dc in 1st sc, * sc bet 2nd and 3rd dc of 4-dc group, 4 dc in next sc, rep from *, ending row with 3 dc in last sc, 1ch, turn.
Rep Row 2-3 for pattern.

14. Multiples of 6 plus 4.

Row 1: Dc in 4th ch from hk, * sk 2 ch, 5 dc in next ch, sk 2 ch, 2 dc in next ch, rep from *, ending row with 2 dc in last ch, ch 3, turn.
Row 2: 2 dc in 1st dc, * 2 dc in 3rd dc of 5-dc group, 5 dc in center sp of 2-dc group, rep from *, ending row with 3 dc in tch, ch 3, turn.
Row 3: Dc in 1st dc, * 5 dc in center sp of 2-dc group, 2 dc in 3rd dc of 5-dc group, rep from *, ending row with dc in last dc, dc in tch, ch 3, turn.
Rep Rows 2-3 for pattern.

15. Multiples of 3.

Row 1: 2 dc in 3rd ch from hk, * sk 2 ch, (sc, 2 dc) in next ch, rep from *, ending row with sc in last ch, ch 2, turn.
Row 2: 2 dc in 1st sc, * (sc, 2 dc) in next sc, rep from *, ending row with (sc, 2 dc) in tch, ch 2, turn.
Rep Row 2 for pattern.

V-Stitch Shell

16. Multiples of 3 plus 6.

Row 1: (Dc, ch 1, dc) in 6th ch from hk, * sk 2 ch, (dc, ch 1, dc) in next ch, rep from *, ending row with sk 2 ch, dc in last ch, ch 3, turn.

Row 2: * (2 dc, ch 1, 2 dc) in next ch-1 sp, rep from *, ending row with dc in tch, ch 3, turn.

Row 3: * (Dc, ch 1, dc) in next ch-1 sp, rep from *, ending row with dc in tch, ch 3, turn.

Rep Rows 2-3 for pattern.

17. Multiples of 6 plus 2.

Row 1: Sc in 2nd ch from hk, * sk 2 ch, 5 dc in next ch, sk 2 ch, sc in next ch, rep from * across row, ch 3, turn.

Row 2: 2 dc in 1st sc, * sk 2 dc, sc through back lp only of next dc, sk 2 dc, 5 dc through back lp only of next sc, rep from *, ending row with 3 dc in last sc, ch 1, turn.

Row 3: Sc in 1st dc, * sk 2 dc, 5 dc through back lp only of next sc, sk 2 dc, sc through back lp only of next dc, rep from *, ending row with sc in tch, ch 3, turn.

Rep Rows 2-3 for pattern.

18. Multiples of 7 plus 5.

Row 1: Sc in 2nd ch from hk, sk 2 ch, 3 dc in next ch, * ch 3, sk 3 ch, sc in next ch, sk 2 ch, 3 dc in next ch, rep from * across row, ch 1, turn.

Row 2: Sc in 1st dc, sk 2 dc, 3 dc in next sc, * ch 3, sc in next ch-3 sp, sk 3 dc, 3 dc in next sc, rep from * across row, 1ch, turn.

Rep Row 2 for pattern.

19. Multiples of 6 plus 7.

Row 1: 2 dc in 4th ch from hk, * sk 2 ch, dc in next ch, sk 2 ch, 5 dc in next ch, rep from *, ending row with sk 2 ch, dc in last ch, ch 3, turn.

Row 2: 2 dc in 1st dc, * sk 2 dc, dc in next dc, sk 2 dc, 5 dc in next dc, rep from *, ending row with dc in tch, ch 3, turn.
Rep Row 2 for pattern.

20. Multiples of 6 plus 7.

Row 1: 3 dc in 4th ch from hk, * sk 2 ch, sc in next ch, sk 2 ch, 5 dc in next ch, rep from *, ending row with sc in last ch, ch 3, turn.
Row 2: 3 dc in back lp only of 1st sc, * sk 2 dc, sc in back lp only of next dc, sk 2 dc, 5 dc in back lp only of next sc, rep from *, ending row with sc in tch, ch 3, turn.
Rep Row 2 for pattern.

21. Multiples of 6 plus 5.

Row 1: Dc in 4th ch from hk, * sk 2 ch, (3 dc, ch 2, 3 dc) in next ch, sk 2 ch, dc in next ch, rep from *, ending row with dc in last 2 ch, ch 3, turn.
Row 2: Dc in 2nd dc, * (3 dc, ch 2, 3 dc) in next ch-2 sp, sk 3 dc, dc in next dc, rep from *, ending row with dc in last dc, dc in tch, ch 3, turn.
Rep Row 2 for pattern.

22. Multiples of 8 plus 5.

Row 1: Dc in 5th ch from hk, * sk 3 ch, (dc, ch 3, dc) in next ch, sk 3 ch, (dc, ch 1, dc) in next ch, rep from * across row, ch 4, turn.
Row 2: Dc in ch-1 sp, * 6 dc in next ch-3 sp, (dc, ch 1, dc) in next ch-1 sp, rep from *, ending row with (dc, ch 1, dc) in tch sp, ch 4, turn.
Row 3: Dc in ch-1 sp, * sk 1st 2 dc of 6-dc group, dc in next dc, ch 3, dc in next dc, (dc, ch 1, dc) in next ch-1 sp, rep from *, ending row with (dc, ch 1, dc) in tch sp, ch 4, turn.
Rep Rows 2-3 for pattern.

V-Stitch **Shell**

23. Multiples of 6 plus 2.

Row 1: Sc in 2nd ch from hk, ch 5, sc in same ch, * sk 2 ch, 5 dc in next ch, sk 2 ch, (sc, ch 5, sc) in next ch, rep from *, ending row with (sc, ch 2, dc) in last ch, ch 1, turn.
Row 2: Sc in 1st dc, ch 5, sc in 1st ch-2 sp, * sk 2 dc, 5 dc in next dc, (sc, ch 2, dc) in next ch-5 sp, rep from * across row, ch 1, turn.
Rep Row 2 for pattern.

24. Multiples of 6 plus 2.

Row 1: Sc in 2nd ch from hk, sc in next ch, * ch 3, sk 3 ch, sc in next 3 ch, rep from *, ending row with sc in last 2 ch, ch 1, turn.
Row 2: Sc in 1st sc, * 5 dc in next ch-3 sp, sc in 2nd sc of 3-sc group, rep from *, ending row with sc in last sc, ch 5, turn.
Row 3: * Sc in 3 center dc of 5-dc group, ch 3, rep from *, ending row with ch 2, dc in last sc, ch 3, turn.
Row 4: 2 dc in ch-2 sp, * sc in 2nd sc of 3-sc group, 5 dc in next ch-3 sp, rep from *, ending row with sc in 2nd sc of 3-sc group, 3 dc in tch sp, ch 1, turn.
Row 5: Sc in 1st 2 dc, * ch 3, sc in 3 center dc of 5-dc group, rep from *, ending row with ch 3, sc in last dc, sc in tch, ch 1, turn.
Rep Rows 2-5 for pattern.

25. Multiples of 8 plus 6.

Row 1: Sc in 10th ch from hk, * ch 3, sk 3 ch, dc in next ch, ch 3, sk 3 ch, sc in next ch, rep from *, ending row with ch 3, dc in last ch, ch 6, turn.
Row 2: * Sc in 2nd ch of next ch-3 sp, ch 3, sc in 2nd ch of next ch-3 sp, ch 1, dc in next dc, ch 1, rep from

*, ending row with ch 3, sc in 2nd ch of tch, ch 3, dc in 4th ch of tch, ch 3, turn.

Row 3: 2 dc in 1st ch-3 sp, dc in next sc, * 7 dc in next ch-3 sp, dc in next dc, rep from *, ending row with dc in last sc, 2 dc in tch arch, dc in 4th ch of tch, ch 6, turn.

Row 4: * Sk 3 dc of next 7-dc group, sc in next dc, ch 3, sk 3 dc, dc in next dc, ch 3, rep from *, ending row with ch 3, dc in tch, ch 3, turn.

Rep Rows 2-4 for pattern.

26. Multiples of 12 plus 2.

Row 1: Dc in 6th ch from hk, * sk 2 ch, 5 dc in next ch, sk 2 ch, dc in next ch, (ch 1, sk 1 ch, dc in next ch) 3 times, rep from *, ending row with sk 2 ch, dc in next ch, ch 1, dc in last ch, ch 4, turn.

Row 2: Sk 1st dc, dc in next dc, * dc in next 5 dc, dc in next dc, (ch 1, dc in next dc) 3 times, rep from *, ending row with ch 1, dc in 2nd ch of tch, ch 4, turn.

Row 3: Sk 1st dc, * sk next dc, dc in next 5 dc, ch 2, sk next dc, dc in next dc, ch 1, dc in next dc, ch 2, rep from *, ending row with ch 2, dc in 2nd ch of tch, ch 6, turn.

Row 4: Sk 1st dc, * sk 2 ch and next dc, dc in next 3 dc, ch 3, sk next dc and 2 ch, dc in next dc, ch 1, dc in next dc, ch 3, rep from *, ending row with ch 3, dc in 3rd ch of tch, ch 7, turn.

Row 5: Sk 1st dc, * dc in 2nd dc of 3-dc group, ch 4, dc in next dc, ch 1, dc in next dc, ch 4, rep from *, ending row with ch 4, dc in 4th ch of tch, ch 4, turn.

Row 6: * Sk 1 ch, dc in next ch, 5 dc in next dc, sk next 2 ch, dc in next ch, (ch 1, dc in next dc) 2 times, ch 1, rep from *, ending row with ch 1, dc in 5th ch of tch, ch 4, turn.

Rep Rows 2-6 for pattern.

27. Multiples of 10 plus 4.

Row 1: 7 dc in 9th ch from hk, * ch 1, sk 4 ch, dc in next ch, ch 1, sk 4 ch, 7 dc in next ch, rep from *, ending row with ch 1, dc in last ch, ch 4, turn.

Row 2: Dc in 1st dc, * ch 1, sk 2 dc, dc in next 3 dc, ch 1, sk 2 dc, (dc, ch 3, dc) in next dc, rep from *, ending row with ch 1, (dc, ch 1, dc) in 2nd ch of tch, ch 3, turn.

Row 3: 3 dc in 1st ch-1 sp, * ch 1, dc in 2nd dc of 3-dc group, ch 1, 7 dc in ch-3 sp, rep from *, ending row with ch 1, 4 dc in last ch sp, ch 4, turn.

Row 4: Dc in 1st dc, sk next 3 dc, * (dc, ch 3, dc) in next dc, sk 2 dc, dc in next 3 dc, sk next 2 dc, rep from *, ending row with (dc, ch 1, dc) in tch, ch 4, turn.

Row 5: *7 dc in next ch-3 sp, ch 1, dc in 2nd dc of 3-dc group, ch 1, rep from *, ending row with ch 1, dc in 2nd ch of tch, ch 4, turn.

Rep Rows 2-5 for pattern.

28. Multiples of 4 plus 7.

Row 1: In 5th ch from hk * (yo, insert hk, yo, pull through, yo, pull through 2 lps) 2 lps on hk, rep ( ), in next ch, yo, pull through 3 lps on hk, ch 1, rep from *, in next 2 ch and in each ch across, ending row with dc in last ch, ch 3, turn.

Row 2: Dc in top of next closing st of 3 lps, * sk ch-1 sp, 5 dc in top of next closing st, sk ch-1 sp, dc in top of next closing st, rep from *, ending row with dc in tch, ch 4, turn.

Row 3: Rep from (*) of Row 1 in next 2 dc, sk next dc, rep from *, ending row with dc in tch, ch 3, turn.

Rep Rows 2-3 for pattern.

29. Multiples of 14 plus 2.

Row 1: Sc in 2nd ch from hk, * sk 6 ch, 1 elongated dc in next ch (yo, insert hk, pull up a lp 1/2" long, yo, pull through 2 lps, yo, pull through 2 lps), 12 more elongated dc in same ch, sk 6 ch, sc in next ch, rep from *, ending row with sc in last ch, ch 4, turn.

Row 2: 1 elongated dc in 1st sc, *ch 5, sk 6 dc, sc in next dc, ch 5, sk 6 dc, 2 dc in sc bet 13-dc group, rep from *, ending row with 2 elongated dc in last sc, ch 1, turn.

Row 3: Sc bet 1st 2 elongated dc, *13 elongated dc in next sc, sc bet next 2 dc, rep from *, ending row with sc bet last dc and tch, ch 4, turn.

Rep Rows 2-3 for pattern.

30. Multiples of 10 plus 1.

Row 1: Dc in 4th ch from hk, * sk 2 ch, 5 dc in next ch, sk 2 ch, dc in next ch, sk 1 ch, (dc, ch 1, dc) in next ch, sk 1 ch, dc in next ch, rep from *, ending row with last 5-dc group, sk 2 ch, dc in last 2 ch, ch 3, turn.
Row 2: Sk 1st dc, dc in next dc, * ch 2, (yo, insert hk in next dc, yo, pull lp through, yo, pull through 2 lps on hk) 5 times, yo, pull through 6 lps on hk (inverted v-st made), ch 2, dc in next dc, (dc, ch 1, dc) in next ch-1 sp, dc in next dc, rep from *, ending row with dc in last dc, dc in tch, ch 3, turn.
Row 3: Sk 1st dc, dc in next dc, * 5 dc in top of inverted v-st, dc in next dc, (dc, ch 1, dc) in next ch-1 sp, dc in next dc, rep from *, ending row with dc in last dc, dc in tch, ch 3, turn.
Rep Rows 2-3 for pattern.

31. Multiples of 4 plus 4.

Row 1: (2 dc, ch 1, dc) in 4th ch from hk, * sk 3 ch, (3 dc, ch 1, dc) in next ch, rep from *, ending row with sk 3 ch, dc in last ch, ch 3, turn.
Row 2: (2 dc, ch 1, dc) in 1st ch-1 sp, *(3 dc, ch 1, dc) in next ch-1 sp, rep from *, ending row with dc in tch, ch 3, turn.
Rep Row 2 for pattern.

32. Multiples of 5 plus 2.

Row 1: Sc in 2nd ch from hk, * ch 3, 5 dc in ch just worked, sk 4 ch, sc in next ch, rep from *, ending row with sc in last ch, ch 5, turn.
Row 2: *Sk 4 dc, sc in next dc, sc in top of ch-3 sp, ch 3, rep from *, ending row with sc in last dc, sc in last ch-3 sp, ch 3, turn.
Row 3: Sk 1st sc, dc in next sc, * ch 3, dc in next 2 sc, rep from *, ending row with ch 2, dc in 3rd ch of tch, ch 3, turn.
Row 4: Dc in ch-2 sp, * ch 3, 2 dc in next ch-3 sp, rep from *, ending row with ch 3, dc in tch, ch 1, turn.

Row 5: Sc in 1st dc, * ch 3, 5 dc in sp just worked, sk next dc, sc in next dc, rep from *, ending row with sc in tch, ch 5, turn.
Rep Rows 2-5 for pattern.

33. Multiples of 10 plus 12.

Row 1: 2 dc in 6th ch from hk, * sk 5 ch, (2 dc, ch 2, dc) in next ch, (ch 1, sk next ch, dc in next ch) 2 times, ch 2, 2 dc in ch just worked, rep from *, ending row with (2 dc, ch 2, dc) in last ch, ch 5, turn.
Row 2: 2 dc in 1st dc, * sk 4 dc, (2 dc, ch 2, dc) in next dc, (ch 1, dc in next dc) 2 times, ch 2, 2 dc in st just worked, rep from *, ending row with (2 dc, ch 2, dc) in 3rd ch of tch, ch 5, turn.
Rep Row 2 for pattern.

34. Multiples of 16 plus 6.

Row 1: Sc in 9th ch from hk, ch 3, 3 dc in same ch, * sk 4 ch, dc in next ch, sk 4 ch, (3 dc, ch 3, sc) in next ch, ch 3, sk 2 ch, dc in next ch, ch 3, sk 2 ch, (sc, ch 3, 3 dc) in next ch, rep from *, ending row with (3 dc, ch 3, sc) in next ch, ch 3, sk 2 ch, dc in last ch, ch 1, turn.
Row 2: Sc in 1st dc, ch 3, sk next ch-3 sp, * sc in top of next ch-3 sp, ch 3, sk 3 dc, sc in next dc, ch 3, sc in top of next ch-3 sp, ch 3, sc in next dc, ch 3, rep from *, ending row with ch 3, sc in 4th ch of tch, ch 6, turn.
Row 3: *(Sc, ch 3, 3 dc) in next sc, dc in next sc, (3 dc, ch 3, sc) in next sc, ch 3, dc in next sc, ch 3, rep from *, ending row with ch 3, dc in last sc, ch 1, turn.
Rep Rows 2-3 for pattern.

35. Multiples of 6 plus 3.

Row 1: Sc in 2nd ch from hk, sc in next ch, * ch 4, sk 4 ch, sc in next 2 ch, rep from * across row, ch 3, turn.
Row 2: *(2 dc, ch 2, 2 dc) in next ch-4 sp, rep from *, ending row with dc in last sc, ch 5, turn.
Row 3: * 2 sc in next ch-2 sp, ch 4, rep from *, ending row with ch 2, dc in tch, ch 4, turn.
Row 4: 2 dc in next ch-2 sp, * (2 dc, ch 2, 2 dc) in next ch-4 sp, rep from *, ending row with dc in 1st 2 ch of tch, ch 1, dc in 3rd ch of tch, ch 1, turn.
Row 5: Sc in 1st dc, sc in ch-1 sp, * ch 4, 2 sc in next ch-2 sp, rep from *, ending row with 2 sc in tch, ch 3, turn.
Rep Rows 2-5 for pattern.

36. Multiples of 4 plus 9.

Row 1: 2 dc in 5th ch from hk, * ch 2, sk 3 ch, sc in next ch, (ch 2, 1 tr, 2 dc) in same ch, rep from *, ending row with ch 2, sk 3 ch, sc in last ch, ch 4, turn.
Row 2: 2 dc in 1st sc, * ch 2, sk next ch-2 sp, sc in top of next ch-2 sp, ch 2, (tr, 2 dc) in next sc, rep from *, ending row with ch 2, sc in 2nd ch of tch, ch 4, turn.
Row 3: 2 dc in 1st sc, * ch 2, sk next ch-2 sp, (sc, ch 2, tr, 2 dc) in next ch-2 sp, rep from *, ending row with ch 2, sc in 2nd ch of tch, ch 4, turn.
Rep Rows 2-3 for pattern.

37. Multiples of 16 plus 14.

Row 1: Sc in 8th ch from hk, * ch 5, sk 3 ch, sc in next ch, rep from *, ending row with ch 2, sk 1 ch, dc in last ch, ch 1, turn.
Row 2: Sc in 1st dc, * (ch 5, sc in center of next ch-5 arch) 2 times, 8 dc in next ch-5 arch, sc in next ch-5 arch, rep from *, ending row with ch 5, sk 2 ch, sc in next tch, ch 5, turn.
Row 3: Sc in next ch-5 arch, * ch 5, sc in next ch-5 arch, ch 4, sk next dc, dc in next 6 dc, ch 4, sc in next ch-5 arch, ch 5, sc in next ch-5 arch, rep from *, ending row with ch 2, dc in sc, ch 8, turn.
Row 4: Sc in next ch-5 arch, * ch 5, sc in next ch-4 arch, ch 3, sk next dc, dc in next 4 dc, ch 3, sc in ch-4 arch, ch 5, sc in next ch-5 arch, rep from *, ending row with ch 5, dc in 3rd ch of tch, ch 5, turn.
Row 5: *Sc in next ch-5 arch, ch 5, sc in next ch-5 arch, ch 5, sc in next ch-3 arch, ch 3, sk next dc, dc in next 2 dc, ch 3, sc in ch-3 arch, ch 5, sc in next ch-5 arch, ch 5, rep from *, ending row with ch 2, dc in 6th ch of tch, ch 1, turn.
Row 6: Sc in 1st dc, * 8 dc in next ch-5 arch, sc in next ch-5 arch, ch 5, sc in center of 2-dc group, ch 5, sc in next ch-5 arch, rep from *, ending row with 8 dc, sc in 3rd ch of tch, ch 4, turn.
Row 7: * Sk 1st dc, dc in next 6 dc, ch 4, sc in next ch-5 arch, ch 5, sc in next ch-5 arch, ch 4, rep from *, ending row with 6 dc, ch 1, dc in last sc, ch 5, turn.

Row 8: * Sk 1st dc of 6-dc group, dc in next 4 dc, ch 3, sc in next ch-4 arch, ch 5, sc in next ch-5 arch, ch 5, sc in next ch-4 arch, ch 3, rep from *, ending row with 4 dc, ch 2, sk 1 ch, dc in next tch, ch 6, turn.

Row 9: * Sk 1st dc of 4-dc group, dc in next 2 dc, ch 3, sc in next ch-3 arch, (ch 5, sc in next ch-5 arch) 2 times, ch 5, sc in next ch-3 arch, ch 3, rep from *, ending row with ch 3, dc in 3rd ch of tch, ch 5, turn.

Row 10: * Sc in center of 2-dc group, (ch 5, sc in next ch-5 arch) 3 times, ch 5, rep from *, ending row with ch 2, dc in 4th ch of tch, ch 1, turn.

Rep Rows 2-10 for pattern.

38. Multiples of 7 plus 5.

Row 1: Dc in 5th ch from hk, * ch 2, sk 6 ch, (dc, ch 3, dc) in next ch, rep from *, ending row with (dc, ch 1, dc) in last ch, ch 3, turn.

Row 2: 3 dc in ch-1 sp, * 8 dc in next ch-3 sp, rep from *, ending row with 4 dc in bet last dc and tch, ch 4, turn.

Row 3: Dc in 1st dc, * ch 2, sk next 7 dc, (dc, ch 3, dc) in sp before next dc, rep from *, ending row with ch 2, (dc, ch 1, dc) in bet last dc and tch, ch 3, turn.

Rep Rows 2-3 for pattern.

39. Multiples of 12 plus 4.

Row 1: 2 dc in 4th ch from hk, * ch 3, sk 3 ch, sc in next ch, ch 5, sk 3 ch, sc in next ch, ch 3, sk 3 ch, (2 dc, ch 1, 2 dc) in next ch, rep from *, ending row with ch 3, 3 dc in last ch, ch 3, turn.

Row 2: 2 dc in 1st dc, * dc in next ch-3 arch, ch 3, sc in next ch-5 arch, ch 3, dc in next ch-3 arch, (2 dc, ch 1, 2 dc) in next ch-1 sp, rep from *, ending row with 3 dc in tch, ch 3, turn.

Row 3: 2 dc in 1st dc, * ch 3, sc in next ch-3 arch, ch 5, sc in next ch-3 arch, ch 3, (2 dc, ch 1, 2 dc) in next ch-1 sp, rep from *, ending row with ch 3, 3 dc in tch, ch 3, turn.

Rep Rows 2-3 for pattern.

40. Multiples of 11 plus 8.

Row 1: Dc in 5th ch from hk, * ch 2, sk 2 ch, sc in next ch, sk 3 ch, (dc, ch 1 in next ch) 4 times, dc in same

sp, sk 3 ch, sc in next ch, rep from *, ending row with ch 2, (dc, ch 1, dc) in last ch, ch 1, turn.

Row 2: Sc in 1st dc, (sc, ch 3, sc) in next ch-1 sp (picot made), * ch 3, (sc, ch 3, sc) in each ch-1 sp of 5-dc group, ch 3, (dc, ch 1, dc) in next ch-2 sp, rep from *, ending row with sk last ch-2 sp, ch 3, (sc, ch 3, 2 sc) in tch, ch 4, turn.

Row 3: Dc in 1st sc, * ch 3, sk 1st picot of 5-dc group, sc in next picot, ch 3, sc in next picot, ch 3, (dc, ch 1, dc) in next ch-1 sp, rep from *, ending row with ch 3, (dc, ch 1, dc) in last sc, ch 4, turn.

Row 4: Dc in 1st dc, ch 2, sc in next ch-3 sp, * (dc, ch1 in next ch-3 sp) 4 times, dc in same sp, ch 2, (dc, ch 1, dc) in next ch-1 sp, ch 2, sk next ch-3 sp, rep from *, ending row with sc in last ch-3 sp, ch 2, (dc, ch 1, dc) in tch, ch 1, turn.

Rep Rows 2-4 for pattern.

Patterns Using V-Stitch and Shell

Christening Gown Set

Materials Needed: *Approximately 21 ounces sport-weight white cotton yarn; size H crochet hook; 6 yards of 1/2" white ribbon; 5 ribbon roses; small button.*

Finished Size: *Chest = 10"; Skirt length = 20"; Bootie Sole = 4"; Hat width = 13"*

Gauge: *3 sc = 1"*
2 rows sc = 1/2"

Christening Gown Yoke:
Ch 2.

Row 1: Sc in 2nd ch from hk, ch 1, turn. (1 sc)

Row 2: 2 sc in sc, ch 1, turn. (2 sc)

Row 3: 2 sc in each sc, ch 1, turn. (4 sc)

Row 4: 2 sc in next sc, sc in next 2 sc, 2 sc in last sc, ch 1, turn. (6 sc)

Rows 5-8: Continue working 2 sc in first and last sc, sc in each sc bet. (14 sc at end of Row 8)

Rows 9-10: Sc in each sc across, ch 1, turn. (14 sc)

Row 11: 2 sc in next sc, sc in each of next 12 sc, 2 sc in last sc, ch 1, turn. (16 sc)

Row 12: Sc in each sc across, ch 1, turn. (16 sc)

Rows 13-15: Rep Row 5, (22 sc at end of Row 15)

Row 16: Sc in each sc across, ch 1, turn. (22 sc)

Rows 17-31: Rep Rows 5 and 9 alternately. (38 sc at end of Row 31)

Neck shaping:

Row 32: 2 sc in next sc, sc in next 10 sc, sl st in next sc, ch 1, turn.

Row 33: Work 1 sc over next 2 sc (dec made), sc in next 11 sc, ch 1, turn. (12 sc)

Row 34: Sc in next 10 sc, dec in last 2 sc, ch 1, turn. (11 sc)

Row 35: Dec in 1st 2 sc, sc in next 9 sc, ch 1, turn. (10 sc)

Rows 36-41: Sc in each sc across, ch 1, turn. (10 sc)

Row 42: 2 sc in 1st sc, sc in next 9 sc, ch 1, turn. (11 sc)

Row 43: Sc in next 10 sc, 2 sc in last sc, ch 1, turn. (12 sc)

Row 44: 2 sc in 1st sc, sc in next 11 sc, ch 1, turn. (13 sc)

Row 45: Dec over 1st 2 sc, sc in next 10 sc, 2 sc in last sc, ch 1, turn. (13 sc)

Row 46: 2 sc in 1st sc, sc in next 10 sc, dec in last 2 sc, ch 1, turn. (13 sc)

Row 47: Sc in next 12 sc, 2 sc in last sc, ch 1, turn. (14 sc)

Row 48: 2 sc in 1st sc, sc in next 13 sc, ch 1, turn. (15 sc)

Row 49: Dec in 1st 2 sc, sc in next 12 sc, 2 sc in last sc, ch 1, turn. (15 sc)

Row 50: 2 sc in 1st sc, sc in next 14 sc, ch 1, turn. (16 sc)

Row 51: Dec in 1st 2 sc, sc in next 13 sc, 2 sc in last sc, ch 1, turn. (16 sc)

Row 52: Sc in each sc across, ch 1, turn. (16 sc)

Row 53: Dec in 1st 2 sc, sc in next 14 sc, ch 1, turn. (15 sc)

Row 54: Rep Row 52. (15 sc)

Row 55: Dec in 1st 2 sc, sc in next 13 sc, ch 1, turn. (14 sc)

Row 56: Rep Row 52. (14 sc)

Row 57: Dec in 1st 2 sc, sc in next 12 sc, ch 1, turn. (13 sc)

Row 58: Rep Row 52. (13 sc) **F.O.** Attach thread with sl st to last sc of Row 31. Rep instructions for Rows 32-58 except do not **F.O.**

Row 59: Sc in each sc across both pieces, ch 1, turn. (26 sc)

Row 60: Sc in each sc across, ch 1, turn. (26 sc)

Row 61: Dec in 1st 2 sc, sc in next 22 sc, dec in last 2 sc, ch 1, turn. (24 sc)

Row 62: Rep Row 60. (24 sc)

Row 63: Dec in 1st 2 sc, sc in next 20 sc, dec in last 2 sc, ch 1, turn. (22 sc)

Row 64: Rep Row 60. (22 sc)

Row 65: Dec in 1st 2 sc, sc in next 18 sc, dec in last 2 sc, ch 1, turn. (20 sc)

Row 66: Rep Row 60. (20 sc)

Row 67: Dec in 1st 2 sc, sc in next 16 sc, dec in last 2 sc, ch 1, turn. (18 sc)

Row 68: Rep Row 67 except sc in next 14 sc. (16 sc)

Row 69: Rep Row 67 except sc in next 12 sc. (14 sc)

Rows 70-71: Sc in each sc across, ch 1, turn. (14 sc)

Row 72: Dec in 1st 2 sc, sc in next 10 sc, dec in last 2 sc, ch 1, turn. (12 sc)

Rows 73-78: Rep Row 72: dec at beg and end of each row. You will have 1 sc at end of Row 78. Do not **F.O.**

Edging

Row 1: Ch 6 (counts as dc, ch 3), dc in sm sp (corner st made), * ch 1, dc, rep from * placing dc at evenly spaced intervals, work corner st (dc, ch 3, dc) at other tip of yoke, end with ch 1, join with sl st to 3rd ch of beg ch 6.

Row 2: Work (Sc, dc, sc) in corner sp and each ch-1 sp around, join with sl st to beg sc, **F.O.**

Chest: Ch 91.

Row 1: Sc in 2nd ch from hk and in each ch across, ch 1, turn. (90 sc)

Rows 2-3: Sc in each sc across, ch 1, turn, **F.O.** at end of Row 3. (90 sc)

Row 4: Sk 1st 27 sc, join with sc in next sc, sc in next 35 sc, ch 1, turn. (36 sc)

Rows 5-10: Sc in each of next 36 sc, ch 1, turn.

Neck Shaping

Row 11: Sc in next 18 sc, sl st in next, ch 1, turn.

Row 12: Work 1 sc over next 2 sc (dec made), sc in rem 16 sc, ch 1, turn. (17 sc)

Row 13: Sc in next 15 sc, dec over last 2 sc, ch 1, turn. (16 sc)

Rows 14-21: Continue following pattern of Row 12

(dec in 1st 2 sc) and Row 13 (dec in last 2 sc) alternately until only 8 sc remain.

Rows 22-25: Sc in each sc across, ch 1, turn. (8 sc)

Row 26: 2 sc in next sc (inc made), sc in next 7 sc, ch 1, turn. (9 sc)

Row 27: Sc in next 8 sc, 2 sc in last sc, ch 1, turn. (10 sc)

Rows 28-34: Continue following pattern of Row 26 (inc in 1st sc) and Row 27 (inc in last sc) alternately. (17 sc at end of Row 34)

Rows 35-42: Sc in each sc across, ch 1, turn, **F.O.** at end of Row 42. (17 sc)

Join thread to beg sc of Row 10 and follow instructions for Neck Shaping. Using same thread, sew Row 42 tog with Row 10, matching 17 sc to 1st 17 sc on either side. (This will form back and arm opening.) Sl st around back opening and neck.

Skirt: Join with sl st to bottom of Row 1 on chest.

Rnd 1: Sc in each st around, join with sl st to beg sc. (90 sc)

Rnd 2: Ch 4, dc in sm sp, * sk next sc, (dc, ch 1, dc) in next sc (V-st made), rep from * around, join with sl st to third ch of beg ch 4. (45 V-st)

Rnd 3: Sl st to ch-1 sp, ch 4, dc in sm sp, * V-st in next ch-1 sp, rep from * around, join as above. (45 V-st)

Rnds 4-6: Rep Rnd 3.

Rnd 7: Sl st to ch-1 sp, ch 4, dc in sm sp, (V-st in next ch-1 sp) 7 times, * (dc, ch 1, dc, ch 1, dc) in next ch-1 sp (inc made), (V-st in next ch-1 sp) 8 times, rep from * around, join as above. (50 V-st)

Rnds 8-12: V-st in each ch-1 sp around, join as above. (50 V-st)

Rnd 13: Rep Rnd 7 except inc in every 10th ch-1 sp. (55 V-st)

Rnds 14-20: V-st in each ch-1 sp around, join. (55 V-st)

Rnd 21: Rep Rnd 7 except inc in every 11th ch-1 sp. (60 V-st)

Rnds 22-33: V-st in each ch-1 sp around, join. (60 V-st)

Rnd 34: Sl st to ch-1 sp, ch 5, * dc in next ch-1 sp, ch 2, rep from * around, join with sl st to 3rd ch of beg ch-5.

Rnd 35: (Sc, dc, sc) in each 2-ch sp around, **F.O.**

Sleeve (Make 2): Join with sl st to arm opening.

Rnd 1: Work 36 sc around opening, join with sl st to beg sc.

Rnd 2: Rep Rnd 2 of skirt.(18 -st)

Rnd 3: Rep Rnd 3 of skirt. (18 V-st)

Rnds 4-6: V-st in each ch-1 sp around, join as above. (18 V-st)

Rnd 7: Rep Rnd 34 of skirt.

Rnd 8: Rep Rnd 35 of skirt, **F.O.**

Sew button to top of back opening.
Optional: Button loop—attach thread to other side of dress back opening with sl st, ch 10, sl st to beg sl st, **F.O.**

Hat (Back): Ch 19.
Row 1: Sc in 2nd ch from hk and in each ch across, ch 1, turn. (18 sc)
Rows 2-11: Sc in each sc across, ch 1, turn. (18 sc)
Row 12: Work 1 sc over 1st 2 sc (dec made), sc in next 14 sc, dec over last 2 sc. (16 sc)
Rows 13-17: Rep Row 12, dec at beg and end of each row. (6 sc at end of Row 17)**F.O.**

Sides and Top: Join with sl st to beg of Row 1.
Row 1: Work 36 sc across sides of Rows 1-16, across top of Row 17 and down other side of Rows 1-16.
Rows 2-4: Rep Rnd 2 of skirt except do not join, turn work, sl st to ch-1 sp. (18 V-st)
Row 5: Ch 4, dc in sm sp, (V-st in next ch-1 sp) 5 times, * inc in next ch-1 sp, (V-st in next ch-1 sp) 6 times, rep from * across, turn as above. (22 V-st)
Rows 6-8: V-st in each ch-1 sp across, turn work as before. (22 V-st)
Row 9: Rep Rnd 34 of skirt except do not join, turn work.
Row 10: Rep Rnd 35 of skirt except work (sc, dc, sc) around entire hat, on sides work in post of end dc and on bottom of back, work (sc, dc, sc) in every other sc, **F.O.**

Booties (Make 2):
Sole: Ch 13.
Rnd 1: Sc in each ch, turn work and sc in bottom of each ch, join with sl st to beg sc. (24 sc)
Rnd 2: 2 sc in 1st sc, sc in next 10 sc, 2 sc in next 2 sc, sc in next 10 sc, 2 sc in last sc, join. (28 sc)
Rnd 3: 2 sc in each sc around, join. (56 sc)
Rnds 4-5: Sc in each sc around, join. (56 sc)
Rnd 6: Ch 4, * sk next sc, dc in next sc, ch 1, rep from * around, join with sl st to 3rd ch of beg ch 4, **F.O.**

Top: Ch 8.
Row 1: Sc in 2nd ch from hk and in each ch across, ch 1, turn. (7 sc)
Row 2: 2 sc in beg sc, sc in next 5 sc, 2 sc in last sc, ch 1, turn. (9 sc)
Rows 3-5: Sc in each sc, ch 1, turn, **F.O.** at end of Row 5. Leave 12" strand of thread to attach top to sole by lining up edges of top with 10 sc posts at tip of sole, sew with whip stitch.

Bootie Sock: Join with sl st to Rnd 6 of sole.
Rnd 1: Work 30 sc around, including 9 sc in Row 5 of top piece.
Rnd 2: Rep Rnd 6 of sole, except do not **F.O.**
Rnd 3: Sl st to ch-1 sp, V-st in each ch-1 sp around, join. (15 V-st)
Rnd 4: (Sc, dc, sc) in each ch-1 sp around, **F.O.**
Finishing: Weave ribbon over and under dc posts on (dc, ch 1, dc) of each piece. Sew ribbon roses to bootie tops, tips of yoke, and bottom front edges of hat.

Tailored Trellis Placemat
Materials Needed: *Approximately 300 yards of #30 ecru cotton thread; #10 steel crochet hook.*
Finished Size: 20" x 15"
Gauge:10 dc = 1"
3 rows of dc = 1"
Ch 284.
Row 1: (Dc, ch 3, dc) in 4th ch from hk, * ch 3, sk 3 ch, sc in next 3 ch, ch 3, sk 3 ch, (dc, ch 3, dc) in next ch, rep from * across row, ch 3, turn.
Row 2: * 7 dc in next ch-3 sp, ch 3, sc in 2nd sc of 3-sc group, ch 3, sk next ch-3 sp, rep from *, ending row with 7 dc, dc in tch, ch 1, turn.
Row 3: * Sc in each dc of next 7-dc group, ch 5, rep from *, ending row with 7 sc, ch 6, turn.
Row 4: * Sk 2 sc, sc in next 3 sc, ch 3, (dc, ch 3, dc) in

3rd ch of next ch-5 sp, ch 3, rep from *, ending row with sc in next 3 sc, ch 3, dc in last sc, ch 6, turn.
Row 5: * Sc in 2nd sc of 3-sc group, ch 3, sk next ch-

3 sp, 7 dc in next ch-3 sp, ch 3, rep from *, ending row with ch 3, sc in 2nd sc of last 3-sc group, ch 3, dc in 4th ch of tch, ch 1, turn.

Row 6: Sc in dc, ch 5, * sc in next 7 dc, ch 5, rep from *, ending row with sc in 4th ch of tch, ch 3, turn.

Row 7: * (Dc, ch 3, dc) in 3rd ch of next ch-5 sp, ch 3, sk 2 sc, sc in next 3 sc, ch 3, rep from *, ending row with (dc, ch 3, dc) in 3rd ch of last ch-5 sp, dc in last sc, ch 3, turn.

Rows 8-63: Rep Rows 2-7, ending with Row 3 of pattern, ch 1, turn.

Edging:

Row 64: Sc evenly across row and rem 3 edges, work 3 sc in each corner, join with sl st to beg sc, ch 1, turn.

Rows 65-68: Sc in each sc of edging, 3 sc in center sc of each corner, join with sl st to beg sc, ch 1. (**F.O.** at end of Row 68)

Chapter 7

Relief Stitch

1. Multiples of 4 plus 2.

Row 1: Sc in 2nd ch from hk and in each ch across row, ch 3, turn.
Row 2: Sk 1st 2 sc, * (dc, ch 1, dc) in next sc, sk next sc, dc in next sc, sk next sc, rep from *, ending row with dc in last sc, ch 3, turn.
Row 3: * (Dc, ch 1, dc) in next ch-1 sp, sk next dc,1 relief dc around post of next dc (working from the front)(dc/rf made), rep from *, ending row with dc in tch, ch 3, turn.
Row 4: Rep Row 3, except work relief st around back of dc post (dc/rb made).
Rep Rows 3-4 for pattern.

2. Multiples of 2.

Row 1: Dc in 4th ch from hk and in each ch across row, ch 3, turn.
Row 2: Sk 1st dc, * dc/rf around next dc, rep from *, ending row with dc in tch, ch 3, turn.
Rep Row 2 for pattern.

3. Multiples of 4 plus 1.

Row 1: Dc in 4th ch from hk and in each ch across row, ch 3, turn.
Row 2: Sk 1st dc, dc in next 2 dc, * dc/rf around next dc, dc in next 3 dc, rep from *, ending row with dc in last 2 dc, dc in tch, ch 3, turn.
Row 3: Sk 1st dc, dc in each dc across row, dc in tch, ch 3, turn.

Row 4: Sk 1st dc, dc/rf around next dc, * dc in next 3 dc, dc/rf around next dc, rep from *, ending row with dc in tch, ch 3, turn.
Row 5: Rep Row 3.
Rep Rows 2-5 for pattern.

4. Multiples of 2 plus 1.

Row 1: Dc in 4th ch from hk and in each ch across row, ch 1, turn.
Row 2: Sc in each dc across row, sc in tch, ch 2, turn.
Row 3: Hdc/rf around 1st dc in Row 1, * sk next sc, dc in next sc, sk next dc of Row 1, hdc/rf around next dc of Row 1, rep from *, ending row with dc in last sc, ch 1, turn.
Row 4: * Sc in each st across row, sc in tch, ch 2, turn.
Row 5: * Hdc/rf around next hdc/rf of Row 3, sk next sc, dc in next sc, rep from *, ending row with dc in last sc, ch 1, turn.
Rep Rows 4-5 for pattern.

5. Multiples of 4 plus 3.

Row 1: Dc in 4th ch from hk and in each ch across row, ch 1, turn.
Row 2: Sc in each dc across row, sc in tch, ch 4, turn.
Row 3: * Dc/rf around next dc of Row 1 (leave 2 lps on hk), sk next dc of Row 1, dc/rf around next dc, yo, pull through 2 lps on hk, yo, pull through rem 3 lps, ch 1, sk next sc, dc in next sc, ch 1, sk next dc of Row 1, rep from *, ending row with dc in last sc, ch 1, turn.
Row 4: Sc in each st and ch across row, 2 sc in tch, ch 3, turn.
Row 5: Sk 1st sc, dc in each sc across row, dc in tch, ch 1, turn.
Rep Rows 2-5 for pattern.

6. Multiples of 4 plus 2.

Row 1: Dc in 4th ch from hk and in each ch across row, ch 2, turn.
Row 2: Sk 1st dc, dc/rf around next 2 dc, * dc in next 2 dc, dc/rf around next 2 dc, rep from *, ending row

with dc in tch, ch 2, turn.
Row 3: Sk 1st dc, dc/rb around next 2 dc, * dc in next 2 dc, dc/rb around next 2 dc, rep from *, ending row with dc in tch, ch 2, turn.
Rep Rows 2-3 for pattern.

7. Multiples of 8 plus 4.

Row 1: Dc in 4th ch from hk and in each ch across row, ch 3, turn.
Row 2: Sk 1st dc, * dc/rf around next 4 dc, dc/rb around next 4 dc, rep from *, ending row with dc in tch, ch 3, turn.
Rep Row 2 for pattern.

8. Multiples of 6 plus 3.

Row 1: Sk 5 ch, * (2 dc, ch 1, 2 dc) in next ch, sk 2 ch, dc in next ch, sk ch 2, rep from *, ending row with dc in last ch, ch 3, turn.
Row 2: Sk 3 dc, * (2 dc, ch 1, 2 dc) in next ch-1 sp, sk 2 dc, dc/rf around next dc, sk 2 dc, rep from *, ending row with dc in tch, ch 3, turn.
Row 3: Sk 3 dc, * (2 dc, ch 1, 2 dc) in next ch-1 sp, sk 2 dc, dc/rb around next dc, sk 2 dc, rep from *, ending row with dc in tch, ch 3, turn.
Rep Rows 2-3 for pattern.

9. Multiples of 6 plus 1.

Row 1: Dc in 4th ch from hk and in each ch across row, ch 3, turn.
Row 2: Sk 1st dc, * dc/rf around next 3 dc, dc/rb around next 3 dc, rep from *, ending row with dc/rf around last 3 dc, dc in tch, ch 3, turn.
Row 3: Rep Row 2.
Row 4: Sk 1st dc, * dc/rb around next 3 dc, dc/rf around next 3 dc, rep from *, ending row with dc/rb around last 3 dc, dc in tch, ch 3, turn.

Row 5: Rep Row 4.
Rep Rows 2-5 for pattern.

10. Multiples of 7 plus 6.

Row 1: Dc in 4th ch from hk, dc in next ch, * sk 2 ch, (2 dc, ch 2, 2 dc) in next ch, sk 2 ch, dc in next 2 ch, rep from *, ending row with dc in last 3 ch, ch 3, turn.
Row 2: Sk 1st dc, dc/rf around next 2 dc, * (2 dc, ch 2, 2 dc) in next ch-2 sp, sk 2 dc, dc/rf around next 2 dc, rep from *, ending row with 2 dc/rf around last 2 dc, dc in tch, ch 3, turn.
Row 3: Sk 1st dc, dc/rb around next 2 dc, * (2 dc, ch 2, 2 dc) in next ch-2 sp, sk 2 dc, dc/rb around next 2 dc, rep from *, ending row with 2 dc/rb around last 2 dc, dc in tch, ch 3, turn.
Rep Rows 2-3 for pattern.

Patterns Using Relief Stitch

Lacy Winter Scarf

Materials Needed: *Approximately 7 ounces of worsted weight off-white yarn; size H crochet hook.*
Finished Size: *8" x 47"*
Gauge: *4 dc = 1"*
 2 rows dc = 1"
Ch 30 (Multiples of 4 plus 2).
Row 1: Sc in 2nd ch from hk and in each ch across row, ch 3, turn.
Row 2: Sk 1st 2 sc, * (dc, ch 1, dc) in next sc, sk next sc, dc in next sc, sk next sc, rep from *, ending row with dc in last sc, ch 3, turn.
Row 3: * (Dc, ch 1, dc) in next ch-1 sp, sk next dc, 1 relief dc around post of next dc (working from the front)(dc/rf made), rep from *, ending row with dc in tch, ch 3, turn.
Row 4: Rep Row 3, except work relief st around back of dc post (dc/rb made).
Rows 5-102: Rep Rows 3 and 4 alternately or continue for desired length, F.O.
Finishing: Sc evenly around all sides, **F.O.** Cut strands of yarn approximately 10" long, attach to both ends of scarf for fringe.

Lacy Winter Hat

Materials Needed: *Approximately 3-1/2 ounces of worsted weight off-white yarn; size H crochet hook; yarn needle.*
Finished Size: *22" circumference*
Gauge: *Same as scarf.*
Ch 70 (Multiples of 4 plus 2).

Row 1: Sc in 2nd ch from hk and in each ch across row, ch 3, turn.
Row 2: Sk 1st 2 sc, * (dc, ch 1, dc) in next sc, sk next sc, dc in next sc, sk next sc, rep from *, ending row with dc in last sc, ch 3, turn.
Row 3: *(Dc, ch 1, dc) in next ch-1 sp, sk next dc, 1 relief dc around post of next dc (working from the front)(dc/rf made),rep from *, ending row with dc in tch, ch 3, turn.
Row 4: Rep Row 3, except work relief st around back of dc post (dc/rb).
Rows 5-22: Rep Rows 3 and 4 alternately.

Hat Cuff

Rows 23-26: Rep Rows 4 and 3 alternately, (textured pattern will be on opposite side of hat, **F.O.**
Finishing: Sew side edges tog, placing one edge over the other to make a raised ridge. This continues textured look of pattern. Gather Row 1 and sew closed. Make a 3" pom-pon to attach at top of hat. Turn hat cuff up to edge of hat.

Chapter 8

Puff Stitch

1. Multiples of 2 plus 4.

Row 1: 4-lp puff st in 4th ch from hk, * ch 1, sk 1 ch, 4-lp puff st in next ch, rep from *, ending row with ch 1, sk 1 ch, dc in last ch, ch 3, turn.
Row 2: 4-lp puff st in 1st ch-1 sp, * ch 1, 4-lp puff st in next ch-1 sp, rep from *, ending row with ch 1, dc in tch, ch 3, turn.
Rep Row 2 for pattern.

2. Multiples of 8 plus 3.

Row 1: Dc in 4th ch from hk and in next 2 ch, * ch 1, sk 1 ch, dc in next 7 ch, rep from *, ending row with dc in last 4 ch, ch 3, turn.
Row 2: Sk 1st dc, dc in next 3 dc, * 4-lp puff st around next ch-1 sp, dc in next 7 dc, rep from *, ending row with dc in last 3 dc, dc in tch, ch 3, turn.
Row 3: Sk 1st dc, dc in each dc and puff st across row, dc in tch, ch 3, turn.
Row 4: Sk 1st dc, dc in next 6 dc, * ch 1, sk next dc, dc in next 7 dc, rep from *, ending row with ch 1, sk next dc, dc in tch, ch 3, turn.
Row 5: * 4-lp puff st around next ch-1 sp, dc in next 7 dc, rep from *, ending row with 6 dc, dc in tch, ch 3, turn.
Row 6: Rep Row 3.
Row 7: Sk 1st dc, dc in next 3 dc, * ch 1, sk 1 dc, dc in next 7 dc, rep from *, ending row with dc in last 3 dc, dc in tch, ch 3, turn.
Rep Rows 2-7 for pattern.

3. Multiples of 6 plus 4.

Row 1: Sc in 5th ch from hk, * ch 3, sk 2 ch, sc in next ch, rep from *, ending row with ch 1, sk 1 ch, hdc in last ch, ch 1, turn.

Row 2: Sc in hdc, * 7 dc in next ch-3 sp, sc in next ch-3 sp, rep from *, ending row with sc in 2nd ch of tch, ch 6, turn.

Row 3: * Sk 3 dc, sc in next dc, ch 3, sk 3 dc, 4-lp puff st in next sc, ch 3, rep from *, ending row with ch 3, dc in last sc, ch 4, turn.

Row 4: * Sc in center of next ch-3 sp, ch 3, rep from *, ending row with ch 1, hdc in 4th ch of tch, ch 3, turn.

Row 5: 3 dc in next ch-1 sp, * sc in next ch-3 sp, 7 dc in next ch-3 sp, rep from *, ending row with sc in last ch-3 sp, 4 dc in tch sp, ch 1, turn.

Row 6: Sc in 1st dc, * ch 2, sk 3 dc, 4-lp puff st in next sc, ch 2, sk next 3 dc, sc in next dc, rep from *, ending row with ch 2, sc in tch, ch 4, turn.

Row 7: Sk 1st sc and next ch, sc in next ch, ch 3, * sk next 4-lp puff st and 1 ch, sc in next ch, ch 3, sk next sc and 1 ch, sc in next ch, ch 3, rep from *, ending row with ch 1, hdc in last sc, ch 1, turn.

Rep Rows 2-7 for pattern.

4. Multiples of 14 plus 7.

Row 1: Dc in 4th ch from hk, dc in next 3 ch, * (ch 1, sk next ch, dc in next ch) 5 times, dc in next 4 ch, rep from *, ending row with dc in last 4 ch, ch 3, turn.

Row 2: Sk 1st dc, dc in next 4 dc, * (ch 1, sk next ch, dc in next dc) 5 times, dc in next 4 dc, rep from *, ending row with dc in last 3 dc, dc in tch, ch 3, turn.

Row 3: Sk 1st dc, * dc in next 4 dc, (ch 1, sk next ch, dc in next dc) 2 times, 4-lp puff st in next ch-1 sp, dc in next dc, (ch 1, sk next ch, dc in next dc) 2 times, rep from *, ending row with dc in last 3 dc, dc in tch, ch 3, turn.

Row 4: Sk 1st dc, dc in next 4 dc, * ch 1, dc in next dc, 4-lp puff st in next ch-1 sp, dc in next dc, ch 1, dc in next dc, 4-lp puff st in next ch-1 sp, dc in next dc, ch 1, dc in next 5 dc, rep from *, ending row with dc in last 4 dc, dc in tch, ch 3, turn.

Row 5: Sk 1st dc, dc in next 4 dc, * (ch 1, dc in next dc) 2 times, 4-lp puff st in next ch-1 sp, dc in next dc, (ch 1, dc in next dc) 2 times, dc in next 4 dc, rep from *, ending row with dc in last 3 dc, dc in tch, ch 3, turn.

Row 6: Sk 1st dc, dc in next 4 dc, * (ch 1, dc in next dc) 5 times, dc in next 4 dc, rep from *, ending row with dc in last 3 dc, dc in tch, ch 3, turn.

Rep Rows 2-6 for pattern.

5. Multiples of 10 plus 3.

Row 1: Dc in 4th ch from hk, * ch 2, sk next 3 ch, 5 dc in next ch, ch 2, sk 3 ch, dc in next 3 ch, rep from *, ending row with dc in last 2 ch, ch 5, turn.

Row 2: Sk 1st 2 dc, * dc in next dc, 2 dc in next dc, dc in next dc, 2 dc in next dc, dc in next dc, ch 2, dc in center dc of next 3-dc group, ch 2, sk next dc and 2-ch sp, rep from *, ending row with ch 2, dc in tch, ch 5, turn.

Row 3: Sk 1st dc, * 4-lp puff st in next dc, (ch 2, sk next dc, 4-lp puff st in next dc) 3 times, sk next (ch 2, dc, ch 2), rep from *, ending row with ch 2, dc in tch, ch 5, turn.

Row 4: Sk 1st ch-2 sp and puff st, * dc in next ch-2 sp, ch 2, (dc, ch 2, dc) in next ch-2 sp, ch 2, dc in next ch-2 sp, ch 3, sk next 2 puff st, rep from *, ending row with ch 2, dc in tch, ch 3, turn.

Row 5: Dc in 1st ch-2 sp, * ch 2, sk next ch-2 sp, 5 dc in next ch-2 sp, ch 2, 3 dc in next ch-3 sp, rep from *, ending row with ch 2, dc in 2nd and 3rd ch of tch, ch 5, turn.

Rep Rows 2-5 for pattern.

6. Multiples of 6 plus 2.

Row 1: Sc in 2nd ch from hk, * ch 3, sk 2 ch, 4-lp puff st in next ch, ch 3, sk 2 ch, sc in next ch, rep from * across row, ch 6, turn.

Row 2: Sc in next ch-3 sp, ch 3, * 4-lp puff st around next ch-3 sp, ch 3, sc in next ch-3 sp, ch 3, rep from *, ending row with 4-lp puff st in last ch-3 sp, ch 3, dc in last sc, ch 6, turn.

Row 3: Sk 1st ch-3 sp, sc in next ch-3 sp, * ch 3, 4-lp puff st in next ch-3 sp, ch 3, sc in next ch-3 sp, rep from *, ending row with ch 3, 4-lp puff st in 3rd ch of tch, dc in 4th ch of tch, ch 6, turn.

Rep Rows 2-3 for pattern.

7. Multiples of 8 plus 1.

Row 1: Dc in 4th ch from hk, dc in next ch, * 3-lp puff st in next ch, dc in next 3 ch, ch 1, sk next ch, dc in next 3 ch, rep from *, ending row with dc in last 3 ch, ch 4, turn.

Row 2: Sk 1st dc, * dc in next 2 dc, dc in top of 3-lp puff st and next 2 dc, ch 1, dc in next ch-1 sp, ch 1, sk next dc, rep from *, ending row with dc in last 2 dc, ch 1, dc in tch, ch 3, turn.

Row 3: * Dc in ch-1 sp, ch 1, sk next dc, dc in next 3 dc, ch 1, dc in next ch-1 sp, dc in next dc, rep from *, ending row with ch 1, sk last dc, dc in 1st and 2nd ch of tch, ch 3, turn.

Row 4: Sk 1st dc, dc in next dc, * dc in next ch-1 sp, ch 1, sk next dc, dc in next dc, ch 1, dc in next ch-1 sp, dc in next 3 dc, rep from *, ending row with dc in last ch-1 sp, dc in last dc, dc in tch, ch 3, turn.

Row 5: Sk 1st dc, dc in next 2 dc, dc in next ch-1 sp, * ch 1, dc in next ch-1 sp, dc in next 2 dc, 3-lp puff st in next dc, dc in next 2 dc, dc in next ch-1 sp, rep from *, ending row with ch 1, dc in last ch-1 sp, dc in last 2 dc, dc in tch, ch 3, turn.

Row 6: Sk 1st dc, dc in next 2 dc, * ch 1, dc in next ch-1 sp, ch 1, sk next dc, dc in next (2 dc, 3-lp puff st, 2 dc), rep from *, ending row with ch 1, dc in last ch-1 sp, ch 1, dc in last 2 dc, dc in tch, ch 3, turn.

Row 7: Sk 1st dc, dc in next dc, * ch 1, dc in next ch-1 sp, dc in next dc, dc in next ch-1 sp, ch 1, sk next dc, dc in next 3 dc, rep from *, ending row with ch 1, dc in last dc, dc in tch, ch 4, turn.

Row 8: * Dc in next ch-1 sp, dc in next 3 dc, dc in next ch-1 sp, ch 1, sk next dc, dc in next dc, ch 1, rep from *, ending row with dc in last ch-1 sp, ch 1, dc in tch, ch 3, turn.

Row 9: Sk 1st dc, * dc in next 2 dc, 3-lp puff st in next dc, dc in next 2 dc, dc in next ch-1 sp, ch 1, dc in next ch-1 sp, rep from *, ending row with dc in tch, ch 3, turn.

Rep Rows 2-9 for pattern.

8. Multiples of 6 plus 5.

Row 1: (Dc, ch 2, dc) in 4th ch from hk, * ch 1, sk 2 ch, 4-lp puff st in next ch, ch 1, sk 2 ch, (dc, ch 2, dc) in next ch, rep from * across row, dc in last ch, ch 3, turn.

Row 2: * 4-lp puff st in next ch-2 sp, ch 1, (dc, ch 2, dc) in top of next 4-lp puff st, ch 1, rep from *, ending row with 4-lp puff st in last ch-2 sp, dc in tch, ch 3, turn.

Row 3: (Dc, ch 2, dc) in top of next 4-lp puff st, * ch 1, 4-lp puff st in ch-2 sp, ch 1, (dc, ch 2, dc) in top of next 4-lp puff st, rep from *, ending row with dc in tch, ch 3, turn.

Rep Rows 2-3 for pattern.

9. Multiples of 10 plus 6.

Row 1: Dc in 6th ch from hk, * ch 1, sk next ch, dc in next ch, rep from * across row, ch 4, turn.

Row 2: Sk 1st dc, * dc in next dc, ch 1, rep from *, ending row with dc in 2nd ch of tch, ch 4, turn.

Row 3: Sk 1st dc, dc in next dc, * ch 3, 3-lp puff st in next dc (leave 2 lps on hk), sk next dc, 3-lp puff st in next dc, yo, pull through 3 lps on hk (2 puff st tog), ch 3, dc in next dc, ch 1, dc in next dc, rep from *, ending row with ch 1, dc in 2nd ch of tch, ch 4, turn.

Row 4: Sk 1st dc, dc in next dc, * ch 2, 3-lp puff st in top of next 2 puff st tog, ch 3, 3-lp puff st in same sp, ch 2, dc in next dc, ch 1, dc in next dc, rep from *, ending row with ch 1, dc in 2nd ch of tch, ch 4, turn.

Row 5: Sk 1st dc, dc in next dc, * ch 1, dc in top of next 3-lp puff st, ch 1, dc in center of next ch-3 sp, ch 1, dc in top of next 3-lp puff st, (ch 1, dc in next dc) 2 times, rep from *, ending row with ch 1, dc in 2nd ch of tch, ch 4, turn.

Rep Rows 2-5 for pattern.

10. Multiples of 4 plus 1.

Row 1: Hdc in 5th ch from hk, * ch 1, sk next ch, hdc in next ch, rep from * across row, ch 2, turn.

Row 2: * Hdc in next ch-1 sp, ch 1, 4-lp puff st in next ch-1 sp, ch 1, rep from *, ending row with hdc in 1st and 2nd tch, ch 3, turn.

Row 3: * Hdc in next ch-1 sp, ch 1, rep from *, ending row with hdc in tch, ch 2, turn.

Row 4: * 4-lp puff st in next ch-1 sp, ch 1, hdc in next ch-1 sp, ch 1, rep from *, ending row with 4-lp puff st, hdc in 2nd ch of tch, ch 3, turn.

Row 5: Rep Row 3.

Rep Rows 2-5 for pattern.

Patterns Using Puff Stitch

Boudoir Bolster Pillow

Materials Needed: Approximately 5 ounces of white cotton worsted weight yarn; size F crochet hook; 18" oblong bolster pillow; sewing needle and thread; 1/2 yard of 2" white satin ribbon.

Finished Size: 25" length

Gauge: 5 dc = 1"
2 rows of dc = 1"

Pillow Cover

Ch 104.

Row 1: 4-lp puff st in 4th ch from hk, * ch 1, sk 1 ch, 4-lp puff st in next ch, rep from *, ending row with ch 1, sk 1 ch, dc in last ch, ch 3, turn.

Row 2: 4-lp puff st in 1st ch-1 sp, * ch 1, 4-lp puff st in next ch-1 sp, rep from *, ending row with ch 1, dc in tch, ch 3, turn. Rep Row 2 until work wraps comfortably around pillow form, **F.O.**

Finishing

Sew pillow cover edges along 1st and last rows tog (tube shape formed). Insert pillow in tube. Cut ribbon in 2 equal lengths and tie in bow around each side of pillow.

Note: Our pattern uses stitch design #1 in this chapter. You can create an entirely different look by using thread. Customize the pillow to your own personal decor by covering the form with material that compliments your furniture! Add an edging from chapter 16 to the ends for a Victorian feel. Attach silk flowers to the ribbon ties. The design possibilities are endless!

Chapter 9

Popcorn Stitch

1. Multiples of 4 plus 2.

Row 1: Sc in 2nd ch from hk, sc in next ch, * 3-dc pc st in next ch, sc in next 3 ch, rep from *, ending row with sc in last 2 ch, ch 1, turn.
Row 2: * Sc in each sc and pc st across row, ch 1, turn.
Row 3: Sc in next 4 sc, * 3-dc pc st in next sc, sc in next 3 sc, rep from *, ending row with sc in last 4 sc, ch 1, turn.
Row 4: Rep Row 2.
Row 5: Sc in 1st 2 sc, * pc st in next sc, sc in next 3 sc, rep from *, ending row with sc in last 2 sc, ch 1, turn.
Rep Rows 2-5 for pattern.

2. Multiples of 6 plus 4.

Row 1: 2 dc in 4th ch from hk, * sk 2 ch, sc in next ch, sk 2 ch, 5 dc in next ch, rep from *, ending row with 3 dc in last ch, ch 1, turn.
Row 2: Sc in 1st dc, * sk next dc, 2 dc in next dc, 4-dc pc st in next sc, 2 dc in next dc, sk next dc, sc in next dc, rep from *, ending row with sc in tch, ch 3, turn.
Row 3: 2 dc in 1st sc, * sk next 2 dc, sc in top of next pc st, sk next 2 dc, 5 dc in next sc, rep from *, ending row with 3 dc in last sc, ch 1, turn.
Rep Rows 2-3 for pattern.

3. Multiples of 6 plus 2.

Row 1: Dc in 6th ch from hk, * ch 1, sk next ch, dc in next ch, rep from * across row, ch 4, turn.

Row 2: Sk 1st dc, * 4-dc pc st in next dc, (ch 1, dc in next dc) 2 times, ch 1, rep from *, ending row with 4-dc pc st in last dc, ch 1, dc in 2nd ch of tch, ch 4, turn.

Row 3: Sk 1st dc, * dc in next pc st, (ch 1, dc in next dc) 2 times, ch 1, rep from *, ending row with ch 1, dc in 2nd ch of tch, ch 4, turn.

Rep Rows 2-3 for pattern.

4. Multiples of 12 plus 2.

Row 1: Sc in 2nd ch from hk, * ch 3, sk 2 ch, 4-dc pc st in next ch, ch 3, sk 2 ch, sc in next ch, rep from *, ending row with sc in last ch, ch 1, turn.

Row 2: Sc in 1st sc, * 3 sc in next ch-3 sp, rep from *, ending row with sc in last sc, ch 2, turn.

Row 3: Dc in 1st sc, * ch 3, sc in sp bet next 2 3-sc group (over pc st), ch 3, sk 3 sc, 4-dc pc st in sp bet 2 3-sc group, rep from *, ending row with 2-dc pc st in last sc, ch 1, turn.

Row 4: Sc in pc st, * 3 sc in next ch-3 sp, rep from *, ending row with sc in last dc and tch, ch 1, turn.

Row 5: Sc in 1st sc, * ch 3, 4-dc pc st in sp bet next 2 3-sc group, ch 3, sk 3 sc, sc in sp bet 2 3-sc group, rep from *, ending row with sc in last sc, ch 1, turn.

Rep Rows 2-5 for pattern.

5. Multiples of 14 plus 2.

Row 1: 4-dc pc st in 6th ch from hk, * ch 3, 4-dc pc st in same sp, sk 2 ch, dc in next 2 ch, sk 2 ch, 4-dc pc st in next ch, rep from *, ending row with sk 2 ch, dc in last ch, ch 6, turn.

Row 2: * Sc in center of next ch-3 sp, ch 3, dc in next 2 dc, ch 3, rep from *, ending row with ch 3, dc in tch, ch 5, turn.

Row 3: * 4-dc pc st in next sc, ch 3, dc in next 2 dc, ch 3, rep from *, ending row with 4-dc pc st, ch 2, dc in 4th ch of tch, ch 3, turn.

Row 4: * 4-dc pc st in top of next pc st, ch 3, 4-dc pc st in sm sp, dc in next 2 dc, rep from *, ending row with dc in 3rd ch of tch, ch 6, turn.

Rep Rows 2-4 for pattern.

6. Multiples of 14 plus 5.

Row 1: Dc in 4th ch from hk and in each ch across row, ch 3, turn.

Row 2: Sk 1st dc, dc in next 2 dc, * (ch 1, sk next dc, dc in next dc) 6 times, dc in next 2 dc, rep from *, ending row with dc in last 2 dc, dc in tch, ch 3, turn.

Row 3: Sk 1st dc, dc in next 2 dc, * ch 1, 5-dc pc st in next dc, ch 1, (dc in next dc, ch 1) 3 times, 5-dc pc st in next dc, ch 1, dc in next 3 dc, rep from *, ending row with dc in last 2 dc, dc in tch, ch 3, turn.

Row 4: Sk 1st dc, dc in next 2 dc, * ch 1, dc in top of next 5-dc pc st, ch 1, 5-dc pc st in next dc, ch 1, dc in next dc, ch 1, 5-dc pc st in next dc, ch 1, dc in top of next pc st, ch 1, dc in next 3 dc, rep from *, ending row with dc in last 2 dc, dc in tch, ch 3, turn.

Row 5: Sk 1st dc, dc in next 2 dc, * ch 1, dc in next dc, ch 1, dc in top of next pc st, ch 1, 5-dc pc st in next dc, ch 1, dc in top of next pc st, ch 1, dc in next dc, ch 1, dc in next 3 dc, rep from *, ending row with dc in last 2 dc, dc in tch, ch 3, turn.

Row 6: Sk 1st dc, dc in next 2 dc, * (ch 1, dc in next dc) 2 times, ch 1, dc in top of next pc st, (ch 1, dc in next dc) 2 times, ch 1, dc in next 3 dc, rep from *, ending row with dc in last 2 dc, dc in tch, ch 3, turn.

Row 7: Sk 1st dc, dc in each dc and ch-1 sp across, dc in tch, ch 3, turn.

Rep Rows 2-7 for pattern.

7. Multiples of 12 plus 6.

Row 1: Sc in 9th ch from hk, * ch 3, sk 2 ch, 4-dc pc st in next ch, ch 3, sk 2 ch, sc in next ch, rep from *, ending row with ch 3, sk 2 ch, dc in last ch, ch 3, turn.

Row 2: Dc in 1st dc, * ch 5, (dc, ch 1, dc) in top of next pc st, rep from *, ending row with ch 5, 2 dc in 4th ch of tch, ch 6, turn.

Row 3: * Sc in center of next ch-5 sp, ch 3, pc st in next ch-1 sp, ch 3, rep from *, ending row with sc in last ch-5 sp, ch 3, dc in tch, ch 3, turn.

Rep Rows 2-3 for pattern.

8. Multiples of 8 plus 1.

Row 1: Dc in 4th ch from hk and in next 5 ch, * ch 1, sk 1 ch, dc in next 7 ch, rep from * across row, ch 3, turn.
Row 2: Sk 1st dc, dc in next 2 dc, * 4-dc pc st in next dc, dc in next 3 dc, ch 1, dc in next 3 dc, rep from *, ending row with dc in last 2 dc, dc in tch, ch 3, turn.
Row 3: Sk 1st dc, dc in next 2 dc, * dc in top of next pc st, dc in next 3 dc, ch 1, dc in next 3 dc, rep from *, ending row with dc in last 2 dc, dc in tch, ch 4, turn.
Row 4: Sk 1st 2 dc, dc in next dc, * ch 1, sk next st, dc in next st, rep from *, ending row with ch 1, dc in tch, ch 3, turn.
Row 5: Sk 1st dc, * (dc in next ch-1 sp and dc) 3 times, ch 1, dc in next dc, rep from *, ending row with ch 1, dc in tch, ch 3, turn.
Rep Rows 2-5 for pattern.

9. Multiples of 16 plus 7.

Row 1: Dc in 4th ch from hk and in next 3 ch, * ch 5, sk 4 ch, sc in next ch, ch 3, sk 1 ch, sc in next ch, ch 5, sk 4 ch, dc in next 5 ch, rep from *, ending row with dc in last 5 ch, ch 3, turn.
Row 2: Sk 1st dc, dc in next 4 dc, * ch 3, dc in center of next ch-5 sp, ch 1, 4-dc pc st in ch-3 sp, ch 1, dc in center of next ch-5 sp, ch 3, dc in next 5 dc, rep from *, ending row with dc in last 4 dc, dc in tch, ch 3, turn.
Row 3: Sk 1st dc, dc in next 4 dc, * ch 5, sc in next dc, ch 3, sc in next dc, ch 5, dc in next 5 dc, rep from *, ending row with dc in last 4 dc, dc in tch, ch 3, turn.
Rep Rows 2-3 for pattern.

10. Multiples of 16 plus 5.

Row 1: Dc in 4th ch from hk, * ch 3, sk 3 ch, 4-dc pc st in next ch, (ch1, sk 1 ch, 4-dc pc st in next ch) 4 times, ch 3, sk 3 ch, dc in next ch, rep from *, ending row with dc in last 2 ch, ch 3, turn.

Row 2: Sk 1st dc, dc in next dc, dc in next ch-3 sp, * ch 3, (4-dc pc st in next ch-1 sp, ch 1) 3 times, 4-dc pc st in next ch-1 sp, ch 3, dc in next ch-3 sp, dc in next dc, dc in next ch-3 sp, rep from *, ending row with dc in last dc, dc in tch, ch 3, turn.

Row 3: Sk 1st dc, dc in next 2 dc, dc in next ch-3 sp, * ch 3, (4-dc pc st in next ch-1 sp, ch 1) 2 times, 4-dc pc st in next ch-1 sp, ch 3, dc in next ch-3 sp, dc in next 3 dc, dc in next ch-3 sp, rep from *, ending row with dc in last ch-3 sp, dc in last 2 dc, dc in tch, ch 3, turn.

Row 4: Sk 1st dc, dc in next 3 dc, dc in next ch-3 sp, * ch 3, 4-dc pc st in next ch-1 sp, ch 1, 4-dc pc st in next ch-1 sp, ch 3, dc in next ch-3 sp, dc in next 5 dc, dc in next ch-3 sp, rep from *, ending row with dc in last ch-3 sp, dc in last 3 dc, dc in tch, ch 3, turn.

Row 5: Sk 1st dc, dc in next 4 dc, dc in next ch-3 sp, * ch 3, 4-dc pc st in next ch-1 sp, ch 3, dc in next ch-3 sp, dc in next 7 dc, dc in next ch-3 sp, rep from *, ending row with dc in last ch-3 sp, dc in last 4 dc, dc in tch, ch 3, turn.

Row 6: Sk 1st dc, 4-dc pc st in next dc, (ch 1, sk next dc, 4-dc pc st in next dc) 2 times, * ch 3, dc in top of next pc st, ch 3, 4-dc pc st in next dc, (ch 1, sk next dc, 4-dc pc st in next dc) 4 times, rep from *, ending row with dc in tch, ch 4, turn.

Row 7: 4-dc pc st in next ch-1 sp, ch 1, 4-dc pc st in next ch-1 sp, * ch 3, dc in next ch-3 sp, dc in next dc, dc in next ch-3 sp, ch 3, 4-dc pc st in next ch-1 sp, (ch 1, 4-dc pc st in next ch-1 sp) 2 times, ch 1, 4-dc pc st in next ch-1 sp, rep from *, ending row with ch 1, dc in tch, ch 3, turn.

Row 8: 4-dc pc st in next ch-1 sp, ch 1, 4-dc pc st in next ch, * ch 3, dc in next ch-3 sp, dc in next 3 dc, dc in next ch-3 sp, ch 3, 4-dc pc st in next ch, (ch 1, 4-dc pc st in next ch-1 sp) 2 times, rep from *, ending row with 4-dc pc st in 1st ch of tch, dc in next ch of tch, ch 4, turn.

Row 9: 4-dc pc st in next ch-1 sp, * ch 3, dc in next ch-3 sp, dc in next 5 dc, dc in next ch-3 sp, ch 3, 4-dc pc st in next ch-1 sp, ch 1, 4-dc pc st in next ch-1 sp, rep from *, ending row with 4-dc pc st in last ch-1 sp, ch 1, dc in tch, ch 3, turn.

Row 10: 4-dc pc st in next ch-1 sp, * ch 3, dc in next ch-3 sp, dc in next 7 dc, dc in next ch-3 sp, ch 3, 4-dc pc st in next ch-1 sp, rep from *, ending row with 4-dc pc st in 1st ch of tch, dc in next ch of tch, ch 3, turn.

Row 11: * Dc in top of next pc st, ch 3, 4-dc pc st in next dc, (ch 1, sk next dc, 4-dc pc st in next dc) 4 times, ch 3, rep from *, ending row with dc in top of last pc st, dc in tch, ch 3, turn.

Rep Rows 2-11 for pattern.

Patterns Using Popcorn Stitch

Victorian Accent Afghan

Materials Needed: *Worsted weight yarn: 50 ounces dark green, 10 ounces dark rose; size H crochet hook.*
Finished Size: *63" x 63"*
Gauge: *3 sc = 1"*
4 rows of sc = 1"
Color Sequence:
      5 rows dark green
      1 row dark rose
      1 row dark green
      1 row dark rose
Note: Work last 5 rows with dark green.

Ch 206.
Row 1: Sc in 2nd ch from hk, * ch 3, sk 2 ch, 4-dc pc st in next ch, ch 3, sk 2 ch, sc in next ch, rep from *, ending row with sc in last ch, ch 1, turn.
Row 2: Sc in 1st sc, * 3 sc in next ch-3 sp, rep from *, ending row with sc in last sc, ch 2, turn.
Row 3: Dc in 1st sc, * ch 3, sc in sp bet next 2 3-sc group (over pc st), ch 3, sk 3 sc, 4-dc pc st in sp bet 2 3-sc group, rep from *, ending row with 2-dc pc st in last sc, ch 1, turn.
Row 4: Sc in pc st, * 3 sc in next ch-3 sp, rep from *, ending row with sc in last dc and tch, ch 1, turn.
Row 5: Sc in 1st sc, * ch 3, 4-dc pc st in sp bet next 2 3-sc group, ch 3, sk 3 sc, sc in sp bet 2 3-sc group, rep from *, ending row with sc in last sc, ch 1, turn.
Rows 6-65: Rep Rows 2-5 alternately, end with pattern of Row 2, **F.O.**
Edging
Color sequence: 2 rows dark green, 1 row dark rose
Note: Work last 2 rows in dark green.
Join with sl st to any corner.
Row 1: Ch 1, 3 sc in corner, sc evenly around edges, work 3 sc in each corner, join with sl st to beg sc.
Rows 2-8: Ch 1, sc in each sc around, work 3 sc in center sc of each corner, join with sl st to beg sc, **F.O.** at end of Row 8.

Popcorn Trivet

Materials Needed: *Worsted weight yarn: 30 yards medium blue, 30 yards variegated blue; size F crochet hook.*
Finished Size: *8" x 8"*
Gauge: *3 sc = 1"*
3 rows sc = 1"
Ch 26.
Row 1: Sc in 2nd ch from hk, sc in next ch, * 3-dc pc st in next ch, sc in next 3 ch, rep from *, ending row with sc in last 2 ch, ch 1, turn.
Row 2: * Sc in each sc and pc st across row, ch 1, turn.
Row 3: Sc in next 4 sc, * 3-dc pc st in next sc, sc in next 3 sc, rep from *, ending row with sc in last 4 sc, ch 1, turn.
Row 4: Rep Row 2.
Row 5: Sc in 1st 2 sc, * pc st in next sc, sc in next 3 sc, rep from *, ending row with sc in last 2 sc, ch 1, turn.
Rows 6-17: Rep Rows 2-5 alternately.

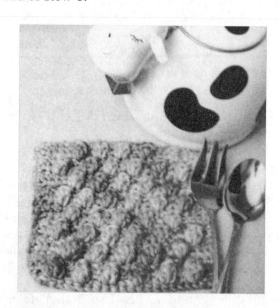

Edging: Sc evenly around all edges, 3 sc in each corner, join with sl st to beg sc, **F.O.**

Chapter 10

Cluster Stitch

1. Multiples of 2 plus 1.

Row 1: 2-lp cl st in 4th ch from hk, * sk next ch, cl st in next ch, rep from *, ending row with dc in last ch, ch 2, turn.
Row 2: 2-lp cl st in each cl st across, ending row with dc in tch, ch 2, turn.
Rep Row 2 for pattern.

2. Multiples of 2.

Row 1: 3-lp cl st in 6th ch from hk, * ch 1, sk 1 ch, cl st in next ch, rep from *, ending row with ch 1, dc in last ch, ch 3, turn.
Row 2: * 3-lp cl st in next ch-1 sp, ch 1, rep from *, ending row with cl st in 1st ch of tch, dc in next ch of tch, ch 4, turn.
Row 3: * 3-lp cl st in next ch-1 sp, ch 1, sk next cl st, rep from *, ending row with ch 1, sk last cl st, dc in tch, ch 3, turn.
Rep Rows 2-3 for pattern.

3. Multiples of any even number plus 1.

Row 1: 4-lp cl st in 4th ch from hk, * ch 1, sk 1 ch, cl st in next ch, rep from *, ending row with dc in last ch, ch 1, turn.
Row 2: Sc in dc, sc in each cl st and ch-1 sp across, ending row with sc in tch, ch 3, turn.
Row 3: Sk 1st sc, * 4-lp cl st in next sc, ch 1, sk next sc, rep from *, ending row with cl st, dc in last sc, ch 3, turn.
Rep Rows 2-3 for pattern.

4. Multiples of 6 plus 5.

Row 1: Sc in 2nd ch from hk, * ch 3, sk 2 ch, sc in next ch, rep from * across row, ch 3, turn.
Row 2: 3-lp cl st in next ch-3 sp, ch 4, * sc in next ch-3 sp, ch 4, 3-lp cl st in next ch-3 sp, rep from *, ending row with dc in last sc, ch 6, turn.
Row 3: * Sc in next ch-4 lp, ch 3, rep from *, ending row with dc in tch, ch 3, turn.
Rep Rows 2-3 for pattern.

5. Multiples of 3 plus 5.

Row 1: 2 dc in 4th ch from hk, * sk 2 ch, 2 dc in next ch, rep from *, ending row with dc in last ch, ch 3, turn.
Row 2: * 2 dc in center sp of next 2-dc group, rep from *, ending row with dc in tch, ch 4, turn.
Row 3: * 4-lp cl st in center sp of next 2-dc group, ch 1, rep from *, ending row with dc in tch, ch 1, turn.
Row 4: Sc in dc, * ch 2, sc in next ch-1 sp, rep from *, ending row with sc in tch, ch 3, turn.
Row 5: 2 dc in each ch-2 sp across row, dc in last sc, ch 3, turn.
Rep Rows 2-5 for pattern.

6. Multiples of 5 plus 2.

Row 1: Sc in 2nd ch from hk, * ch 4, 4-lp cl st in sm ch, sk 4 ch, sc in next ch, rep from *, ending row with sc in last ch, ch 1, turn.
Row 2: * (Sc, ch 4, 4-lp cl st) in next sc, sk (4-lp cl st, ch 4), rep from *, ending row with sc in last sc, ch 1, **turn.**
Row 3: * (Sc, ch 4, 4-lp cl st) in next sc, sk (4-lp cl st, ch 4), rep from *, ending row with sc in last sc, ch 1, turn.
Rep Rows 2-3 for pattern.

7. Multiples of 3 plus 2.

Row 1: * 3 dc in 4th from hk, ch 2, sk 2 ch, 3 dc in next ch, rep from *, ending row with dc in last ch, ch 3, turn.

Row 2: Sk 1st dc, * (yo, insert hk in next dc, yo, pull through 1 lp, yo, pull through 2 lps on hk), rep ( ) in next 2 dc, yo, pull through last 4 lps on hk (cl group formed), ch 2, rep from *, ending row with last cl group, dc in tch, ch 3, turn.

Row 3: * 3 dc in top of next cl group, ch 2, rep from *, ending row with 3 dc in top of last cl group, dc in tch, ch 3, turn.

Rep Rows 2-3 for pattern.

8. Multiples of 12 plus 4.

Row 1: 3 dc in 4th ch from hk, * sk 5 ch, (3 dc, ch 2, 3 dc) in next ch, rep from *, ending row with 4 dc in last ch, ch 3, turn.

Row 2: Sk 1st dc, dc in next dc, * ch 5, 4-lp cl st in next ch-2 sp, rep from *, ending row with dc in last dc, dc in tch, ch 3, turn.

Row 3: * (3 dc, ch 2, 3 dc) in center ch of next ch-5 sp, rep from *, ending row with dc in tch, ch 5, turn.

Row 4: 4-lp cl st in next ch-2 sp, * ch 5, 4-lp cl st in next ch-2 sp, rep from *, ending row with ch 2, dc in tch, ch 3, turn.

Row 5: 3 dc in 1st dc, * (3 dc, ch 2, 3 dc) in center ch of next ch-5 sp, rep from *, ending row with 4 dc in 3rd ch of tch, ch 3, turn.

Rep Rows 2-5 for pattern.

9. Multiples of 4 plus 8.

Row 1: Dc in 6th ch from hk, * ch 1, sk 1 ch, dc in next ch, rep from * across row, ch 4, turn.

Row 2: Sk next (dc, ch-1 sp), * 4-lp cl st in next dc, ch 1, sk 1 ch, dc in next dc, ch 1, sk 1 ch, rep from *, ending row with ch 1, dc in 2nd ch of tch, ch 4, turn.

Row 3: Sk next (dc, ch-1 sp), * dc in top of next cl st, ch 1, sk 1 ch, dc in next dc, ch 1, sk 1 ch, rep from *, ending row with dc in 2nd ch of tch, ch 3, turn.

Row 4: 3-lp cl st in 1st dc, * ch 1, sk ch-1 sp, dc in next dc, ch 1, sk 1 ch, 4-lp cl st in next dc, rep from *, ending row with cl st in 2nd ch of tch, ch 4, turn.

Row 5: Sk (cl st, ch 1), * dc in next dc, ch 1, sk 1 ch, dc in top of next cl st, ch 1, sk 1 ch, rep from *, ending row with ch 1, dc in tch, ch 4, turn.

Rep Rows 2-5 for pattern.

10. Multiples of 8 plus 8.

Row 1: Sc in 8th ch from hk, * ch 3, sk 3 ch, sc in next ch, rep from * across row, ch 1, turn.

Row 2: Sc in sc, ch 3, sc in 1st ch-3 sp, * ch 3, 4-lp cl st in next ch-3 sp, ch 3, sc in next ch-3 sp, rep from *, ending row with sc in 2nd ch of tch, ch 3, sc in 4th ch of tch, ch 1, turn.

Row 3: Sc in 1st sc, ch 3, * cl st in next sc, ch 3, sc in top of next cl st, ch 3, rep from *, ending row with ch 3, sc in last sc, 1 ch, turn.

Row 4: Sc in 1st sc, ch 3, * sc in next cl st, ch 3, cl st in next sc, ch 3, rep from *, ending row with sc in last cl st, ch 3, sc in last sc, ch 1, turn.

Rep Rows 3-4 for pattern.

11. Multiples of 8 plus 7.

Row 1: (Dc, ch 3, dc) in 5th ch from hk, * sk 3 ch, (dc, ch 3, dc) in next ch, rep from *, ending row with sk 1 ch, dc in last ch, ch 1, turn.

Row 2: Sc in 1st dc, * sk 1 dc, 3 sc in next ch-3 sp, sk 1 dc, 3-lp cl st in sp bet next dc, rep from *, ending row with 3 sc in last ch-3 sp, sc in tch, ch 1, turn.

Row 3: Sc in each sc and in top of each cl st across row, ch 3, turn.

Row 4: Sk 1st 2 sc, * (dc, ch 3, dc) in next sc, sk 3 sc, rep from *, ending row with sk next sc, dc in last sc, ch 1, turn.

Rep Rows 2-4 for pattern.

12. Multiples of 12 plus 4.

Row 1: Dc in 6th ch from hk, * ch 1, sk 1 ch, dc in next next ch, rep from *, ending row with dc in last ch, ch 3, turn.

Row 2: 3 tr in 1st dc, * sk next dc, dc in next dc, (ch 1, dc in next dc) 2 times, sk next dc, 7 tr in next dc, rep from *, ending row with 3 tr in 2nd ch of tch, dc in sm sp, ch 3, turn.

Row 3: 3 tr cl group as follows: [yo twice, insert hk in top lps of 1st tr, yo, pull through, (yo, pull through 2 lps on hk) 2 times], rep [ ] in next 2 tr, yo, pull through 4 lps on hk (3 tr cl group), * ch 3, dc in next dc, (ch 1, dc in next dc) 2 times, ch 3, (rep [ ] in next 7 tr, yo, pull through 8 lp on hk) 7 tr cl group made, rep from *, ending row with ch 3, 3 tr cl group in last 3 tr, dc in tch, ch 4, turn.

Row 4: Dc in next tr cl group, * (ch 1, dc in next dc) 3 times, ch 1, dc in next ch-3 sp, ch 1, dc in top of 7 tr cl group, ch 1, dc in next ch-3 sp, rep from *, ending row with ch 1, dc in top of last tr cl group, ch 1, dc in tch, ch 4, turn.

Row 5: Sk 1st dc, dc in next dc, * sk next dc, 7 tr in next dc, sk next dc, dc in next dc, (ch 1, dc in next dc) 2 times, rep from *, ending row with ch 1, dc in 2nd ch of tch, ch 4, turn.

Row 6: Sk 1st dc, dc in next dc, * ch 3, 7 tr cl group in next 7 tr, ch 3, dc in next dc, (ch 1, dc in next dc) 2 times, rep from *, ending row with ch 1, dc in 2nd ch of tch, ch 4, turn.

Row 7: Sk 1st dc, dc in next dc, * ch 1, dc in next ch-3 sp, ch 1, dc in top of 7 tr cl group, ch 1, dc in next ch-3 sp, (ch 1, dc in next dc) 3 times, rep from *, ending row with ch 1, dc in 2nd ch of tch, ch 3, turn.

Rep Rows 2-7 for pattern.

13. Multiples of 18 plus 5.

Row 1: Dc in 8th ch from hk, * ch 2, sk 2 ch, dc in next ch, sk 2 ch, (dc, ch 3, dc) in next ch, sk 2 ch, dc in

next ch, (ch 2, sk 2 ch, dc in next ch) 4 times, rep from *, ending row with (ch 2, sk 2 ch, dc in next ch) 2 times, ch 5, turn.

Row 2: Sk 1st dc, dc in next dc, * ch 2, 6 dc around ch-3 sp, ch 2, sk 2 dc, dc in next dc, (ch 2, dc in next dc) 2 times, rep from *, ending row with ch 2, dc in 3rd ch of tch, ch 5, turn.

Row 3: Sk 1st dc, dc in next dc, ch 2, * (dc in next dc, ch 1) 5 times, dc in last dc of 6-dc group, ch 2, dc in next dc, (ch 2, dc in next dc) 2 times, rep from *, ending row with ch 2, dc in 3rd ch of tch, ch 5, turn.

Row 4: Sk 1st 2 dc, * (3-lp cl st, ch 1 in next dc) 5 times, 3-lp cl st in next dc, ch 2, sk next dc, dc in next dc, ch 2, sk next dc, rep from *, ending row with ch 2, dc in 3rd ch of tch, ch 5, turn .

Row 5: * Sk next 2 ch, dc in next cl st, ch 1, (3-lp cl st, ch 1 in next ch-1 sp) 5 times, dc in next cl st, ch 2, dc in next dc, ch 2, rep from *, ending row with ch 2, dc in 3rd ch of tch, ch 5, turn.

Row 6: Sk 1st dc, * dc in next dc, ch 1, (3-lp cl st, ch 1 in next ch-1 sp) 4 times, dc in next dc, ch 2, dc in next dc, ch 2, rep from *, ending row with ch 2, dc in 3rd ch of tch, ch 5, turn.

Row 7: Sk 1st dc, dc in next dc, * ch 2, sk next (ch 1, cl st), (3-lp cl st, ch 1 in next ch-1 sp) 2 times, 3-lp cl st in next ch-1 sp, (ch 2, dc in next dc) 3 times, rep from *, ending row with ch 2, dc in 3rd ch of tch, ch 5, turn.

Row 8: Sk 1st dc, dc in next dc, * ch 2, dc in top of next cl st, ch 1, (3-lp cl st, ch 1 in next ch-1 sp) 2 times, dc in top of next cl st, (ch 2, dc in next dc) 3 times, rep from *, ending row with ch 2, dc in 3rd ch of tch, ch 5, turn.

Row 9: Sk 1st dc, dc in next dc, ch 2, dc in next dc, ch 2, * sk (1 ch, cl st), (3-lp cl st in next ch-1 sp), (ch 2, dc in next dc) 5 times, rep from *, ending row with ch 2, dc in 3rd ch of tch, ch 5, turn.

Row 10: Sk 1st dc, dc in next dc, ch 2, dc in next dc, * (dc, ch 3, dc) in top of next cl st, dc in next dc, (ch 2, dc in next dc) 4 times, rep from *, ending row with ch 2, dc in 3rd ch of tch, ch 5, turn.

Rep Rows 2-10 for pattern.

14. Multiples of 37 plus 2.

Row 1: Dc in 4th ch from hk, and in each ch across row, ch 7, turn.

Row 2: Sk 1st 2 dc, 4-lp cl st in next dc, * (ch 1, sk 3 dc, 4-lp cl st in next dc) 2 times, ch 4, sk next dc, dc in next dc, (ch 1, sk next dc, dc in next dc) 6 times, ch 4, sk next dc, 4-lp cl st in next dc, rep from *, ending row with ch 4, dc in tch, ch 7, turn.

Row 3: * Sc in top of next 3 cl st, ch 4, dc in next dc, (ch 1, dc in next dc) 6 times, ch 4, rep from *, ending row with ch 4, dc in 5th ch of tch, ch 4, turn.

Row 4: * 4-lp cl st in 1st sc, (ch 3, 4-lp cl st in next sc) 2 times, (ch 1, dc in next dc) 7 times, ch 1, rep from *, ending row with ch 1, dc in 5th ch of tch, ch 3, turn.

Row 5: * Dc in ch-1 sp, (dc in top of cl st, 3 dc in next ch-3 sp) 2 times, dc in top of next cl st, (dc in next ch-1 sp and dc) 7 times, rep from *, ending row with 2 dc in tch, ch 4, turn.

Row 6: Sk 1st 2 dc, dc in next dc, * (ch 1, sk next dc, dc in next dc) 5 times, ch 4, sk next dc, 4-lp cl st in next dc, (ch 1, sk 3 dc, 4-lp cl in next dc) 2 times, ch 4, sk next dc, dc in next dc, (ch 1, sk next dc, dc in next dc) 6 times, rep from *, ending row with ch 1, dc in tch, ch 4, turn.

Row 7: Sk 1st dc, * dc in next dc, (ch 1, dc in next dc) 5 times, ch 4, sc in next 3 4-lp cl st, ch 4, dc in next dc, ch 1, rep from *, ending row with dc in 2nd ch of tch, ch 4, turn.

Row 8: Sk 1st dc, * dc in next dc, (ch 1, dc in next dc) 5 times, ch 1, 4-lp cl st in 1st sc, (ch 3, 4-lp cl st in next sc) 2 times, ch 1, dc in next dc, ch 1, rep from *, ending row with dc in 2nd ch of tch, ch 3, turn.

Row 9: * (Dc in next ch-1 sp and dc) 6 times, dc in next ch-1 sp, (dc in top of next cl st, 3 dc in next ch-3 sp) 2 times, dc in next cl st, dc in next ch-1 sp, dc in next dc, rep from *, ending row with 2 dc in tch, ch 4, turn.
Rep Rows 2-9 for pattern.

15. Multiples of 18 plus 7.

Row 1: Dc in the 4th ch from hk, * ch 1, sk 1 ch, dc in next 2 ch, rep from * across row, ch 5, turn.

Row 2: Sk 1st dc, * tr in next ch-1 sp, ch 1, sk next dc, tr in next dc, ch 1, tr in next dc, ch 3, sk next (dc, ch, 2 dc), (tr, ch 3, tr) in next ch-1 sp, ch 3, sk next (2 dc, ch, dc), tr in next dc, ch 1, tr in next dc, ch 1, rep from *, ending row with ch 1, tr in top of tch, ch 5, turn.

Row 3: Sk 1st tr, tr in next tr, ch 1, tr in next tr, * ch 3, sk next ch-3 sp, (3-lp cl st, ch 3 in next ch-3 sp) 3 times, sk next tr, tr in next tr, (ch 1, tr in next tr) 2 times, rep from *, ending row with tr in tch, ch 5, turn.

Row 4: Sk 1st tr, tr in next tr, * sk next ch-3 sp, (ch 3, 3-lp cl st in next ch-3 sp, ch 3, 3-lp cl st in sm ch-3 sp) 2 times, ch 3, sk next tr, tr in next tr, rep from *, ending row with ch 1, tr in 2nd ch of tch, ch 6, turn.

Row 5: Sk 1st ch-3 sp, * (3-lp cl st in next ch-3 sp, ch 2, 3-lp cl st in sm ch-3 sp, ch 2) 3 times, rep from *, ending row with ch 2, tr in 2nd ch of tch, ch 3, turn.

Row 6: Dc in ch-2 sp, * ch 1, 2 dc in top of next cl st, rep from *, ending row with ch 1, 2 dc in tch, ch 5, turn.
Rep Rows 2-6 for pattern.

Patterns Using Cluster Stitch

Classic Crop Top

Materials Needed: Approximately 366 yards of #20 ecru cotton thread; #10 steel crochet hook.

Finished Size: Ladies small (32" bust, 15" length)

Gauge: 1 multiple repeat = 1-1/2"
5 rows of dc = 2"

Using multiples: Increase or decrease finished size using multiples of 12 plus 4 (refer to Pattern #8). One multiple repeat is equal to gauge size. A ladies small requires 268 ch (12 x 22 + 4) for a measurement of 33" (22 x 1-1/2" = 33") across chest (1" allowed for ease). To increase or decrease size in increments of 1-1/2", add or decrease by one multiple.

Example: Ladies large (38" bust) requires 316 ch (12 x 26 + 4) for a measurement of 39" (26 x 1-1/2") across chest (1" allowed for ease). **Note:** Once the gauge of a pattern stitch is determined, any size can be made according to your needs.

Crop Top Panel (Make 2)
Ch 268.

Rows 1-5: Follow pattern of #8 (see page 87).

Rows 7-41: Rep Rows 2-5, continue to rep Rows 2-5 if a longer length is desired.

Row 42: Sl st to first ch-2 sp, * ch 5, sl st to next ch-2 sp, rep from * across row.

Finishing: Sc evenly around all edges, pin 2 pieces tog at shoulder and sides allowing for desired neck and arm opening size. Join edges with a whip st.

Baby Bunting Blanket

Materials Needed: Worsted weight yarn: 6 ounces each — light green, yellow, pink, white, lavender; size G crochet hook; 30" length of white 1/2" snap tape; 35" x 30" piece of lavender flannel; sewing needle; sewing thread.

Finished Size: 34" x 29"

Gauge: 3 tr = 1"
3 rows of tr = 1"

Color Sequence: 2 rows each of green, yellow, white, pink, lavender.

Ch 111.

Row 1: 4-lp cl st in 4th ch from hk, ch 1, sk 1 ch, cl st in next ch, rep from *, ending row with dc in last ch, ch 1, turn.

Row 2: Sc in dc, sc in each cl st and ch-1 sp across, ending row with sc in tch, ch 3, turn.

Row 3: Sk 1st sc, * 3-lp cl st in next sc, ch 1, sk next sc, rep from *, ending row with cl st, dc in last sc, ch 2, turn.

Rows 4-58: Rep Rows 2 and 3 alternately.

Edging

Rows 1-5: (Rep color sequence except work 1 row only of each color), sc evenly around all edges, work 3 sc in each corner sp.

Finishing: Cut snap tape in two 7-1/2" lengths and one 12" length, unsnap and separate. Sew the 12" pieces of snap tape to each side edge at bottom of the blanket. Sew the remaining 7-1/2" lengths along the bottom edges of the blanket. Cut 1 snap from rem snap tape, sew each side to the top edges of blanket. Pin flannel to blanket, fold edge under and sew in place along 3rd row of edging. For bunting closure directions, refer to diagram.

Diagram

Snap together after closing.
(Armholes made)

Snap together

Snap together   Snap together

Chapter 11

Dropped Stitch

1. Multiples of 10 plus 4.

Row 1: Sc in 2nd ch from hk, sc in next 3 ch, * ch 6, sk 5 ch, sc in next 5 ch, rep from *, ending row with 4 sc, ch 1, turn.
Row 2: Sc in 1st 4 sc, * ch 6, sc in next 5 sc, rep from *, ending row with sc in last 4 sc, ch 1, turn.
Row 3: Rep Row 2.
Row 4: Sc in 1st 4 sc, * ch 3, sl st around center of 3 prev ch-6 lp, ch 3, sc in next 5 sc, rep from *, ending row with 4 sc, ch 1, turn.
Row 5: Rep Row 2.
Rep Rows 2-5 for pattern.

2. Multiple of 6 plus 2.

Row 1: Sc in 2nd ch from hk, * ch 5, sk next 5 ch, sc in next ch, rep from *, ending row with sc in last ch, ch 1, turn.
Row 2: Sc in 1st sc, * ch 5, sc in next sc, rep from *, ending row with sc in last sc, ch 1, turn.
Row 3: Sc in 1st sc, * ch 7, sc in next sc, rep from *, ending row with sc in last sc, ch 1, turn.
Row 4: Rep Row 3 except, ch 5, turn.
Row 5: * Sc around center of 2 prev ch-7 lp, ch 5, rep from *, ending row with ch 2, dc in last sc, ch 1, turn.
Row 6: Sc in 1st dc, ch 2, * sc in next sc, ch 5, rep from *, ending row with ch 2, sc in 3rd ch of tch, ch 1, turn.
Row 7: Sc in 1st sc, ch 3, * sc in next sc, ch 7, rep from *, ending row with ch 3, sc in last sc, ch 1, turn.
Row 8: Sc in 1st sc, * ch 5, sc around center of prev ch-7 and ch-5 lp, rep from *, ending row with ch 5, sc in last sc, ch 1, turn.
Rep Rows 2-8 for pattern.

3. Multiples of 10 plus 2.

Row 1: Sc in 2nd ch from hk, ch 2, sk 2 ch, sc in next 5 ch, * ch 5, sk 5 ch, sc in next 5 ch, rep from *, ending row with ch 2, sk 2 ch, sc in last ch, ch 1, turn.
Row 2: Sc in 1st sc, ch 2, * sc in next 5 sc, ch 5, rep from *, ending row with ch 2, sc in last sc, ch 1, turn.
Row 3: Sc in 1st sc, sc in next 2 ch, * ch 5, sk 5 sc, sc in next 2 ch of ch-5 lp, sc around prev row of ch-5 lp, sc in last 2 ch of sm ch-5 lp, rep from *, ending row with sc in last 2 ch, sc in last sc, ch 1, turn.
Row 4: Sc in 1st 3 sc, * ch 5, sc in next 5 sc, rep from *, ending row with sc in last 3 sc, ch 1, turn.
Row 5: Sc in 1st sc, ch 2, * sc in next 2 ch, sc around prev row of ch-5 lp, sc in last 2 ch of ch-5 lp, ch 5, sk next 5 sc, rep from *, ending row with ch 2, sk next 2 sc, sc in last sc, ch 1, turn.
Rep Rows 2-5 for pattern.

4. Multiples of 8 plus 3.

Row 1: Dc in 4th ch from hk, dc in next ch, * ch 3, sk 3 ch, dc in next 5 ch, rep from *, ending row with dc in last 3 ch, ch 3, turn.
Row 2: Sk 1st dc, dc in next 2 dc, * 3 dc in next ch-3 sp, dc in next 5 dc, rep from *, ending row with dc in last 2 dc, dc in tch, ch 3, turn.
Row 3: Sk 1st dc, dc in next 6 dc, * ch 3, sk 3 dc, dc in next 5 dc, rep from *, ending row with dc in last dc, dc in tch, ch 3, turn.
Row 4: Sk 1st dc, dc in next 6 dc, 3 dc in next ch-3 sp, dc in next 7 dc, rep from *, ending row with dc in last 6 dc, dc in tch, ch 3, turn.
Row 5: Sk 1st dc, dc in next 2 dc, * ch 3, sk 3 dc, dc in next 5 dc, rep from *, ending row with dc in last 2 dc, dc in tch, ch 3, turn.
Rep Rows 2-5 for pattern

5. Multiples of 14 plus 11.

Row 1: Dc in 4th ch from hk, dc in next 6 ch, * ch 7, sk 7 ch, dc in next 7 ch, rep from *, ending row after last 7 dc with dc in last ch, ch 3, turn.
Row 2: Sk 1st dc, * dc in next 7 dc, ch 7, rep from *, ending row with dc in tch, ch 10, turn.
Row 3: * Dc in 1st 3 ch of next ch-7 lp, dc around the next ch of ch-7 lp including prev ch-7 lp, dc in last 3 ch of ch-7 lp, ch 7, rep from *, ending row with dc in tch, ch 10, turn.
Row 4: * Dc in next 7 dc, ch 7, rep from *, ending row with ch 7, dc in 8th ch of tch, ch 3, turn.
Row 5: Rep Row 3.
Rep Rows 2-5 for pattern.

6. Multiples of 7 plus 11.

Row 1: 3 dc in 4th ch from hk, * ch 2, sk 6 ch, (3 dc, ch 1, 3 dc) in next ch, rep from *, ending row with ch 2, sk 6 ch, 4 dc in last ch, ch 3, turn.
Row 2: 3 dc in 1st dc, * ch 2, (3 dc, ch 1, 3 dc) in next ch-1 sp, rep from *, ending row with ch 2, 4 dc in tch, ch 3, turn.
Row 3: 3 dc in 1st dc, * ch 1, sl st around 2 prev ch-2 sp, ch 1, (3 dc, ch 1, 3 dc) in next ch-1 sp, rep from *, ending row with 4 dc in tch, ch 3, turn.
Row 4: Rep Row 2.
Rep Rows 2-4 for pattern. End with Row 3.

7. Multiples of 30 plus 6.

Row 1: Dc in 4th ch from hk and in each ch across row, ch 3, turn.

Row 2: Sk 1st dc, dc in next dc, * ch 10, sk 10 dc, dc in next 10 dc, rep from *, ending row with ch 10, dc in last dc, dc in tch, ch 3, turn.

Row 3: Sk 1st dc, dc in next dc, * ch 10, dc in next 2 dc, (ch 2, sk 2 dc, dc in next 2 dc) 2 times, rep from *, ending row with ch 10, dc in last dc, dc in tch, ch 3, turn.

Row 4: Sk 1st dc, dc in next dc, * ch 10, dc in next 2 dc, 2 dc in next ch-2 sp, ch 2, 2 dc in next ch-2 sp, dc in next 2 dc, rep from *, ending row with ch 10, dc in last dc, dc in tch, ch 3, turn.

Row 5: Sk 1st dc, dc in next dc, * ch 4, 2 sc around 3 prev ch-10 sp, ch 4, dc in next 2 dc, ch 2, 2 dc in next ch-2 sp, ch 2, sk 2 dc, dc in next 2 dc, rep from *, ending row with ch 4, dc in last dc, dc in tch, ch 3, turn.

Row 6: Sk 1st dc, dc in next dc, * ch 10, (dc in next 2 dc, 2 dc in next ch-2 sp) 2 times, dc in next 2 dc, rep from *, ending row with ch 10, dc in last dc, dc in tch, ch 3, turn.

Row 7: Sk 1st dc, dc in next dc, * 10 dc around next ch-10 sp, ch 10, rep from *, ending row with 10 dc in last ch-10 sp, dc in last dc, dc in tch, ch 3, turn.

Rows 8-11: Rep pattern of Rows 3-6.

Rep Rows 2-11 for pattern.

Patterns Using Dropped Stitch

Open Diamond Dresser Scarf

Materials Needed: Approximately 510 yards of #30 white cotton thread; size E crochet hook.

Finished Size: 9" x 49"

Gauge: 3 rows of dc = 4"

Ch 249.

Row 1: 3 dc in 4th ch from hk,* ch 2, sk 6 ch, (3 dc, ch 1, 3 dc) in next ch, rep from *, ending row with ch 2, sk 6 ch, 4 dc in last ch, ch 3, turn.

Row 2: 3 dc in 1st dc, * ch 2, (3 dc, ch 1, 3 dc) in next ch-1 sp, rep from *, ending row with ch 2, 4 dc in tch, ch 3, turn. (34 shells)

Row 3: 3 dc in 1st dc, * ch 1, sl st around 2 prev ch-2 sp, ch 1, (3 dc, ch 1, 3 dc) in next ch-1 sp, rep from *, ending row with 4 dc in tch, ch 3, turn. (34 shells)

Row 4: Rep Row 2.

Rep Rows 2-4 (ending with pattern of Row 3), until work measures 45 inches, ch 6, turn.

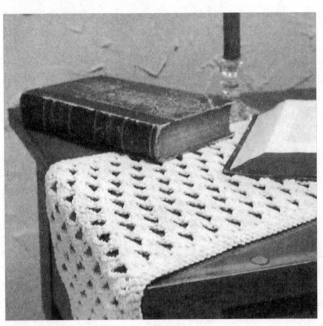

Edging

Rnd 1: Join thread with sl st to any corner sp, (sc, ch 5) evenly spaced around all edges, join with sl st to beg sc.

Rnd 2: Sl st to center of next ch-5 sp, sc in sm sp, * ch 5, sc in center of next ch-5 sp, rep from * around, join with sl st to beg sc.

Rnd 3: Sl st to center of next ch-5 sp, sc in sm sp, * ch 5, sl st in 3rd ch from hk, ch 2, sc in center of next ch-5 rep from *, join with sl st to beg sc, **F.O.**

Pocket Embellishment

Materials Needed: Approximately 100 yards of #20 white cotton thread; #7 steel crochet hook; 2 yards of 1/16" satin ribbon; white sewing thread; sewing needle.

Finished Size: 4-1/2" x 4"

Gauge: 10 sc = 1"

10 rows of sc = 1"

Pocket (Make 2)

Ch 44.

Row 1: Sc in 2nd ch from hk, * ch 5, sk next 5 ch, sc in next ch, rep from *, ending row with sc in last ch, ch 1, turn.

Row 2: Sc in 1st sc, * ch 5, sc in next sc, rep from *, ending row with sc in last sc, ch 1, turn.

Row 3: Sc in 1st sc, * ch 7, sc in next sc, rep from *, ending row with sc in last sc, ch 1, turn.

Row 4: Rep Row 3 except, ch 5, turn.

Row 5: * Sc around center of 2 prev ch-7 lp, ch 5, rep from *, ending row with ch 2, dc in last sc, ch 1, turn.

Rows 6-41: Rep Rows 2-5 alternately, **F.O.** at end of Row 41.

Finishing: Sew side and bottom edges of pocket to clothing article of your choice. Cut ribbon into 14 equal pieces, tie bows randomly around sl st posts of pocket.

Chapter 12

X-Stitch

1. Multiples of 3 plus 4.

Row 1: Dc in 6th ch from hk, * ch 1, dc in 2nd ch behind dc just worked, sk 2 ch, dc in next ch, rep from *, ending row with dc in last ch, ch 3, turn.
Row 2: Dc in next ch-1 sp, * ch 2, dc in sm sp (leave 2 lps on hk), dc in next ch-1 sp, yo, pull through 2 lps on hk, yo, pull through 3 lps on hk (inverted V-st made), rep from *, ending row with 2 dc tog in last ch-1 sp and tch, ch 3, turn.
Row 3: * Sk 2 dc tog, dc in next ch-2 sp, ch 1, dc in skipped 2 dc tog, rep from *, ending row with dc in tch, ch 3, turn.
Rep Rows 2-3 for pattern.

2. Multiples of 12 plus 2.

Row 1: Sc in 2nd ch from hk and in each ch across row, ch 1, turn.
Row 2: Sc in 1st sc, * ch 2, sk 2 sc, sc in next sc, rep from *, ending row with ch 2, sc in last sc, ch 3, turn.
Row 3: Dc in 1st ch-2 sp, * ch 1, dc in next ch-2 sp, dc in prev ch-2 sp, rep from *, ending row with ch 1, dc in last sc, ch 1, turn.
Row 4: Sc in each dc and ch-1 sp across row, sc in tch, ch 1, turn.
Rep Rows 2-4 for pattern.

3. Multiples of 14 plus 3.

Row 1: Dc in 4th ch from hk, dc in next ch, * ch 2, sk 2 ch, dc in next 5 ch, rep from *, ending row with dc in last 3 ch, ch 4, turn.

Row 2: Sk 1st 2 dc, dc in next dc, * ch 2, dc in next dc, (ch 1, sk 1 dc, dc in next dc) 2 times, rep from *, ending row with ch 2, dc in next dc, ch 1, sk last dc, dc in tch, ch 3, turn.

Row 3: Dc in 1st ch-1 sp, dc in next dc, * ch 2, (dc in next dc, dc in next ch-1 sp) 2 times, dc in next dc, rep from *, ending row with ch 2, dc in last dc, 2 dc in tch, ch 4, turn.

Row 4: Sk 1st 2 dc, dc in next dc, * dc in 2nd ch of next ch-2 sp, dc back in 1st ch of sm ch-2 sp, dc in next dc, (ch 1, sk next dc, dc in next dc) 2 times, rep from *, ending row with ch 1, sk last dc, dc in tch, ch 3, turn.

Row 5: Dc in 1st ch-1 sp and next dc, * ch 2, sk next 2 dc, dc in next dc, (dc in next ch-1 sp, dc in next dc) 2 times, rep from *, ending row with ch 2, dc in last dc, 2 dc in tch, ch 4, turn.

Rep Rows 2-5 for pattern.

4. Multiples of 4 plus 4.

Row 1: Tr in 7th ch from hk, * ch 2, tr in 3rd ch behind tr just worked, sk 3 ch, tr in next ch, rep from *, ending row with tr in last ch, ch 1, turn.

Row 2: Sc in 1st tr, * (hdc, dc, hdc) in next ch-2 sp, sc bet next 2 tr, rep from *, ending row with sc in tch, ch 4, turn.

Row 3: Sk 1st sc, tr in next sc, ch 2, tr in skipped sc, * tr in next unworked sc, ch 2, tr back in prev sc, rep from *, ending row with tr in last sc, ch 1, turn.

Rep Rows 2-3 for pattern.

5. Multiples of 6 plus 4.

Row 1: Tr in 7th ch from hk, * ch 1, tr in 2nd ch behind tr just worked, sk 1 ch, 3 tr in next ch, sk 3 ch, tr in next ch, rep from *, ending row with tr in last ch, ch 4, turn.
Row 2: Sk 1st tr, * tr in 3rd tr of 3-tr group, ch 1, tr back in 1st tr of sm 3-tr group, 3 tr in next ch-1 sp, rep from *, ending row with tr in tch, ch 4, turn.
Rep Row 2 for pattern.

6. Multiples of 3 plus 3.

Row 1: Dc in 4th ch from hk and in each ch across row, ch 3, turn.
Row 2: Sk 1st 2 dc, dc in next dc, dc in 2nd dc skipped, * sk 1 dc, dc in next dc, dc in skipped dc, rep from *, ending row with dc in tch, ch 4, turn.
Row 3: Sk 1st dc, * dc in next dc, ch 1, sk next dc, rep from *, ending row with ch 1, dc in tch, ch 3, turn.
Row 4: Sk 1st dc and ch-1 sp, * dc in next dc, dc in skipped ch-1 sp, sk next ch-1 sp, rep from *, ending row with dc in 2nd ch of tch, ch 3, turn.
Row 5: Sk 1st dc, dc in each dc across row, dc in tch, ch 3, turn.
Rep Rows 2-5 for pattern.

7. Multiples of 4 plus 6.

Row 1: Dc in 8th ch from hk, * ch 1, dc in 2nd ch behind dc just worked, ch 1, sk 3 ch, dc in next ch, rep from *, ending row with ch 1, sk 1 ch, dc in last ch, ch 3, turn.
Row 2: Sk 1st dc and ch-1 sp, * dc in next dc, ch 1, dc in skipped dc, ch 1, sk next dc, rep from *, ending row with dc in 2nd ch of tch, ch 1, dc in last skipped dc, dc in 2nd ch of tch, ch 4, turn.

Row 3: Sk 1st 2 dc, * dc in next dc, ch 1, dc in last skipped dc, ch 1, sk next dc, rep from *, ending row with ch 1, sk last dc, dc in tch, ch 3, turn.
Rep Rows 2-3 for pattern.

8. Multiples of 8 plus 5.

Row 1: Dc in 4th ch from hk, dc in next ch, * ch 1, sk 2 ch, (dc, ch 1, dc) in next ch (V-st made), ch 1, sk 2 ch, dc in next 3 ch, rep from * across row, ch 3, turn.
Row 2: Sk 1st dc, dc in next 2 dc, * ch 1, (dc, ch 1, dc) in ch-1 sp of next V-st, ch 1, dc in next 3 dc, rep from *, ending row with dc in last 2 dc, dc in tch, ch 1, turn.
Row 3: Sc in 1st dc, * ch 1, (2 dc, ch 1, 2 dc) in ch-1 sp of next V-st, ch 1, sc in center dc of 3-dc group, rep from *, ending row with sc in tch, ch 3, turn.
Row 4: Dc in 1st sc, * ch 2, sk 2 dc, sc in ch-1 sp, ch 2, dc in 3rd dc of 3-dc group in Row 2, ch 1, dc back in 1st dc of sm 3-dc group, rep from *, ending row with ch 2, 2 dc in last sc, ch 3, turn.
Row 5: 2 dc in 1st dc, * ch 1, sc in sc, ch 1, (2 dc, ch 1, 2 dc) in next ch-1 sp, rep from *, ending row with ch 1, 3 dc in tch, ch 1, turn.
Row 6: Sc in 1st dc, * ch 2, sk ch-1 sp, dc in next ch-1 sp, ch 1, dc in skipped ch-1 sp, ch 2, sc in next ch-1 sp, rep from *, ending row with ch 2, sc in tch, ch 3, turn.
Row 7: * Dc in next sc, dc in ch-2 sp, ch 1, V-st in next ch-1 sp, ch 1, dc in ch-2 sp, rep from *, ending row with dc in last ch-2 sp, 2 dc in last sc, ch 3, turn.
Rep Rows 2-7 for pattern.

9. Multiples of 10 plus 3.

Row 1: Dc in 4th ch from hk and in each ch across row, ch 4, turn.
Row 2: * Sk 4 dc, tr in next dc, ch 2, tr in 3rd dc behind tr just worked, ch 1, rep from *, ending row with tr in tch, ch 3, turn.

Row 3: * 4 dc around next ch-2 sp, rep from *, dc in tch, ch 3, turn.
Row 4: Sk 1st dc, * dc in next 4 dc, ch 1, rep from *, ending row with dc in tch, ch 5, turn.
Row 5: Sk 1st dc, * work next 4 dc tog, ch 5, rep from *, ending row with ch 2, dc in tch, ch 5, turn.
Row 6: * Tr in ch after next 4-dc tog, ch 2, tr back in ch before sm 4-dc tog, ch 1, rep from *, ending row with ch 1, tr in tch, ch 3, turn.
Rep Rows 3-6 for pattern.

10. Multiples of 6 plus 9.

Row 1: Dc in 5th ch from hk, sk 1 ch, dc in next ch, * sk 3 ch, dc in next ch, ch 3, dc in 2nd ch behind dc just worked, sk next ch, dc in next ch, rep from *, ending row with (dc, ch 1, dc) in last ch, ch 3, turn.
Row 2: 3 dc in 1st ch-1 sp, sk next dc, sc in next dc, * 7 dc around next ch-3 sp, sk next dc, sc in next dc, rep from *, ending row with 4 dc in tch, ch 1, turn.
Row 3: Sc in 1st 2 dc, * ch 1, dc in next sc, ch 1, sk 2 dc, sc in next 3 dc, rep from *, ending row with ch 1, sc in last dc, sc in tch, ch 3, turn.
Row 4: * Sk ch-1 sp, dc in next ch-1 sp, ch 3, dc in skipped ch-1 sp, dc in center sc of 3-sc group, rep from *, ending row with dc in last sc, ch 1, turn.
Row 5: Sc in 1st dc, * 7 dc in next ch-3 sp, sk 1 dc, sc in next dc, rep from *, ending row with 7 dc in last ch-3 sp, sc in tch, ch 3, turn.
Row 6: * Sk next 2 dc, sc in next 3 dc, ch 1, dc in next sc, ch 1, rep from *, ending row with ch 1, dc in sc, ch 4, turn.
Row 7: Dc in 1st dc, * dc in center sc of 3-sc group, sk ch-1 sp, dc in next ch-1 sp, ch 3, dc in skipped ch-1 sp, rep from *, ending row with (dc, ch 1, dc) in tch, ch 3, turn.
Rep Rows 2-7 for pattern.

Patterns Using X-Stitch

T-Shirt Trim

Materials Needed: Approximately 250 yards of #20 white cotton thread; #6 steel crochet hook; prewashed T-shirt of desired size; sewing needle; thread.
Finished Size: Measure width of T-shirt edge and determine foundation row by dividing T-shirt width by multiple gauge. Pattern # 4 on page 100 was selected. We used a child's T-shirt that measured 28", (28" ÷ 2" = 14). There are 5 multiple repeats for every 2". (14 x 5 = 70) (We have now determined that 70 repeats of our multiple are needed. (70 x 4 + 4 = 284 ch) A rounding of numbers is sometimes required. Always round up for

clothing items.

Gauge: *Multiples of 4 plus 4.*
5 Multiple repeats = 2"
4 rows = 1"

Ch 284.

Row 1: Tr in 7th ch from hk, * ch 2, tr in 3rd ch behind tr just worked, sk 3 ch, tr in next ch, rep from *, ending row with tr in last ch, ch 1, turn.

Row 2: Sc in 1st tr, * (hdc, dc, hdc) in next ch-2 sp, sc bet next 2 tr, rep from *, ending row with sc in tch, ch 4, turn.

Row 3: Sk 1st sc, tr in next sc, ch 2, tr in skipped sc, * tr in next unworked sc, ch 2, tr back in prev sc, rep from *, ending row with tr in last sc, ch 1, turn.

Rows 4-22: Rep Rows 2-3, end with Row 2, **F.O.**

Finishing: Cut desired length from bottom of T-shirt edge, fold edge for hem and sew trim to edge, using a whip st.

Ladies Jazzy Pearl Tie

Materials Needed: *Approximately 200 yards of #20 white cotton thread; #12 steel crochet hook; approximately 700 4mm pearl beads; needle; jewel clasp.*

Finished Size: *2" x 16"*

Gauge: *10 tr = 1"*
5 rows tr = 1"

Note: Using a needle, string pearl beads onto crochet thread, work in at random intervals by moving the bead close to hook.

Ch 21.

Row 1: Dc in 5th ch from hk, sk 1 ch, dc in next ch, * sk 3 ch, dc in next ch, ch 3, dc in 2nd ch behind dc just worked, sk next ch, dc in next ch, rep from *, ending row with (dc, ch 1, dc) in last ch, ch 3, turn.

Row 2: 3 dc in 1st ch-1 sp, sk next dc, sc in next dc, * 7 dc around next ch-3 sp, sk next dc, sc in next dc, rep from *, ending row with 4 dc in tch, ch 1, turn.

Row 3: Sc in 1st 2 dc, * ch 1, dc in next sc, ch 1, sk 2 dc, sc in next 3 dc, rep from *, ending row with ch 1, sc in last dc, sc in tch, ch 3, turn.

Row 4: * Sk ch-1 sp, dc in next ch-1 sp, ch 3, dc in skipped ch-1 sp, dc in center sc of 3-sc group, rep from *, ending row with dc in last sc, ch 1, turn.

Row 5: Sc in 1st dc, * 7 dc in next ch-3 sp, sk 1 dc, sc in next dc, rep from *, ending row with 7 dc in last ch-3 sp, sc in tch, ch 3, turn.

Row 6: * Sk next 2 dc, sc in next 3 dc, ch 1, dc in next sc, ch 1, rep from *, ending row with ch 1, dc in sc, ch 4, turn.

Row 7: Dc in 1st dc, * dc in center sc of 3-sc group, sk ch-1 sp, dc in next ch-1 sp, ch 3, dc in skipped ch-1 sp, rep from *, ending row with (dc, ch 1, dc) in tch, ch 3, turn.

Rep Rows 2-7 (end with Row 2) until work measures 16 inches, sc evenly around all edges, **F.O.**

Finishing: With wrong side facing you, fold 4" length from beg of work down and over to right side (see diagram), wrap across front, bring edge around to beg

fold, sew edges to secure.

Neck piece: String remaining pearl beads on doubled crochet thread, sew center of strand to top of tie; attach jewel clasp to ends of string.

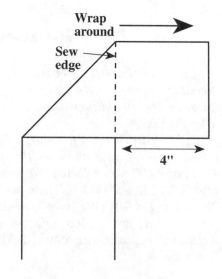

Chapter 13

Wraparound Stitch

1. Multiples of 4 plus 3.

Row 1: Dc in 4th ch from hk, dc in next ch, dc back around post of 1st dc of 2-dc group, * sk 1 ch, dc in next 2 ch, dc back around post of next 2-dc group, rep from *, ending row with sk 1 ch, dc in last ch, ch 3, turn.
Row 2: * Dc in each dc across row, dc in tch, ch 3, turn.
Row 3: Sk 1st dc, * dc in next 2 dc, dc back around post of 1st dc of 2-dc group, sk next dc, rep from *, ending row with dc in tch, ch 3, turn.
Rep Rows 2-3 for pattern.

2. Multiples of 6 plus 1.

Row 1: 2 dc in 5th ch from hk, * sk 2 ch, 3 dc in next ch, rep from *, ending row with sk 1 ch, 2 dc in last ch, ch 3, turn.
Row 2: Sk 1st dc, dc in next 2 dc, * dc back around post of 1st dc of 2-dc group, sk next dc, dc in next 2 dc, rep from *, ending row with dc in tch, ch 4, turn.
Row 3: 2 dc in 2nd dc, * 3 dc bet next 2 dc group, rep from *, ending row with 2 dc in tch, ch 3, turn.
Rep Rows 2-3 for pattern.

3. Multiples of 8 plus 8.

Row 1: Dc in 6th ch from hk, * ch 2, sk 3 ch, dc in next 2 ch, dc back in ch last skipped, ch 2, sk 2 ch, dc in next ch, rep from *, ending row with ch 1, sk 1 ch, dc in last ch, ch 4, turn.
Row 2: Sk 1st dc, dc in next dc, * ch 2, sk ch-2 sp, dc in next 2 dc, dc back in ch-2 sp just skipped, ch 2, dc in next dc, rep from *, ending row with ch 1, dc in 2nd ch of tch, ch 4, turn.
Rep Row 2 for pattern.

4. Multiples of 7 plus 7.

Row 1: Dc in 4th ch from hk, dc in next ch, * dc around post of 1st dc of 2-dc group, sk 2 ch, (dc, ch 1, dc) in next ch, sk 2 ch, dc in next 2 ch, rep from *, ending row with sk 1 ch, dc in last ch, ch 3, turn.
Row 2: Sk 1st 2 dc, * dc in next 2 dc, (dc, ch 1, dc) in next ch-1 sp, sk 2 dc, rep from *, ending row with dc in tch, ch 3, turn.
Row 3: Sk 1st dc, * dc in next 2 dc, dc around post of 1st dc of 2-dc group, (dc, ch 1, dc) in next ch-1 sp, sk next dc, rep from *, ending row with dc in tch, ch 3, turn.
Rep Rows 2-3 for pattern.

5. Multiples of 3 plus 5.

Row 1: Dc in 6th ch from hk, * ch 3, 3 dc tog around post of dc just completed, sk 2 ch, dc in next ch, rep from *, ending row with ch 1, sk 1 ch, dc in last ch, ch 4, turn.
Row 2: * Dc around next ch-3 sp, ch 3, 3 dc tog around post of dc just completed, rep from *, ending row with dc in tch.
Rep Row 2 for pattern.

6. Multiple of 12 plus 3.

Row 1: Dc in 4th ch from hk, dc in next 11 ch, * (ch 3, sk 2 ch, sc in next ch, ch 3, sk 2 ch, dc in next ch) 2 times, dc in next 12 ch, rep from * across row, ch 1, turn.

Row 2: * Sc in next 13 dc, (sk next ch-3 sp, 3 dc in 2nd ch-3 sp, ch 3, 3 dc back in skipped ch-3 sp, sc in next dc) 2 times, sc in next 12 dc, rep from *, ending row with sc in last 11 dc, sc in tch, ch 3, turn.

Row 3: Sk 1st sc, dc in next 12 sc, * (ch 3, sc in next ch-3 sp, ch 3, dc in next sc) 2 times, dc in next 12 sc, rep from * across row, ch 1, turn.

Row 4: Rep Row 2.

Row 5: Sk 1st sc, * dc in next 12 sc, (ch 2, sc in next ch-3 sp, ch 2, dc in next sc) 2 times, rep from *, ending row with dc in last 12 sc, ch 6, turn.

Row 6: Sk 1st 3 dc, * sc in next dc, ch 3, sk next 2 dc, dc in next dc, ch 3, sk 2 dc, sc in next dc, ch 3, sk next 2 dc, dc in next dc, dc in each of next (ch-2 sp, sc, ch-2 sp, dc) 2 times, ch 3, sk next 2 dc, rep from *, ending row with ch 3, dc in tch, ch 1, turn.

Rows 7-11: Rep Rows 2-6, alternating pattern.

Rep Rows 2-11 for pattern.

Patterns Using Wraparound Stitch

Ruffled Eyelet Curtain Valance

Materials Needed: *Approximately 6 ounces of sport weight yarn; size H crochet hook.*
Finished Size: *76" x 8" (fits 18" to 24" wide window). Increase or decrease according to needs using multiples of 4 plus 3. (Refer to Pattern #1)*
Gauge: *10 dc = 2"*
4 rows of dc = 2"
Ch 173.
Rows 1-3: Follow pattern of #1 (page 105).
Rows 4-16: Rep Rows 2-3, do not **F.O.** at end of Row 16, ch 1, turn.
Edging (Chapter 16, #13)
Row 1: Sc in 1st dc, * ch 5, sk 5 ch, sc in next dc, rep from * across, ch 2, turn.
Row 2: (Rep from Pattern 13 of Chapter 16).
Choose any edging pattern from chapter 16 to create a special finishing touch for your designs.

Crocheted Rug

Materials Needed: *Approximately 16 ounces beige worsted weight yarn, beige; size K crochet hook.*
Note: *For heavier texture, use rug yarn or work 2 strands of yarn at the same time.*
Finished Size: *30" x 40"*
Gauge: *3 sc = 1"*
4 rows of sc = 1"

Ch 125.
Row 1: 2 dc in 5th ch from hk, * sk 2 ch, 3 dc in next ch, rep from *, ending row with sk 1 ch, 2 dc in last ch, ch 3, turn.
Row 2: Sk 1st dc, dc in next 2 dc, * dc back around post of 1st dc of 2-dc group, sk next dc, dc in next 2 dc, rep from *, ending row with dc in tch, ch 4, turn.
Row 3: 2 dc in 2nd dc, * 3 dc bet next 2 dc group, rep from *, ending row with 2 dc in tch, ch 3, turn.
Rows 3-36: Rep Row 2.
Row 37: Rep Row 2 except ch 1, turn.
Row 38: Sc in 1st tr, * ch 3, sc in next ch-3 sp, rep from * ,ending row with sc in tch.
Edging: Sc evenly around all edges, work 3 sc in each corner, **F.O.**
Finishing: Cut yarn in equal 9" lengths, attach evenly to side edges of rug for fringe.

Chapter 14

Y-Stitch

1. Multiples of 3 plus 7.

Row 1: Tr in 7th ch from hk, * ch 1, dc around middle of tr post (Y-st made), sk 2 ch, tr in next ch, rep from * across row, ch 4, turn.
Row 2: Rep Row 1, except make Y-st in ch-1 sp of Y-st in prev row, tr in tch, ch 4, turn.
Rep Row 2 for pattern.

2. Multiples of 4 plus 6.

Row 1: Sc in 2nd ch from hk, * ch 3, sk 3 ch, sc in next ch, rep from *, ending row with ch 3, sc in last ch, ch 4, turn.
Row 2: * (Tr, ch 1, dc around middle of tr post) in next ch-3 sp (Y-st made), ch 1, rep from *, ending row with tr in last sc, ch 1, turn.
Row 3: Sc in 1st tr, * ch 3, sc in ch-1 sp bet next 2 Y-st, rep from *, ending row with ch 3, sc in tch, ch 4, turn.
Rep Rows 2-3 for pattern.

Patterns Using Y-Stitch

Sachet Bag

Materials Needed: *Approximately 25 yards of #20 white cotton thread; #7 steel crochet hook; 1/2 yard peach 1/16" satin ribbon; 1/4 yard light green 1/16" satin ribbon; 4mm pearls; 12" square of tulle; small amount potpourri; tacky glue.*

Finished Size: *3" x 5"*

Gauge: *7 tr = 1"*

3 rows of tr = 1"

Side (Make 2)

Ch 34.

Row 1: Tr in 7th ch from hk, * ch 1, dc around middle of tr post (Y-st made), sk 2 ch, tr in next ch, rep from * across row, ch 4, turn.

Row 2: Rep Row 1, except make Y-st in ch-1 sp of Y-st in prev row, tr in tch, ch 4, turn.

Rows 3-12: Rep pattern of Row 2, do not F.O. at end

of 2nd piece.

Edging: Working with both side pieces tog, (sc, hdc, sc) evenly around side and bottom edges, (sc hdc, sc) evenly across each of rem 2 edges, **F.O.**

Finishing: Line sachet bag with tulle, place potpourri inside and weave peach ribbon over and under stitches of Row 10. Pull gently and tie in bow to close. Tie green ribbon in bow, glue ribbon and pearls to sachet bag.

Summer Rose Hat

Materials Needed: *#10 cotton thread: 35 yards light pink, 2 yards leaf green, 2 yards medium pink, 2 yards dark pink; #7 steel crochet hook; wide brim hat; yarn needle.*

Note: Our hat band is for a 20" circumference. Adjust the foundation chain in multiples of 4 for a larger or smaller hat size.

Gauge: *7 tr = 1"*

3 rows of tr = 1"

Hat Band

Using light pink, ch 226.

Row 1: Sc in 2nd ch from hk, * ch 3, sk 3 ch, sc in next ch, rep from *, ending row with ch 3, sc in last ch, ch 4, turn.

Row 2: * (Tr, ch 1, dc around middle of tr post) in next ch-3 sp (Y-st made), ch 1, rep from *, ending row with tr in last sc, ch 1, turn.

Row 3: Sc in 1st dtr, * ch 3, sc in ch-1 sp bet next 2 Y-st, rep from *, ending row with ch 3, sc in tch, ch 4, turn.

Rows 4-5: Rep Rows 2-3, **F.O.** at end of Row 5.

Hat Bow

Using light pink, ch 286.

Rep instructions for hat band.

Hat Bow Center

Ch 18.

Rep Rows 1-3 of hat band.

Rose (Make 6 medium pink-6 dark pink)

Ch 30.

Rep Rows 1-3 of hat band, **F.O.** leaving 6" length for finishing. To form rose, thread yarn needle with finishing length, weave over and under stitches of beg row, pull tight to secure.

Large Leaf (Make 8)

Using green, ch 22.

Rep Rows 1-3 of hat band, **F.O.** leaving 6" length for finishing.

Small Leaf (Make 4)

Using green, ch 10.

Rep Rows 1-3 of hat band, **F.O.** leaving 6" length for finishing.

Shape leaves using same directions as for rose.

Finishing: Sew edges of hat band tog, place on hat. Form 2 loops with bow strip, wrap bow center around, sew to secure. Arrange roses and leaves around hat brim (fold large leaves in half) and sew or glue to secure.

Chapter 15

Motifs

1. Eyelet Square

Ch 8, join with sl st to form a ring.
Rnd 1: 16 sc in ring, join with sl st to beg sc.
Rnd 2: Sc in joining sp, * ch 10, sk 3 sc, sc in next sc, rep from * around, join with sl st to beg sc.
Rnd 3: (11 sc in ch-10 sp, sc in next sc) 4 times, sc in last sc.
Rnd 4: * Sc in next 6 sc, 3 sc in next sc (corner made), sc in next 5 sc, rep from * 3 times, join with sl st to beg sc.
Rnd 5: Sc in each sc, 3 sc in center sc of each corner, sl st in 1st sc.
Rep Rnd 5 for desired size.

2. Puff Stitch Square

Ch 8, join with sl st to form a ring.
Rnd 1: * (4-lp puff st in ring, ch 2) 8 times, sl st to top of 1st 4-lp puff st.
Rnd 2: Sl st to next ch-2 sp, 4-lp puff st in same sp, * ch 2, (dc, ch 2, dc) in next ch-2 sp (corner made), ch 2, 4-lp puff st in next ch-2 sp, rep from *, ending row with (dc, ch 2, dc), ch 2, sl st in 1st 4-lp puff st.
Rnd 3: Sl st to next ch-2 sp, 4-lp puff st in same sp, * ch 2, (dc, ch 2, dc) in corner ch-2 sp, (ch 2, puff st in next ch-2 sp) 2 times, rep from * around, puff st in last ch-2 sp, ch 2, sl st in 1st 4-lp puff st.
Rep Rnd 3, working 1 more puff st on each side of square, until desired size.

3. Flower Square

Ch 5, join with sl st to form a ring.
Rnd 1: 12 sc in ring, sl st in 1st sc.
Rnd 2: (Ch 11, sl st in next sc) 12 times .
Rnd 3: Sl st in 1st 6 ch of 1st ch-11 lp, * ch 4, sc in center of next ch-11 lp, ch 4, (3-lp cl st, ch 2, 3-lp cl st) in next ch-11 lp (corner made), ch 4, sc in center of next ch-11 lp, rep from * 3 times, sl st in top of 1st ch-11 lp.
Rnd 4: Sl st to 1st ch-4 sp, ch 3, 3-lp cl st in same sp, ch 4, sc in next ch-4 sp, ch 4, (3-lp cl st, ch 2, 3-lp cl st) in corner ch-2 sp, ch 4, sc in next ch-4 sp, ch 4, 3-lp cl st in next ch-4 sp, rep from * 3 times, ch 4, sl st in top of 1st 3-lp cl st.

4. Old American Square

Ch 6, join with sl st to form a ring.
Rnd 1: Ch 3, 2 dc in ring, ch 2, (3 dc in ring, ch 2) 3 times, join with sl st in top of beg ch 3.
Rnd 2: Sl st to 1st ch-2 sp, ch 3, (2 dc, ch 2, 3 dc) in same sp to form corner, * ch 1, (3 dc, ch 2, 3 dc in next ch-2 sp) 3 times, ch 1, join with sl st in top of beg ch 3.
Rnd 3: Sl st in 1st ch-2 sp, ch 3, (2 dc, ch 2, 3 dc) in same sp, * ch 1, 3 dc in next ch-1 sp, ch 1, (3 dc, ch 2, 3 dc) in next ch-2 sp, rep from *, ending rnd with ch 1, 3 dc in last ch-1 sp, ch 1, sl st in top of beg ch 3.
Rep Rnd 3 working 1 more 3-dc group on each side of square until desired size.

5. Double-Eyelet Square

Ch 8, join with sl st to form a ring.
Rnd 1: Ch 3, * (3-lp cl st, ch 2, 3-lp cl st) in ring, ch 5, rep from * 3 times, join with sl st to 1st 3-lp cl st.
Rnd 2: Sl st to next ch-2 sp, ch 3, 2 dc in same sp, * ch 2, (3-lp cl st, ch 2, 3-lp cl st) in next ch-5 sp, ch 2, 3 dc in next ch-2 sp, rep from * around, ch 2, join with sl st to top of beg ch 3.
Rnd 3: Ch 3, dc in next 2 dc, 2 dc in next ch-2 sp, ch 2, * (3-lp cl st, ch 2, 3-lp cl st) in next ch-2 sp, ch 2, 2 dc in next ch-2 sp, dc in next 3 dc, 2 dc in next ch-2 sp, ch 2, rep from * around, 2 dc in last ch-2 sp, join with sl st to top of beg ch 3.
Rnds 4 - 6: Rep pattern of Rnd 3 working 2 more dc on each side of dc group.

6. Spoked-Wheel Eyelet Square

Ch 8, join with sl st to form a ring.
Rnd 1: Ch 3, 15 dc in ring, join with sl st to top of beg ch 3.
Rnd 2: Ch 5, (dc in next dc, ch 2) 15 times, join with sl st in 3rd ch of beg ch 5. (16 spokes)
Rnd 3: Ch 3, 2 dc in next ch-2 sp, * ch 1, 3 dc in next ch-2 sp, rep from * around, ch 1, sl st to top of beg ch 3.
Rnd 4: * (Ch 3, sc in next ch-1 sp) 3 times, ch 6, sc in next ch-1 sp, rep from * around, sl st in 1st ch-3 sp to join.
Rnd 5: Ch 3, 2 dc in 1st ch-3 sp, (3 dc in next ch-3 sp) 2 times, * (5 dc, ch 2, 5 dc) in next ch-6 sp, (3 dc in next ch-3 sp) 3 times, rep from * around, end with (5 dc, ch 2, 5 dc) in last ch-6 sp, join with sl st to top of beg ch 3.
Rnd 6: Ch 3, dc in each dc, 4 dc in each ch-2 sp at corners, join with sl st to beg ch 3.

7. Framed Circle

Ch 6, join with sl st to form a ring.
Rnd 1: Ch 3, 15 dc in ring, join with sl st in top of beg ch 3.
Rnd 2: Ch 5, (dc in next dc, ch 2) 15 times, join with sl st to top of beg ch 3. (16 spokes)
Rnd 3: Sl st to next ch-2 sp, ch 3, (dc, ch 3, 2 dc) in same sp, (ch 2, sc in next ch-2 sp) 3 times, * ch 2, (2 dc, ch 3, 2 dc) in next ch-2 sp, (ch 2, sc in next ch-2 sp) 3 times, rep from * around, ch 2, join with sl st to top of beg ch 3.
Rnd 4: Sl st to next ch-3 sp, ch 3, (dc, ch 3, 2 dc) in same sp, (ch 2, sc in next ch-2 sp) 4 times, * ch 2, (2 dc, ch 3, 2 dc) in next ch-3 sp, (ch 2, sc in next ch-2 sp) 4 times, rep from * around, ch 2, join with sl st to top of beg ch 3.
Rnd 5: Sl st to next ch-3 sp, ch 3, (dc, ch 3, 2 dc) in same sp, * (ch 2, sc in next ch-2 sp) 5 times, ch 2, (2 dc, ch 3, 2 dc) in next ch-3 sp, rep from * around, ch 2, join with sl st to top of beg ch 3.

8. Four-Leaf Square

Ch 10, join with sl st to form a ring.
Rnd 1: Ch 4, 3 tr in ring, (ch 7, 4 tr in ring) 3 times, ch 7, join with sl st to top of beg ch 4.
Rnd 2: Ch 4, tr in next 3 tr, tr in next 3 ch, * ch 7, sk 2 ch, tr in next 3 ch, tr in next 4 tr, tr in next 3 ch, rep from * around, ch 7, tr in last 3 ch, join with sl st to top of beg ch 4.
Rnd 3: Ch 4, tr in next 6 tr, tr in next 3 ch, * ch 7, sk 2 ch, tr in next 3 ch, tr in next 10 tr, tr in next 3 ch, rep from * around, ch 7, tr in last 3 ch, tr in next 3 tr, join with sl st to top of beg ch 4.

9. Granny-Square Wheel

Ch 8, join with sl st to form a ring.
Rnd 1: Ch 6 (counts as dc, ch 3), * dc in center of ring, ch 3, rep from * 6 times, join with sl st to 3rd ch of beg ch 6.
Rnd 2: Sl st in next ch-3 sp, ch 3, 3 dc in same ch-3 sp, ch 2, * 4 dc in next ch-3 sp, ch 2, rep from * around, join with sl st to top of beg ch 3.
Rnd 3: Sl st in next 3 dc, ch 3, 5 dc in next ch-2 sp, ch 1, * 6 dc in next ch-2 sp, ch 3, 6 dc in next ch-2 sp, ch 1, rep from * 2 times, end rnd with 6 dc in last ch-2 sp, ch 3, join with sl st to top of beg ch 3.
Rnd 4: Sl st in next 2 dc, sl st in sp before next dc, * ch 3, sc in next ch-1 sp, ch 3, sk 3 dc, sc in sp before next dc, ch 3, (2 dc, ch 3, 2 dc) in next ch-3 sp, ch 3, sk 3 dc, sc in sp before next dc, rep from * around, join with sl st to bottom of beg ch 3.

10. Scalloped Wheel

Ch 5, join with sl st to form a ring.
Rnd 1: Ch 3, 15 dc in center of ring, join with sl st to top of beg ch 3.
Rnd 2: Sc in joining sp, * ch 3, sk next dc, sc in next dc, rep from * 6 times, end with ch 3, sk next dc, join with sl st to 1st sc.
Rnd 3: (Sc, hdc, 2 dc, hdc, sc) in each ch-3 lp around. (8 shells made)
Rnd 4: Sl st in next (sc, hdc, dc), sc in sp before next dc, * ch 4, sc bet 2 dc of next shell, ch 7, sc bet 2 dc of next shell, rep from * 3 times, join with sl st to beg sc.
Rnd 5: Sc in each sc and ch around, work 3 sc in 4th ch of each ch-7 lp to form corners, join with sl st to beg sc.
Rnd 6: Sc in each sc around, 3 sc in center sc of each corner, join with sl st to beg sc.

11. Double Square

Ch 29.

Row 1: Dc in 4th ch from hk, dc in next ch, * ch 3, sk 3 ch, dc in next 3 ch, rep from * across row, ch 5, turn.

Row 2: * 3 dc in next ch-3 sp, ch 3, rep from *, ending row with ch 2, dc in tch, ch 3, turn.

Row 3: 2 dc in ch-2 sp, * ch 3, 3 dc in next ch-3 sp, rep from *, ending row with 3 dc in tch, ch 5, turn.

Rows 4-7: Rep Rows 2-3 for pattern.

Edging: * Ch 3, 3 dc in each sp around, rep from * evenly around all sides, (3 dc, ch 3, 3 dc) in each corner.

12. Framed Star

Ch 5, join with sl st to form a ring.

Rnd 1: Ch 6 (counts as dc, ch 3), * dc in ring, ch 3, rep from * 6 times, join with sl st to 3rd ch of beg ch 6.

Rnd 2: Ch 3 (counts as dc), * 4 dc in next ch-3 sp, dc in next dc, rep from * around, end with 4 dc in last ch-3 sp, join with sl st to top of beg ch 3. (40 dc)

Rnd 3: * Ch 6, sc in 2nd ch from hk, hdc in next ch, dc in next ch, tr in next ch, dtr in last ch, sk next 4 dc, sc in next dc, rep from * 7 times, **F. O.** (8 star points made)

Rnd 4: Join yarn with sl st to beg sc of any star point, ch 4, (tr, ch 3, 2 tr) in same sp, * ch 6, sc in next star point, ch 6, (2 tr, ch 3, 2 tr) in next star point, rep from * 2 times, end with ch 6, sc in next star point, ch 6, join with sl st to top of beg ch 4.

Rnd 5: Ch 3 (counts as 1 dc), dc in next tr, * 5 dc in ch-3 sp, dc in next 2 tr, dc in next 6 ch, dc in next sc, dc in next 6 ch, dc in next 2 tr, rep from * 3 times, join with sl st to top of beg ch 3. (88 dc made)

Rnd 6: Ch 4, sk next dc, dc in next dc, ch 1, sk next dc, (dc, ch 3, dc) in next dc, * (ch 1, sk next dc, dc in next dc) 10 times, ch 1, sk next dc, (dc, ch 3, dc) in next dc, rep from * 3 times, end with ch 1, sk next dc, join with sl st to 2nd ch of beg ch 4.

13. Grape Eyelet Square

Ch 10, join with sl st to form a ring.

Rnd 1: Ch 3, * 5-dc pc st in center of ring, ch 3, rep from * 7 times, join with sl st to top of 1st pc st. (8 pc st made)

Rnd 2: Ch 6, dc in next ch-3 sp, * ch 3, (dc, ch 3, dc) in next ch-3 sp, rep from * around, ch 3, join with sl st to 4th ch of beg ch 6.

Rnd 3: * Ch 3, 5-dc pc st in next ch-3 sp, rep from * around, ch 3, join with sl st to top of 1st pc st.

Rnd 4: Rep Rnd 2.

Rnd 5: Rep Rnd 3.

Rnd 6: Sl st in next ch-3 sp, sc in same sp, * ch 8, sk next ch-3 sp, sc in next ch-3 sp, rep from * around, end with ch 8, join with sl st to beg sc.

Rnd 7: Ch 3, * (5-dc pc st, ch 2) 3 times in next 2 ch-8 sp, 8 tr in next 2 ch-8 sp, ch 2, rep from * around, join with sl st to top of 1st pc st.

Rnd 8: Ch 3, 5-dc pc st in next ch-2 sp, * (ch 2, pc st in next ch-2 sp) 4 times, ch 5, sk next pc st, sc in next tr, (ch 5, sk 1 tr, sc in next tr) 2 times, ch 5, sk 1 tr, tr in next 4 tr, (ch 5, sk 1 tr, sc in next tr) 3 times, ch 5, sk next pc st, 5-dc pc st in next ch-2 sp, rep from * around, end with ch 5, join with sl st to top of 1st pc st.

Rnd 9: Ch 3, 5-dc pc st in next ch-2 sp, * (ch 2, pc st in next ch-2 sp) 3 times, sk next pc st, (ch 5, sc in next ch-5 sp) 3 times, ch 5, sk next ch-5 sp, tr in next tr, (ch 2, tr in next tr) 3 times, ch 5, sk next ch-5 sp, sc in next ch-5 sp, (ch 5, sc in next ch-5 sp) 2 times, ch 5, sk next pc st, pc st in next ch-2 sp, rep from * around, end with ch 5, join with sl st to top of 1st pc st.

Rnd 10: Ch 3, 5-dc pc st in next ch-2 sp, * (ch 2, pc st in next ch-2 sp) 2 times, sk next pc st, (ch 5, sc in next ch-5 sp) 3 times, ch 5, sk next ch-5 sp, 2 tr in next tr, (ch 3, 2 tr in next tr) 3 times, ch 5, sk next ch-5 sp, sc in next ch-5 sp, (ch 5, sc in next ch-5 sp) 2 times, ch 5, sk next pc st, 5-dc pc st in next ch-2 sp, rep from * around, end with ch 5, join with sl st to top of 1st pc st.

Rnd 11: Ch 3, 5-dc pc st in next ch-2 sp, * ch 2, pc st in next ch-2 sp, sk next pc st, (ch 5, sc in next ch-5 sp) 3 times, ch 5, sk next ch-5 sp, (tr in next 2 tr, ch 4) 2 times, pc st in next ch-3 sp, (ch 4, tr in next 2 tr) 2 times, ch 5, sk next ch-5 sp, sc in next ch-5 sp, (ch 5, sc in next ch-5 sp) 2 times, ch 5, sk next pc st, pc st in next ch-2 sp, rep from * around, end with ch 5, join with sl st to top of 1st pc st.

Rnd 12: Ch 3, 5-dc pc st in next ch-2 sp, * sk pc st, (ch 5, sc in next ch-5 sp) 3 times, ch 5, sk next ch-5 sp, (tr in next 2 tr, ch 4) 2 times, pc st in next ch-4 sp, ch 2, sk next pc st, pc st in next ch-4 sp, (ch 4, tr in next 2 tr) 2 times, ch 5, sk next ch-5 sp, sc in next ch-5 sp, (ch 5, sc in next ch-5 sp) 2 times, ch 5, sk next pc st, pc st in next ch-2 sp, rep from * around, end with ch 5, join with sl st to top of 1st pc st.

Rnd 13: Sl st to center of 1st ch-5 sp, sc in same ch-5 sp, ch 5, sc in next ch-5 sp, * ch 5, sc in next ch-5 sp, ch 5, sk next ch-5 sp, (tr in next 2 tr, ch 4) 2 times, pc st in next ch-4 sp, ch 2, pc st in next ch-2 sp, ch 2, pc st in next ch-4 sp, (ch 4, tr in next 2 tr) 2 times, ch 5, sk next ch-5 sp, sc in next ch-5 sp, (ch 5, sc in next ch-5 sp) 2 times, rep from * around, end with ch 5, join with sl st to beg sc.

14. Squared Eyelet

Ch 6, join with sl st to form a ring.

Rnd 1: Ch 2, (yo, insert hk in center of ring, yo, pull through, yo, pull through 1 lp on hk, yo, pull through 2 lps on hk) 2 times, yo, pull through last 3 lps on hk, ch 2, [(yo, insert hk in center of ring, yo, pull through, yo, pull through 1 lp on hk, yo, pull through 2 lps on hk) 3 times, yo, pull through last 4 lps on hk (cluster group made)], * ch 5, (cl group, ch 2, cl group) in center of ring, rep from * 2 times, end with ch 5, join with sl st to top of beg cl group.

Rnd 2: * (Cl group, ch 5, cl group) in next ch-2 sp, ch 2, 3 dc in next ch-5 sp, ch 2, rep from * 3 times, join with sl st to beg cl group.

Rnd 3: * (Cl group, ch 5, cl group) in next ch-5 sp, ch 2, 2 dc in next ch-2 sp, dc in next 3 dc, 2 dc in next ch-2 sp, ch 2, rep from * around, join with sl st to beg cl group.

Rnd 4: * (Cl group, ch 5, cl group) in next ch-5 sp, ch 2, 2 dc in next ch-2 sp, dc in next 7 dc, 2 dc in next ch-2 sp, ch 2, rep from * around, join with sl st to beg cl group.

15. Posey

Ch 6, join with sl st to form a ring.

Rnd 1: Ch 2, 23 sc in ring, join with sl st to top of beg ch 2.

Rnd 2: Ch 5, dc in joining sp, ch 1, * sk 2 sc, (dc, ch 2, dc) in next sc, ch 1, rep from * around, join with sl st to 3rd ch of beg ch 5.

Rnd 3: Sl st in next ch-2 sp, ch 2, (hdc, ch 2, hdc) in same sp, sc in next ch-1 sp, * (2 hdc, ch 2, 2 hdc) in ch-2 sp, sc in next ch-1 sp, rep from * around, sl st in top of beg ch 2.

Rnd 4: Sl st in next ch-2 sp, ch 3, (2 dc, ch 1, 3 dc) in same sp, * sc on each side of next sc, (3 dc, ch 1, 3 dc) in next ch-2 sp, rep from * around, end with sc on each side of last sc, join with sl st to top of beg ch 3.

16. Four-Leaf Clover

Ch 5, join with sl st to form a ring.

Rnd 1: 12 sc in ring, join with sl st to beg sc.

Rnd 2: *Ch 4, (yo twice, insert hk in next sc, pull up lp, yo, pull through 2 lps, yo, pull through 2 lps) 3 times in same st, yo, pull through rem 4 lps, ch 4, sc in next 2 sc, rep from * around.

17. Star

Ch 5, join with sl st to form a ring.

Rnd 1: 10 sc in ring, join with sl st to beg sc.

Rnd 2: *Sc in next sc, 2 sc in next sc, rep from * around, join with sl st to beg sc.

Rnd 3: * Ch 6, sc in 2nd ch from hk, hdc in next ch, dc in next ch, tr in next ch, dtr in last ch, sk 2 sc, sc in next sc, rep from * around, join with sl st to base of beg ch 6.

18. Hexagon

Ch 6, join with sl st to form a ring.
Rnd 1: Ch 3, 2 dc in ring, ch 3, (3 dc in ring, ch 3) 5 times, join with sl st to top of beg ch 3.
Rnd 2: Sl st to next ch-3 sp, ch 4, (2 tr, ch 2, 3 tr) in ch-3 sp, * (3 tr, ch 2, 3 tr) in next ch-3 sp, rep from * around, join with sl st to top of beg ch 4.
Rnd 3: Ch 3, * dc in each tr, (2 dc, ch 2, 2 dc) in next ch-2 sp, rep from * around, join with sl st in top of beg ch 3.
Rnd 4: Ch 3, * sk next st, dc in next st, dc in skipped st, rep from * around, join with sl st in top of beg ch 3.

19. Scalloped Granny Wheel

Ch 6, join with sl st to form a ring.
Rnd 1: Ch 6 (counts as dc, ch 3), * dc in ring, ch 3, rep from * 5 times, join with sl st to 4th ch of beg ch 6.
Rnd 2: Sl st in next ch-3 sp, ch 3, 3 dc in same ch-3 sp, ch 2, * 4 dc in next ch-3 sp, ch 2, rep from * around, join with sl st to top of beg ch 3.
Rnd 3: Sl st to next ch-2 sp, ch 3, 4 dc in same ch-2 sp, ch 3, * 5 dc in next ch-2 sp, ch 3, rep from * around, join with sl st to top of beg ch 3.
Rnd 4: Sl st to next ch-3 sp, ch 3, (4 dc, ch 2, 5 dc) in same sp, * sc in center of next 5-dc group, (5 dc, ch 2, 5 dc) in next ch-3 sp, rep from * around, end with sc in center of last 5-dc group, join with sl st to top of beg ch 3.

20. Dogwood

Ch 2.

Rnd 1: 8 sc in 2nd ch from hk, join with sl st to 1st sc.

Rnd 2: Sc in 1st sc, ch 4, sk next sc, sc in next sc, (ch 4, sk next sc, sc in next sc) 2 times, ch 4, join with sl st to beg sc.

Rnd 3: Sl st in next ch-4 sp, ch 3, 6 dc in same sp, ch 2, * 7 dc in next ch-4 sp, ch 2, rep from * 2 times, join with sl st in top of beg ch 3.

Rnd 4: Ch 1, sc in joining sp, * sc in next 3 dc, 2 sc in next dc, sc in next 3 dc, ch 3, rep from * around, join with sl st to top of beg sc.

Rnd 5: Ch 3, dc in next 2 sc, * (2 dc in next sc) 2 times, dc in next 3 sc, 3 dc in ch-3 sp, dc in next 3 sc, rep from * around, join with sl st to beg ch 3.

Rnd 6: Sk 1st dc, * sc in next dc, ch 2, sk next dc, dc in next 4 dc, ch 2, sk next dc, rep from * around, join with sl st to beg sc.

21. Paddle Wheel

Ch 5, join with sl st to form a ring.

Rnd 1: (Ch 6, sc in ring) 6 times.

Rnd 2: Sl st to top of 1st ch-6 lp, * ch 4, sc in top of next ch-6 lp, rep from * around, join with sl st to top of 1st ch-6 lp.

Rnd 3: Sc in joining sp, * sc in next ch, ch 4, sc in next sc, rep from * around, join with sl st to beg sc.

Rnd 4: Sc in joining sp, sc in next sc, * sc in next ch, ch 4, sc in next 2 sc, rep from * around, end with ch 4, join with sl st to beg sc.

Rep Rnd 4 as many times as desired, adding 1 sc to each sc-group.

22. Wagon Wheel

Ch 4, join with sl st to form a ring.
Rnd 1: Ch 2, (5-lp puff st in ring, ch 1) 8 times, sl st in top of beg puff st.
Rnd 2: Sl st to next ch-1 sp, ch 3, dc in same sp, ch 2, * 2 dc in next ch-1 sp, ch 2, rep from * around, join with sl st to beg ch 3.
Rnd 3: Sl st to next ch-2 sp, ch 3, (dc, ch 1, 2 dc) in same sp, ch 1, * (2 dc, ch 1, 2 dc) in next ch-2 sp, ch 1, rep from * around, join with sl st to beg ch 3.
Rnd 4: Sl st to next ch-1 sp, ch 3, 2 dc in same sp, * ch 1, 3 dc in next ch-1 sp, ch 1, rep from * around, join with sl st to beg ch 3.
Rep Rnd 4 as many times as desired, after 5th rnd, ch 2 bet each dc group.

23. Geometric Circle

Ch 10, join with sl st to form a ring.
Rnd 1: Ch 3, 29 dc in ring, join with sl st to top of beg ch 3.
Rnd 2: Ch 6, * sk 2 dc, dc in next dc, ch 3, rep from * 8 times, join with sl st to 4th ch of beg ch 6.
Rnd 3: Ch 3, 2 dc in joining sp, * ch 3, 3 dc in next dc, rep from * around, end with ch 3, join with sl st to top of beg ch 3.
Rnd 4: Ch 3, dc in next 2 dc, * ch 4, dc in next 3 dc, rep from * around, end with ch 4, join with sl st to top of beg ch 3.

Rnd 5: Ch 3, dc in next 2 dc, * ch 5, dc in next 3 dc, rep from * around, end with ch 5, join with sl st to top of beg ch 3.

24. Sunflower

Ch 6, join with sl st to form a ring.
Rnd 1: Ch 1, 12 sc in ring, join with sl st to 1st sc.
Rnd 2: Ch 1, * sc in next sc, 2 sc in next sc, rep from * around, join with sl st to 1st sc. (18 sc)
Rnd 3: Ch 1, * sc in next 2 sc, 2 sc in next sc, rep from * around, join with sl st to 1st sc. (24 sc)
Rnd 4: Ch 1, * sc in next 3 sc, 2 sc in next sc, rep from * around, join with sl st to 1st sc. (30 sc)
Rnd 5: Ch 1, * sc in next 4 sc, 2 sc in next sc, rep from * around, join with sl st to 1st sc. (36 sc)
Rnd 6: Ch 1, * sc in next 5 sc, 2 sc in next sc, rep from * around, join with sl st to 1st sc. (42 sc)
Rnd 7: Ch 1, * sc in next 6 sc, 2 sc in next sc, rep from * around, join with sl st to 1st sc. (48 sc)
Rnd 8: Ch 4, [yo twice, insert hk in joining sp, yo, pull through, (yo, pull through 2 lps on hk) 2 times] 2 times, yo, pull through last 3 lps on hk (2-tr cl-st made), * ch 5, sk 2 sc, [yo twice, insert hk in next sc, yo, pull through, (yo, pull through 2 lps on hk) 2 times] 3 times, yo, pull through last 4 lps on hk (3-tr cl-st made), rep from * around, end with ch 5, join with sl st to top of 1st cl st.
Rnd 9: Sl st to center of next ch-5 sp, sc in same sp, ch 6, * sc in next ch-5 sp, ch 6, rep from * around, join with sl st to 1st sc.

25. Six-Spoked Wheel

Ch 6, join with sl st to form a ring.

Rnd 1: Ch 1, 12 sc in ring, join with sl st to 1st sc.

Rnd 2: Ch 4, 2 tr in joining sp, * ch 3, sk next sc, 3 tr in next sc, rep from * around, end with ch 3, join with sl st to top of beg ch 4.

Rnd 3: Ch 4, tr in joining sp, * tr in next tr, 2 tr in next tr, (ch 6, sc in 4th ch from hk) (picot made), ch 2, 2 tr in next tr, rep from * around, end with tr in next tr, 2 tr in next tr, (picot), ch 2, join with sl st to top of beg ch 4.

Rnd 4: Ch 4, tr in joining sp, * tr in next 3 tr, 2 tr in next tr, ch 9, 2 tr in next tr, rep from * around, end with tr in next 3 tr, 2 tr in next tr, ch 9, join with sl st to top of beg ch 4.

Rnd 5: Ch 4, yo twice, insert hk in next tr sp, yo, pull through, (yo, pull through 2 lps on hk) 2 times, yo, pull through last 3 lps on hk (2 tr inverted V-st made), * ch 5, sl st in next tr, ch 5, [yo twice, insert hk in next tr, yo, pull through, (yo, pull 2 lps on hk) 2 times] 3 times, yo, pull through last 4 lp on hk (3 tr inverted V-st made), ch 6, sk 4 ch, (sc, ch 4, sc) in next ch, ch 6, tr V-st in next 3 tr, rep from * around, end with ch 6, join with sl st to top of beg V-st.

26. Lacy Hexagon

Ch 8, join with sl st to form a ring.

Rnd 1: Ch 4 (counts as dc, ch 1), * dc in ring, ch 1, rep from * 10 times, join with sl st to 2nd ch of beg ch 4. (12 dc)

Rnd 2: Sc in 1st ch-1 sp, ch 4, * sk (dc, ch-1 sp, dc), sc in next ch-1 sp, ch 4, rep from * 5 times, join with sl st to 1st sc. (6 ch-4 sp)

Rnd 3: Ch 1, sc in same sc as joining sp, * ch 1, (dc, ch 1) 4 times in next ch-4 sp, sc in next sc, rep from * around, join with sl st to 1st sc.

Rnd 4: Ch 4, tr in joining sp, ch 1, (tr, ch 1) 2 times in same sp, * sk next ch-1 sp, sc in next ch-1 sp, ch 1, (tr, ch 1) 4 times in next sc, rep from * around, end with sk next ch-1 sp, sc in next ch-1 sp, ch 1, join with sl st to 3rd ch of beg ch 4.

Rnd 5: Ch 1, * (sc, ch 1, sc in next ch-1 sp) 3 times, (ch 1, sc in next ch-1 sp) 2 times, ch 1, rep from * around, join with sl st to 1st sc.

27. Grape

Ch 5.

Row 1: 2 dc in 5th ch from hk, ch 3, 3 dc in same ch, turn.

Row 2: Sl st in 1st 3 dc, sl st in next ch-3 sp, (ch 3, 2 dc) in same ch-3 sp, (ch 3, 3 dc in same ch-3 sp) 2 times, turn.

Row 3: Sl st in 1st 3 dc, sl st in next ch-3 sp, (ch 3, 2 dc, ch 2, 3 dc) in same ch-3 sp, sk 3 dc, (3 dc, ch 2, 3 dc) in next ch-3 sp, turn.

Row 4: Sl st in 1st 3 dc, sl st in next ch-2 sp, (ch 3, 2 dc, ch 2, 3 dc) in same ch-2 sp, sk 3 dc, dc in sp before next dc, sk 3 dc, (3 dc, ch 2, 3 dc) in next ch-2 sp (shell made), turn.

Row 5: Sl st in 1st 3 dc, sl st in next ch-2 sp, (ch 3, 2 dc, ch 2, 3 dc) in same ch-2 sp, sk 3 dc, (dc, ch 3, dc) in next dc, sk 3 dc, shell in next ch-2 sp, turn.

Row 6: Sl st in 1st 3 dc, sl st in next ch-2 sp, (ch 3, 2 dc, ch 2, 3 dc) in same ch-2 sp, ch 1, 9 dc in next ch-3 sp, ch 1, shell in next ch-2 sp, turn.

Row 7: Sl st in 1st 3 dc, sl st in next ch-2 sp, (ch 3, 2 dc, ch 2, 3 dc) in same ch-2 sp, ch 1, sk (3 dc, ch 1), (dc, ch 1 in next dc) 9 times, sk (ch 1, 3 dc), shell in next ch-2 sp, turn.

Row 8: Sl st in 1st 3 dc, sl st in next ch-2 sp, (ch 3, 2 dc, ch 2, 3 dc) in same ch-2 sp, ch 2, sk (3 dc, ch 1), (3-lp puff st in next ch-1 sp, ch 2) 8 times, sk (ch 1, 3 dc), shell in next ch-2 sp, turn.

Row 9: Sl st in 1st 3 dc, sl st in next ch-2 sp, (ch 3, 2 dc, ch 2, 3 dc) in same ch-2 sp, ch 2, sk (3 dc, ch 2), (3-lp puff st in next ch-2 sp, ch 2) 7 times, sk (puff st, ch 2, 3 dc), shell in next ch-2 sp, turn.

Rows 10-15: Rep pattern of row 9 decreasing 1 puff st for each row.

Row 16: Sl st in 1st 3 dc, sl st in next ch-2 sp, (ch 3, 2 dc, ch 2, 3 dc) in same ch-2 sp, sk (3 dc, ch 2, puff st, ch 2, 3 dc), shell in next ch-2 sp, turn.

Row 17: Sl st in 1st 3 dc, sl st in next ch-2 sp, (ch 3, 2 dc) in same ch-2 sp, sk 6 dc, 3 dc in next ch-2 sp.

28. Rose

Ch 4, join with sl st to form a ring.
Rnd 1: Ch 6, (dc in ring, ch 3) 6 times, join with sl st to 3rd ch of beg ch 6.
Rnd 2: Ch 1, (sc, hdc, 3 dc, hdc, sc) in each ch-3 sp around, join with sl st to 1st sc. (7 petals)
Rnd 3: Ch 1, sc in joining sp, ch 5, * sc in sp bet next 2 petals, ch 5, rep from * around, join with sl st to 1st sc. (Place ch-5 lp behind petals)
Rnd 4: Ch 1, (sc, hdc, 5 dc, hdc, sc) in each ch-5 lp around, join with sl st to 1st sc.
Rnd 5: Ch 1, sc in joining sp, ch 7, * sc in sp bet next 2 petals, ch 7, rep from * around, join with sl st to 1st sc. (Place ch-7 lp behind petals)
Rnd 6: Ch 1, (sc, hdc, dc, 4 tr, dc, hdc, sc) in each ch-7 lp around, join with sl st to 1st sc.

29. Spoked Hexagon

Ch 8, join with sl st to form a ring.
Rnd 1: Ch 3 (counts as dc), 17 dc in ring, join with sl st to top of beg ch 3.
Rnd 2: Ch 1, sc in joining sp, * ch 5, sk 2 dc, sc in next dc, rep from * 5 times, join with sl st to 1st sc.
Rnd 3: Sl st to next ch-5 sp, ch 3 (counts as dc), 8 dc in same ch-5 sp, * 8 dc in next ch-5 sp, rep from * around, join with sl st to top of beg ch 3. (49 dc)

Rnd 4: Working through back lp only, ch 3 (counts as dc), dc in joining sp, * sk next dc, (ch 1, dc in next dc) 5 times, ch 1, sk next dc, 2 dc in next dc, rep from * 4 times, end with sk next dc, (ch 1, dc in next dc) 5 times, ch 1, join with sl st to top of beg ch 3.

Rnd 5: Ch 6 (counts as dc, ch 3), dc in joining sp (corner made), * (ch 1, dc in next dc) 6 times, ch 1, (dc, ch 3, dc) in next dc, rep from * 4 times, end with (ch 1, dc in next dc) 6 times, ch 1, join with sl st to 4th ch of beg ch 6.

Rnd 6: Sl st to next ch-3 sp, ch 6, dc in same sp, * (ch 1, sk next dc, dc in next ch-1 sp) 7 times, ch 1, (dc, ch 3, dc) in corner ch-3 sp, rep from * 4 times, end with (ch 1, sk next dc, dc in next ch-1 sp) 7 times, ch 1, join with sl st in 4th ch of beg ch 6.

30. Flower In Hexagon

Ch 6, join with sl st to form a ring.

Rnd 1: Ch 4, 23 tr in ring, join with sl st to top of beg ch 4.

Rnd 2: Ch 4, (yo, insert hk horizontally from right to left under ch 4 of prev rnd, yo, pull up a long lp) 4 times, yo, pull through 9 lps on hk (puff st made), ch 1, * sk next tr, (2 dc, tr, 2 dc) in next tr, ch 1, sk next tr, (puff st from right to left around next tr), ch 1, rep from * around, end with sk next tr, (2 dc, tr, 2 dc) in next tr, ch 1, sk last tr, join with sl st to top of 1st puff st. (6 puff st made)

Rnd 3: Sc in each (ch-1 sp, puff st and dc) around, 3 sc in each tr around (corner made), join with sl st to 1st sc.

31. Snowflake

Ch 6, join with sl st to form a ring.

Rnd 1: Ch 4, (keeping last lp of each tr on hk) 2 tr in ring, yo, pull through 3 lp on hk, * ch 5, (keeping last lp of each tr on hk) 3 tr into ring, yo, pull through 4 lp on hk (cl st made), rep from * 3 times, ch 5, join with sl st to top of 1st cl st.

Rnd 2: * Ch 7, sl st in 3rd ch from hk (picot made), ch 4, sl st in same cl st, ch 7, sl st in 3rd ch from hk, (ch 3, sl st in 3rd ch from hk) 2 times (picot cl made), ch 4, sl st in next cl st, rep from * around, join with sl st in bottom of beg ch 7.

32. Six-Point Snowflake

Ch 15, join with sl st to form a ring.

Rnd 1: (Ch 4, tr in ring, ch 4, sl st in ring) 12 times.

Rnd 2: Sl st to top of beg ch 4, ch 1, sc in tr, (ch 11, sk next tr, sc in next tr) 5 times, ch 11, sk next tr, join with sl st to beg sc.

Rnd 3: Ch 1, (sc in 1st 5 ch of next ch-11 lp, 3 sc in next ch, sc in next 5 ch) 6 times, join with sl st to beg sc.

Rnd 4: Ch 1, sc in joining sp, sc in each sc around, 3 sc in center sc of each 3-sc group, join with sl st to beg sc.

Rnd 5: Ch 1, sc in joining sp, sc in each sc around, 3 sc in center sc of each 3-sc group, join with sl st to beg sc.

Rnd 6: Ch 1, sc in joining sp, * ch 6, tr in center sc of next 3-sc group, ch 5, sl st in 3rd ch from hk (picot made), ch 2, (tr in same sp, picot, ch 2) 3 times, tr in same sp, ch 6, sk next 7 sc, sc in next 2 sc, rep from * around, end with sc in last sc, join with sl st to beg of sc.

33. Daisy

Ch 6, join with sl st to form a ring.

Rnd 1: (5-lp puff st in ring, ch 3) 6 times, join with sl st to top of beg puff st.

Rnd 2: * 5 sc in next ch-3 lp, sc in next puff st, rep from * around, end with 5 sc in last ch-3 lp, sc in last puff st, join with sl st to 1st sc at beg of rnd.

Rnd 3: Ch 1, sc in joining sp, * ch 4, 5-lp puff st in next sc, (ch 1, sk next sc, puff st in next sc) 2 times, ch 4, sc in next sc, rep from * around, join with sl st to 1st sc at beg of rnd.

Rnd 4: Ch 1, sc in joining sp, * ch 2, (5-lp puff st in top of next puff st, ch 1) 2 times, puff st in next puff st, ch 2, sc in next sc, rep from * around, join with sl st in 1st sc at beg of rnd.

Rnd 5: Ch 8, * sk next puff st, sc in next puff st, ch 5, dc in next sc, ch 5, rep from * around, end with ch 5, sl st in 6th ch of beg ch 8.

Rnd 6: Ch 1, sc in joining sp, * 5 sc in next ch-5 lp, 3 sc in next dc, 5 sc in next ch-5 lp, sc in next dc, rep from * around, join with sl st to 1st sc at beg of rnd.

Rnd 7: Ch 1, sc in joining sp, * ch 3, sc in 3rd ch from hk (picot made), sk next sc, sc in next sc, rep from * around, join with sl st to 1st sc at beg of rnd.

34. Wreath

Ch 50, join with sl st to form a ring.

Rnd 1: Ch 5 (counts as dc, ch 2), sk next ch, dc in next ch, (ch 2, sk next ch, dc in next ch) 23 times, end with ch 2, join with sl st in 3rd ch of beg ch 5.

Rnd 2: Sl st in next ch-2 sp, ch 3 (counts as dc), 2 dc in same sp, ch 2, (3 dc in next ch-2 sp, ch 2) 24 times, join with sl st to top of beg ch 3.

Rnd 3: Ch 4 (counts as tr), [yo twice, pull up lp in next dc, (yo, pull through 2 lp on hk) 2 times] 2 times, yo, pull through rem 3 lp on hk, ch 4, sc in next ch-2 sp, ch 4, * [yo twice, pull up lp in next dc, (yo, pull through 2 lp in hk) 2 times] 3 times, yo, pull through rem 4 lp on hk (3-tr inverted V-st made), ch 4, sc in next ch-2 sp, ch 4, rep from * 23 times, join with sl st to top of beg inverted V-st.

Rnd 4: (Ch 6, sl st in top of next inverted V-st) 24 times, join with sl st to bottom of beg ch 6.

Rnd 5: Sl st in next 3 ch of ch-6 sp, (ch 8, sl st in center of next ch-6 sp) 24 times, end with ch 8, join with sl st in bottom of beg ch 8.

35. Five-Point Snowflake

Ch 2.

Rnd 1: 10 sc in 2nd ch from hk, sl st in 1st sc.

Rnd 2: Ch 6 (counts as tr, ch 2), (tr in next sc, ch 2) 9 times, sl st in 3rd ch of beg ch 6.

Rnd 3: Ch 3 (counts as dc), 2 dc in next ch-2 sp, dc in tr, 2 dc in next ch-2 sp, * ch 3, (dc in next tr, 2 dc in ch-2 sp) 2 times, rep from * around, end with ch 3, join with sl st to beg ch 3.

Rnd 4: Ch 4 (counts as tr), [yo twice, pull up lp in next dc, (yo, pull through 2 lp on hk) 2 times] 5 times, yo, pull through rem 6 lp on hk, 14 ch, * [yo twice, pull up lp in next dc, (yo, pull through 2 lp on hk) 2 times] 6 times, yo, pull through rem 7 lp on hk (6 tr inverted V-st made), 14 ch, rep from * around, join with sl st to top of 1st inverted V-st.

Rnd 5: * (3 sc, 3 dc, 4 tr, ch 3, 4 tr, 3 dc, 3 sc) in next ch-14 sp, ch 1, rep from * around, join with sl st to 1st sc at beg of rnd.

Rnd 6: Sl st in last ch-1 sp made, ch 12 (counts as tr, ch 8), * 5 tr in next ch-3 sp, ch 8, tr in next ch-1 sp, ch 8, rep from * around, end with 5 tr in last ch-3 sp, ch 8, join with sl st to 4th ch of beg ch 12.

Rnd 7: * (Ch 5, sl st in 3rd ch from hk, ch 2, sl st in ch-8 sp) 2 times, ch 5, 5 tr inverted V-st in next 5 tr, (ch 3, sl st in 3rd ch from hk) (picot made), ch 5, sl st in next ch-8 sp, (ch 5, sl st in 3rd ch from hk, ch 2, sl st in ch-8 sp) 2 times, rep from * around, join with sl st to beg picot.

36. Four-Point Snowflake

Ch 12, join with sl st to form a ring.

Rnd 1: Ch 3 (counts as dc), 23 dc in ring, sl st in top of beg ch 3.

Rnd 2: Ch 3 (counts as dc), dc in next 4 dc, * ch 5, sk next dc, dc in next 5 dc, rep from * around, end with ch 5, sl st in top of beg ch 3.

Rnd 3: Sl st in next dc, ch 3 (counts as dc), dc in next 2 dc, * ch 5, dc in center of next ch-5 sp, ch 5, sk next dc, dc in next 3 dc, rep from * around, end with ch 5, join with sl st in top of beg ch 3.

Rnd 4: Sl st in next dc, ch 9 (counts as dc, ch 3), dc in same sp as sl st, * ch 4, sc in next ch-5 sp, ch 6, sc in next ch-5 sp, ch 4, sk next dc, (dc, ch 6, dc) in next dc, rep from * around, end with ch 4, join with sl st to 7th ch of beg ch 9.

Rnd 5: Sl st in next ch-6 sp, ch 3 (counts as dc), 4 dc in same ch-6 sp, * ch 8, (2 dc, ch 3, 2 dc) in next ch-6 sp, ch 8, 5 dc in next ch-6 sp, rep from * around, end with (2 dc, ch 3, 2 dc) in last ch-6 sp, ch 8, join with sl st in top of beg ch 3.

Rnd 6: Ch 3 (counts as dc), dc in next 4 dc, * ch 8, (2 dc, ch 3, 2 dc) in next ch-3 sp, ch 8, dc in next 5 dc, rep from * around, end with (2 dc, ch 3, 2 dc) in last ch-3 sp, ch 8, join with sl st in top of beg ch 3.

Rnd 7: Ch 4 (counts as tr), [yo twice, pull up lp in next dc, (yo, pull through 2 lp on hk) 2 times] 4 times, yo, pull through rem 5 lp on hk, * ch 8, sc tog both ch-8 sp of Rnds 5 and 6, ch 8, (2 tr, ch 3, 2 tr) in next ch-3 sp, ch 8, sc tog both ch-8 sp of Rnds 5 and 6, ch 8, [yo twice, pull up lp in next dc, (yo, pull through 2 lp on hk) 2 times] 5 times (4 tr inverted V-st made), yo, pull through rem 6 lp on hk, rep from * around, end with ch 8, join with sl st to beg ch 4.

Rnd 8: Sl st in next ch-8 sp, * (8 sc in next ch-8 sp) 2 times, sc in next 2 dc, (2 sc, ch 3, 2 sc) in next ch-3 sp, sc in next 2 dc, (8 sc in next ch-8 sp) 2 times, rep from * around, join with sl st to beg sc.

Rnd 9: * (Ch 3, sk next sc, sl st in next sc) 10 times, (2 sc, ch-3 picot, 2 sc) in next ch-3 sp, (ch 3, sk next sc, sl st in next sc) 10 times, rep from * around, join with sl st to beg ch 3.

37. Twelve Petal Flower

Ch 4, join with sl st to form a ring.
Rnd 1: Ch 3 (counts as dc), 11 dc in ring, join with sl st to top of beg ch 3.
Rnd 2: Ch 3 (counts as dc), dc in joining sp, * 2 dc in next dc, rep from * around, join with sl st to 3rd ch of beg ch 3. (24 dc)
Rnd 3: Ch 6, * sk next dc, dc in next dc, ch 3, rep from * around, join with sl st to 3rd ch of beg ch 6.
Rnd 4: Sl st in next ch-3 sp, ch 3, (dc, tr, 2 dtr, tr, dc) in next ch-3 sp, * (dc, tr, 2 dtr, tr, dc) in next ch-3 sp, rep from * around, join with sl st to top of beg ch 3.

38. Plain Octagon

Ch 10, join with sl st to form a ring.
Rnd 1: Ch 3 (counts as dc), 23 dc in ring, sl st to top of beg ch 3. (24 dc)
Rnd 2: Ch 3, dc in next 2 dc, * ch 2, dc in next 3 dc, rep from * 6 times, end with ch 2, join with sl st in top of beg ch 3. (8 3-dc groups)
Rnd 3: Ch 3, dc in joining sp, dc in next dc, 2 dc in next dc, * ch 2, 2 dc in next dc, dc in next dc, 2 dc in next dc, rep from * 6 times, ch 2, join with sl st to top of beg ch 3.
Rnd 4: Ch 3, dc in joining sp, dc in next 3 dc, 2 dc in next dc, * ch 2, 2 dc in next dc, dc in next 3 dc, 2 dc in next dc, rep from * 6 times, ch 2, join with sl st to top of beg ch 3.
Rnd 5: Ch 3, dc in joining sp, dc in next 5 dc, 2 dc in next dc, * ch 2, 2 dc in next dc, dc in next 5 dc, 2 dc in next dc, rep from * 6 times, ch 2, join with sl st top of beg ch 3.

39. Framed Flower

Ch 6, join with sl st to form a ring.
Rnd 1: Ch 1, 8 sc in ring, join with sl st to beg sc.
Rnd 2: * Ch 9, sc in 2nd ch from hk, hdc in next ch, dc in next 5 ch, hdc in next ch, sl st in next sc of Rnd 1, rep from * 7 times, **F.O.** (8 petals made)
Rnd 3: Join thread with sl st to point of any petal, * ch 10, sc in beg sc of next petal, rep from *, join with sc to beg sl st .
Rnd 4: Ch 1, sc in each ch and sc around, join with sl st to beg sc, **F.O.**

40. Shamrock

Ch 21.
Rnd 1: Sc in 20th ch from hk to form a lp, (21 ch, sc in 20th ch from hk) 2 times, join with sl st to beg sc. (3 ch-20 lp formed)
Rnd 2: 24 sc in each ch-20 lp, join with sl st to beg sc.
Rnd 3: Sc in each sc around, join with sl st to beg sc.
Rnd 4: Sl st in 1st 4 sc, * sc in next sc, * (ch 4, sc in 3rd ch from hk, ch 5, sc in 3rd ch from hk, ch 1) (picot

lp formed), sk next 4 sc, sc in next sc, (picot lp, sk next 4 sc, sc in next sc) 2 times, picot lp, sk next 9 sc, sc in next sc, rep from * around, join with sl st in beg sc.

Rnd 5: Sl st to center ch-2 sp of picot lp, ch 1, 5 sc in same sp, ch 4, * 5 sc in ch-2 sp of next picot lp, ch 4, rep from * around, join with sl st to beg picot lp.

Rnd 6: Sl st back to last ch-4 lp of prev rnd, * ch 8, sc in next ch-4 lp, rep from * around, join with sc to bottom of beg ch 8.

Patterns Using Motifs

Quick And Easy Tote Bag

Materials Needed: Approximately 6 ounces worsted weight tweed-look yarn; size H crochet hook, two 15" squares of fabric lining; 15" strip of 1" Velcro; sewing needle and thread.

Finished Size: 14" square
Shoulder Strap: 48" length
Gauge: 4 dc = 1"
2 rows of dc = 1"

Tote Bag Panel (make 2)

Ch 8, join with a sl st to form a ring.

Rnd 1: Ch 3, * (3-lp cl st, ch 2, 3-lp cl st) in ring, ch 5, rep from * 3 times, join with sl st to 1st 3-lp cl st.

Rnd 2: Sl st to next ch-2 sp, ch 3, 2 dc in sm sp, * ch 2, (3-lp cl st, ch 2, 3-lp cl st) in next ch-5 sp, ch 2, 3 dc in next ch-2 sp, rep from * around, ch 2, join with sl st to top of beg ch 3.

Rnd 3: Ch 3, dc in next 2 dc, 2 dc in next ch-2 sp, ch 2, * (3-lp cl st, ch 2, 3-lp cl st) in next ch-2 sp, ch 2, 2 dc in next ch-2 sp, dc in next 3 dc, 2 dc in next ch-2 sp, ch 2, rep from * around, 2 dc in last ch-2 sp, join with sl st to top of beg ch 3.

Rnds 4-13: Rep Rnd 3 working 2 more dc on both sides of each dc group.

Shoulder Strap

Ch 143.

Row 1: Dc in 3rd ch from hk, dc in each ch across row, ch 3, join with sl st to sp of last dc, ch 3, turn and work along bottom of dc row just completed.

Row 2: Dc in each dc, ch 3, join with sl st to sp of last dc, **F.O.**

Finishing

Place panels right side tog, sc panels tog along 3 sides only. Using tote bag as a pattern, sew fabric lining along 3 sides, turn top edge under for hem and sew inside bag. Place shoulder strap ends approximately 1" inside bag and sew securely. Separate Velcro strip and sew each piece to top inside edge of bag.

Our tote bag pattern uses stitch design #5 in this chapter. The motif square was increased following the design to create a bag the desired size. Choose another motif of your choice and create a personalized gift.

Boutique Sweater

Materials Needed: Approximately 18 ounces of #3 black thread; size D crochet hook; #4 steel crochet hook; four 1/2" buttons; tapestry needle.

Finished Size: Ladies small to medium: sleeve length = 20"; chest = 36". (If you need a larger size, use larger hook to increase motif size.)

Gauge: Motif = 5" x 5" (when blocked)

Note: Read joining instructions before starting project. The following are two stitch variations used in pattern:

Stitch Variation #1 — 3 dc tog: (yo, insert hk in next dc, yo, pull thro, yo, pull thro 2 lps) 3 times, yo, pull thro rem 4 lps on hk. When starting a new rnd, you will beg with ch 3, complete above directions 2 times, yo, pull thro rem 3 lps on hk.

Stitch Variation #2 — 3 tr tog: * [yo twice, insert hk in next tr, yo, pull thro, (yo, pull thro 2 lps) 2 times], rep [ ] 3 times, yo, pull thro rem 4 lps on hk.

Motif A

Ch 5, join with sl st to form ring.

Rnd 1: Ch 5 (counts as dc, ch 2), (dc in ring, ch 2) 7 times, join with sl st to 3rd ch of beg ch 5. (8 dc, 8 ch-2 sp)

Rnd 2: (Sc, hdc, 3 dc, hdc, sc) in each ch-2 sp around. (8 petals)

Rnd 3: Sl st in next (sc, hdc, 2 dc), ch 1, sc in sm sp, * ch 15, sk next petal, sc in 2nd dc of next petal, rep from * around, join with sl st in beg sc. (4 sc, 4 ch-15 lp)

Rnd 4: Ch 2, * in next ch-15 lp work (hdc in next 6 ch, sc in next ch, sl st around next ch, sc in next ch, hdc in rem 6 ch), ch 1, rep from * around, join with sl st to top of beg ch 2. (4 ch-1 sp, 4-leaf groups begun)

Rnd 5: [Sl st back into last ch-1 sp of Rnd 4, ch 3, 2 dc in sm sp, ch 4, 3 tr in sm sp, ch 4, 3 dc in sm sp, * ch 5, sk next 7 st, sl st in sl st, ch 5, (3 dc, ch 4, 3 tr, ch 4, 3 dc) in next ch-1 sp], rep from * around, end with ch 5, sk next 7 st, sl st in sl st, ch 5, join with sl st to top of beg ch 3. (8 ch-5 lp, 8 ch-4 lp, 4-leaf groups)

Rnd 6: * 3 dc tog, ch 4, dc in center of next ch-4 lp, ch 4, 3 tr tog, ch 4, dc in center of next ch-4 lp, ch 4, 3 dc tog, (ch 4, dc in center of next ch-5 lp) 2 times, ch 4, rep from * around, join with sl st to top of beg 3-dc tog, **F.O.** (28 ch-4 lp, 4-leaf groups completed)

Joining Instructions: All Motifs will be joined during Rnd 6. Refer to the diagram as needed. All motifs are numbered in order of assembly and joined edges darkened. Unless noted, all joining will begin with a sl st in the completed motif at the corner ch-4 lp made before 3-tr tog. The term "join" refers to the following instructions (sl st to next ch-4 lp of completed motif). Each joined edge should have 7 sl st. **Hint:** Pin motifs tog so that sts match during joining rnd.

Motif B

Rnds 1-5: Follow instructions for the first 5 rnds of

Sweater Joining Diagrams

F 24	E 22	B 17	C 18	C 19	C 20	E 21	F 23
C 16	D 14	B 9	C 10	C 11	C 12	D 13	C 15
A 1	B 2	B 3	B 4	B 5	B 6	B 7	B 8

Sleeve Joining Diagrams

A 1	B 2	B 3
B 4	C 5	C 6
G 9	B 7	G 8
	B 10	H 11

Motif A.

Rnd 6: 3 dc tog, ch 4, dc in center of next ch-4 lp, ch 4, 3 tr tog, [ch 2, join to next motif, ch 2, dc in next ch-4 lp of uncompleted motif, ch 2, join, ch 2, 3 dc tog in uncompleted motif, (ch 2, join, ch 2, dc in next ch-5 lp of uncompleted motif) 2 times, ch 2, join, ch 2, 3 dc tog in uncompleted motif, ch 2, join, ch 2, dc in next ch-4 lp of uncompleted motif, ch 2, join, ch 2, 3 tr tog in uncompleted motif], ch 4, dc in next ch-4 lp of uncompleted motif, ch 4, 3 dc tog, (ch 4, dc in next ch-5 lp of uncompleted motif) 2 times, ch 4, rep from * of Rnd 6 instructions for Motif A.

Motif C

Rnds 1-5: Follow instructions for the first 5 rnds of Motif A.

Rnd 6: [Ch 2, join to next motif, ch 2, dc in next ch-4 lp of uncompleted motif, ch 2, join, ch 2, 3 dc tog in uncompleted motif, (ch 2, join, ch 2, dc in next ch-5 lp of uncompleted motif) 2 times, ch 2, join, ch 2, 3 dc tog in uncompleted motif, ch 2, join, ch 2, dc in next ch-4 lp of uncompleted motif, ch 2, join, ch 2, 3 tr tog in uncompleted motif], follow [ ] instructions of Motif B, ch 2, join, ch 2, dc in next ch-4 lp of uncompleted motif, ch 2, join, ch 2, 3 dc tog, (ch 2, join, ch 2, dc in next ch-5 lp) 2 times, ch 4, rep from * Rnd 6 of Motif A.

Motif D (Armhole Opening)

Rnds 1-5: Follow instructions for the first 5 rnds of **Motif A.**

Rnd 6: Rep Rnd 6 of Motif A from *, 3 dc tog, ch 4, dc in next ch-4 lp, ch 4, 3 tr tog, ch 4, dc in next ch-4 lp, 3 dc tog, ch 2 (**Note:** Join in ch-4 lp following dc of completed motif), ch 2, dc in next ch-5 lp, ch 2, join, ch 2, dc in next ch-5 lp, ch 2, join, ch 2, 3 dc tog, ch 2, join, ch 2, dc in next ch-4 lp, ch 2, join, ch 2, 3 tr tog, rep [ ] of Motif B, rep instructions in Motif B following [ ], join with sl st to beg 3 dc tog.

Motif E (Armhole Opening)

Rnds 1-5: Follow instructions for the first 5 rnds of Motif A.

Rnd 6: * 3 dc tog, ch 4, dc in center of next ch-4 lp, ch 4, 3 tr tog, (follow [ ] instructions of Motif B), ch 4, dc in next ch-4 lp, ch 4, 3 dc tog, (4 ch, dc in next ch-5 lp) 2 times, ch 4 * fold wrong sides tog, join at top of #20 or #17 as follows: rep instructions bet * *, join with sl st to beg 3 dc tog, **F.O.**

Motif F

Ch 5, join with sl st to form a ring.

Rnd 1: Ch 5 (counts as dc, ch 2), (dc, ch 2 in ring) 4 times, dc in ring, sl st across bottom of motif by working 2 sl st in side of dc just completed, 2 sl st in ring, 2 sl st in side of beg dc. (6 dc, 5 ch-2 sp)

Rnd 2: (3 dc, hdc, sc) in next ch-2 sp, (sc, hdc, 3 dc, hdc, sc) in next 3 ch-2 sp, (sc, hdc, 3 dc) in last ch-2 sp, ch 1, turn. (5 petals)

Rnd 3: Sc in last dc of Rnd 2, ch 15, sk next petal, sc in 2nd dc of next petal, ch 15, sk next petal, sc in last dc of rem petal. (2 ch-15 lp)

Rnd 4: Ch 3 (counts as hdc, ch 1), turn, (hdc in next 6 ch, sc in next ch, sl st around next ch, sc in next ch, hdc in rem 6 ch, ch 1 in next 15-ch lp) 2 times, hdc in beg sc of Rnd 3. (3 ch-1 sp)

Rnd 5: Ch 4 (counts as tr), turn, 2 tr in ch-1 sp, ch 4, 3 dc in sm sp, ch 5, sk next 7 st, sl st in sl st, ch 5, (3 dc, ch 4, 3 tr, ch 4, 3 dc) in next ch-1 sp, ch 5, sk next 7 st, sl st in sl st, ch 5, (3 dc, ch 4, 3 tr) in last ch-1 sp, turn. (4 ch-5 sp, 3 leaf groups)

Rnd 6: 3 tr tog, (follow [ ] instructions of Rnd 6 for Motif B) 2 times, across diagonal edge after last 3 tr tog: ch 4, dc to bottom edge of 3 tr tog just completed, ch 4, dc in last ch-1 sp of Rnd 4, (4 ch, dc in bottom of next petal) 2 times, ch 4, dc in beg ch-1 sp of Rnd 4, ch 4, dc in bottom edge of beg 3 tr tog, ch 4, join with sl st to top of 3 tr tog, **F.O.**

Motif G (Sleeve Decrease)

Rnds 1-4: Follow instructions for first 4 rnds of Motif A.

Rnd 5: Follow [ ] instructions for Rnd 5 of Motif A, (ch 5, sk next 7 st, sl st in sl st, ch 5, sl st in next ch-1 sp) 2 times, ch 5, sk next 7 st, sl st in sl st, ch 5, sl st to top of beg ch 3.

Rnd 6: 3 dc tog, ch 2, (**Note:** Join to corresponding ch-4 lp of completed motif), ch 2, dc in center of next ch-4 lp, ch 2, join, ch 2, 3 tr tog, follow [ ] instructions of Motif B, ch 4, dc in next ch-4 lp of uncompleted motif, ch 4, 3 dc tog, (ch 4, dc in ch-5 lp) 2 times, ch 4, dc in ch-1 sp, (ch 4, dc in ch-5 lp) 2 times, (ch 4, dc in next ch-1 sp) 3 times, (ch 4, dc in next ch-5 lp) 2 times, ch 4, join with sl st to top of beg ch 3, **F.O.**

Motif H

Rnds 1-5: Follow instructions for first 5 rnds of Motif A.

Rnd 6: Follow [ ] instructions of Motif B, place G Motifs wrong sides tog, ch 2, join to #9 Motif (see diagram), ch 2, dc in next ch-4 lp of uncompleted motif, ch 2, join, ch 2, 3 dc tog, (ch 2, join, ch 2, dc in next ch-5 lp) 2 times, ch 2, join to #8 in ch-4 lp after 3 tr tog, ch 2, dc in next ch-4 lp of uncompleted motif, ch 2, join, ch 2, 3 dc tog, (ch 2, join, ch 2, dc in next ch-5 lp) 2 times, ch 2, join, ch 2, dc tog, ch 2, join, ch 2, dc in next ch-4 lp of uncompleted motif, ch 2, join, ch 2, 3 tr tog, ch 4, dc in next ch-4 lp, ch 4, rep from * of Rnd 6 of Motif A. (Bottom of sleeve joined)

Sleeve Joining

Fold sleeve wrong sides tog, match motif sts, and begin at top of sleeve: join thread with sl st to corner ch-4 lp, ch 2, join to corresponding motif, ch 2, sl st in top of dc, ch 2, join, ch 2, sl st in top of 3-dc tog, (ch 2, join, ch 2, sl st in dc) 2 times, ch 2, join, ch 2, sl st in 3-dc tog, ch 2, join, ch 2, sl st in dc, ch 2, join, ch 2, sl st in 3-tr tog, ch 2, join, **F.O.** Rep in rem motifs, ease sleeve into armhole opening (match motif designs), sew in place with whip st and tapestry needle.

Sleeve Edging

Using a #4 steel crochet hook, join with sl st to any ch-4 lp at edge of sleeve.

Rnd 1: Ch 1, work 3 sc in each lp around, do not join, mark beg of each rnd. (54 sc)

Rnds 2-5: Sc in each sc around, **F.O.** (54 sc)

Sweater Edging

Join with sl st to left front corner at bottom edge.

Rnd 1: Ch 1, 4 sc in each ch-4 lp around, 2 sc in each

corner, do not join, mark beg of each rnd. (540 sc)
Rnd 2: Sc in each sc around, 3 sc in center sc of each corner. (546 sc)
Rnd 3: Sc in each sc until reaching right front at bottom edge, work 3 sc in center sc of each corner.
Button Holes: Sc in next 2 sc, ch 4, sk next 4 sc, (sc in next 17 sc, ch 4, sk next 4 sc) 3 times, sc in each sc around. (4 button holes - 552 sc)
Rnd 4: Sc in each sc and ch around.
Rnd 5: Sc in each sc around, **F.O.**
Button Covers (Make 4)
Rnd 1: Ch 3, using #4 hk, 6 sc in 3rd ch from hk, do not join, mark beg of each rnd. (6 sc)

Rnd 2: 2 sc in each sc around. (12 sc)
Rnd 3: Sc in each sc around. (12 sc)
Rnd 4: * Sk next sc, sc in next sc, rep from * around, placing button on work as the rnd gets tighter, join with sl st to beg sc, **F.O.** Leave 6" length of thread to sew button in place.
Optional: The following instructions are for a small motif to fill in 8 ch-2 sp where 4 motifs join:
Using D hk, ch 5, join with sl st to form a ring, * ch 3, join with sl st to ch-2 sp in center of 4 joined motifs, ch 3, sl st in ring, rep from * in each ch-2 sp around, **F.O.** (8 spokes)
Block if desired.

Sunflower Bouquet Vest

Materials Needed: Worsted weight yarn: 1 ounce bright yellow, 2 ounces medium brown, 6 ounces dark green; size E crochet hook.
Finished Size: 42" chest
Gauge: 5 sc = 1"
5 rows of sc = 1"
Sunflower Motif (make ten)
Using brown yarn, ch 6, join with sl st to form a ring.
Rnd 1: Ch 1, 12 sc in ring, join with sl st to 1st sc.
Rnd 2: Ch 1, * sc in next sc, 2 sc in next sc, rep from * around, join with sl st to 1st sc. (18 sc)
Rnd 3: Ch 1, * sc in next 2 sc, 2 sc in next sc, rep from * around, join with sl st to 1st sc. (24 sc)
Rnd 4: Ch 1, * sc in next 3 sc, 2 sc in next sc, rep from * around, join with sl st to 1st sc. (30 sc)
Rnd 5: Ch 1, * sc in next 4 sc, 2 sc in next sc, rep from * around, join with sl st to 1st sc. (36 sc)
Rnd 6: Ch 1, * sc in next 5 sc, 2 sc in next sc, rep from * around, join with sl st to 1st sc. (42 sc)
Rnd 7: Ch 1, * sc in next 6 sc, 2 sc in next sc, rep from * around, join with sl st to 1st sc, **F.O.** (48 sc)
Using yellow yarn, join with sl st to joining sp of Rnd 7.
Rnd 8: Ch 4, [yo twice, insert hk in joining sp, yo, pull through, (yo, pull through 2 lps on hk) 2 times] 2 times, yo, pull through last 3 lps on hk (3-tr cl st made), * ch 5, sk 2 sc, [yo twice, insert hk in next sc, yo, pull through, (yo, pull through 2 lps on hk) 2 times] 3 times, yo, pull through last 4 lps on hk (3-tr cl st made), rep from * around, end with ch 5, join with sl st to top of 1st cl st, **F.O.** Using green yarn, join with sl st to any ch-5 sp.
Rnd 9: Sc in sm sp, ch 6, * sc in next ch-5 sp, ch 6, rep from * around, join with sl st to 1st sc, **F.O. Note:** Each front panel has 5 sunflower motifs. Refer to dia-

gram. Each sunflower motif is joined at two petals, after 1st motif is complete, join remaining motifs tog during Rnd 9 as follows: Join with sl st to any ch-5 sp of Rnd 8, sc in sm sp, ch 3, join with sl st to any ch-6 lp of finished motif, ch 3, sc in next ch-5 sp of unfinished motif, ch 3, join with sl st to next ch-6 sp of finished motif, ch 3, sc in next ch-5 sp of unfinished motif, * ch 6, sc in next ch-5 sp, rep from * around, join with sl st to 1st sc.
Small Flower Motif (make 4)
(Used to fill sp in center of four joined sunflowers.)
Using green, Ch 8, join with sl st to form a ring.
Ch 5, join with sl st to any unworked ch-6 sp of sunflower motif, ch 5, sc in ring, * ch 5, join with sl st to next unworked ch-6 sp, ch 5, sc in ring, rep from * 6 times, **F.O.**
Note: 2 small flower motifs near the neckline line will not have as many 6 ch-sp to join, work (ch 10, sc in

ring) 2 times, these 2 lps will be worked during the edging.

Half Flower Motif (make 8)
(Used to fill sp slong edges where sunflower motifs were joined.) **Using green, Ch 4**, join with sl st to form a ring. Begin at right, * ch 5, join with sl st to unworked ch-6 sp, ch 5, sc in ring, rep from * 3 times, **F.O.**

Sunflower Panel Edging
Join with sl st to any ch-6 sp, sc in sm sp, *ch 5, sc in next ch-6 sp, rep from * except at half flower motif, (sc in center of ch-10 sp, ch 5) 2 times, at bottom corners and at shoulder corners of panels, ch 10 instead of 5 (corners made), join with sl st to beg sc, **F.O.**

Vest Back
Using dark green, ch 86.
Row 1: Sc in 2nd ch from hk, * ch 5, sk 3 ch, sc in next ch, rep from *, ending row with sc in last ch, ch 5, turn.
Row 2: * Sc in center of next ch-5 sp, ch 5, rep from *, ending row with sc in last ch-5 sp, ch 2, dc in last sc, ch 1, turn.
Row 3: Sc in dc, * ch 5, sc in center of next ch-5 sp, rep from *, ending row with sc in 3rd ch of last ch-5 sp, ch 5, turn.
Row 4: * Sc in center of next ch-5 sp, ch 5, rep from *, ending row with ch 2, dc in last sc, ch 1, turn.
Row 5: Sc in dc, * ch 5, sc in center of next ch-5 sp, rep from *, ending row with sc in 3rd ch of last ch-5

sp, ch 3, turn.
Rows 6-31: Rep Rows 2-5 alternately.
Shoulder Shaping (you will be joining back to each front panel at shoulders during the following directions)
Join with sl st to 5th ch of front panel ch-10 sp, * ch 2, sl st to next ch-5 sp of back, ch 2, sl st to next ch-5 sp of front panel, rep from * 4 times, ch 2, sl st to next ch-5 sp of back, ch 3, join with sl st to ch-10 sp at end of front panel, **F.O.** Rep to other side, reversing shaping.
Side Joining
Join with sl st to bottom side edge of back, ch 2, sl st to ch-5 sp of front panel, * ch 2, sl st to next ch-5 sp of back edge, rep from * 7 times, **F.O.** (9" opening left for arm) Rep to other side.
Vest Edging
Join with sl st.
Row 1: Ch 1, sc evenly around all edges, work 3 sc in each front bottom corner, join with sl st to beg sc.
Rows 2-3: Ch 1, sc in each sc around, work 3 sc in center of sc of each corner, **F.O.**
Armhole Edging
Join with sl st.
Rnd 1: Ch 1, sc evenly around, join with sl st to beg sc.
Rnds 2-3: Ch 1, sc in each sc around, join with sl st to beg sc, **F.O.**

Right   **Left**

Chapter 16

Edgings and Trims

1. Multiples of 3.

Row 1: * 3 tr in 3rd ch from hk, ch 3, sl st in same ch, * sk next 2 ch, (3 tr, ch 3, sl st) in next ch, rep from * across.

2. Multiples of 3 plus 1.

Row 1: Sc in 7th ch from hk, * ch 3, sk 2 ch, sc in next ch, rep from * across row, ch 5, turn.
Row 2: * Sc in next ch-3 lp, ch 3, rep from * across row, end with sc in last ch-3 lp, ch 2, dc in 4th ch of tch, ch 1, turn.
Row 3: Sc in dc, * ch 6, sc in 4th ch from hk (picot made), ch 2, sc in next ch-3 lp, rep from * across, ending row with picot, ch 2, sl st in 3rd ch of tch.

3. Multiples of 12 plus 9.

Row 1: Tr in 9th ch from hk, * ch 2, sk 2 ch, tr in next ch, rep from * across row, ending with tr in last ch, turn.
Row 2: Sl st to 1st ch-2 sp, ch 5, (2 dtr, ch 2, 3 dtr) in same sp, * ch 5, sk next ch-2 sp, sc in next ch-2 sp, ch 5, sk next ch-2 sp, (3 dtr, ch 2, 3 dtr) in next ch-2 sp, rep from * across, ch 1, turn.
Row 3: * Sc in next 3 dtr, (sc, ch 3, sc) in next ch-2 sp, sc in next 3 dtr, (5 sc in next ch-5 sp) 2 times, rep from * across, ending row with sc in tch.

4. Chain 5.

Join with sl st to form a ring.

Row 1: Ch 3, 4 tr in ring, ch 2, sl st in same ring, * ch 3, turn, 4 tr in ch-2 sp, ch 2, sl st in same sp, rep from * for desired length.

Optional Edging (not pictured): When desired length is made, start at edge of last 4-tr group, * ch 5, sl st in next 4-dtr group, rep from *. Edging row allows you to sew trim onto material.

5. Chain 5.

Row 1: 3 dc, ch 2, 3 dc in 5th ch from hk (shell made), turn.

Row 2: Sl st to ch-2 sp, (ch 3, 2 dc, ch 2, 3 dc) in same ch-2 sp, turn.

Rep Row 2 until an odd number of shells is made to desired length.

Row 3: Working along edge, * ch 3, sc in side of next shell, rep from *, ending row with ch 3, join with sc to bottom edge of 1st shell made, turn.

Row 4: Sl st in 1st ch-3 sp, ch 4, 6 tr in same ch, * sc in next ch-3 sp, 6 tr in next ch-3 sp, rep from * across.

6. Multiples of 4 plus 11.

Row 1: Dc in 11th ch from hk, * ch 3, sk 3 ch, dc in next ch, rep from * across, ch 1, turn.

Row 2: Sc in dc, sc in next 2 ch, * ch 5, sc in center of next ch-3 sp, rep from * ending row with sk 1st ch of tch, sc in next 3 ch, ch 3, turn.

Row 3: * 9 sc in next ch-5 sp, rep from *, ending row with ch 3, sl st in last sc, ch 3, turn.
Row 4: * Dc in 1st sc of 9-sc group, (ch 2, sk next sc, dc in next sc) 4 times, rep from *, ending row with ch 3, join with sl st in tch.

7. Multiples of 13 plus 12.

Row 1: Sc in 2nd ch from hk, sc in next 10 ch, * ch 2, sk 2 ch, sc in next 11 ch, rep from * across, ch 6, turn.
Row 2: * Sk next sc, sc in next 9 sc, (ch 3, dc, ch 3) in next ch-2 sp, rep from *, ending row with sk next sc, sc in next 9 sc, ch 3, dc in last sc, ch 6, turn.
Row 3: Dc in next ch-3 sp, ch 3, * sk next sc, sc in next 7 sc, (ch 3, dc in next ch-3 sp) 2 times, ch 3, rep from *, ending row with sk next sc, sc in next 7 sc, (ch 3, dc in tch) 2 times, ch 6, turn.
Row 4: (Dc in next ch-3 sp, ch 3) 2 times, * sk next sc, sc in next 5 sc, (ch 3, dc in next ch-3 sp) 3 times, ch 3, rep from *, ending row with sk next sc, sc in next 5 sc, ch 3, dc in next ch-3 sp, (ch 3, dc in tch) 2 times, ch 6, turn.
Row 5: (Dc in next ch-3 sp, ch 3) 3 times, * sk next sc, sc in next 3 sc, (ch 3, dc in next ch-3 sp) 4 times, ch 3, rep from *, ending row with sk next sc, sc in next 3 sc, (ch 3, dc in next ch-3 sp) 2 times, (ch 3, dc in tch) 2 times, ch 6, turn.
Row 6: (Dc in next ch-3 sp, ch 3) 4 times, * sk next sc, sc in next sc, (ch 3, dc in next ch-3 sp) 5 times, ch 3, rep from *, ending row with sk next sc, sc in next sc, (ch 3, dc in next ch-3 sp) 3 times, (ch 3, dc in tch) 2 times.

8. Chain 21.

Row 1: Tr in 5th ch from hk, ch 2, sk 2 ch, (tr, ch 2, tr) in next ch, ch 2, sk 4 ch, 3 tr in next ch, ch 2, sk 4 ch, (tr, ch 2, tr) in next ch, ch 2, sk 2 ch, (tr, ch 2, tr) in last ch, ch 4, turn.
Row 2: 5 tr in next ch-2 sp, ch 2, sk next ch-2 sp, 5 tr in next ch-2 sp, ch 2, tr in next ch-2 sp, tr in next 3 tr, tr in next ch-2 sp, ch 2, 5 tr in next ch-2 sp, ch 2, tr in last tr, tr in tch, ch 4, turn.
Row 3: Sk 1st tr, tr in next tr, ch 2, (tr, ch 2, tr) in 3rd tr of 5 tr group, ch 2, tr in next ch-2 sp, tr in next 5 tr, tr in next ch-2 sp, [(ch 2, tr, ch 2, tr) in 3rd tr of 5 tr group)] 2 times, ch 4, turn.
Row 4: (5 tr in next ch-2 sp, ch 2, sk next ch-2 sp) 2 times, tr in next ch-2 sp, tr in next 7 tr, tr in next ch-2 sp, ch 2, sk next ch-2 sp, 5 tr in next ch-2 sp, ch 2, tr in last tr, tr in tch, ch 4, turn.
Row 5: Sk 1st tr, tr in next tr, ch 2, (tr, ch 2, tr) in 3rd tr of 5 tr group, ch 2, (tr, ch 2, tr) in 1st tr of 9 tr group, ch 2, sk 3 tr, 3 tr in next tr, ch 2, (tr, ch 2, tr) in last tr of 9 tr group, ch 4, turn.
Rep pattern of Rows 2-5 for desired length.

9. Chain 7.

Row 1: Tr in 7th ch from hk (counts as tr, ch 2), (ch 2, tr in sm sp) 2 times, ch 6, turn.

Row 2: Sk 1st ch-2 sp, tr in next ch-2 sp, (ch 2, tr in same sp) 3 times, ch 5, join with sl st to last tr of prev row, ch 1, turn.

Row 3: 9 sc in ch-5 sp, ch 2, turn.

Row 4: Sk 1st ch-2 sp, tr in next ch-2 sp, (ch 2, tr in same sp) 3 times, ch 6, turn.

Rep Rows 2-4 until desired length.

10. Chain 4.

Row 1: (2 dc, ch 1, 3 dc) in 4th ch from hk, ch 5, turn.

Row 2: (3 dc, ch 1, 3 dc) in next ch-1 sp, ch 1, turn.

Row 3: Sk 1st dc, sl st in next 2 dc, sl st in ch-1 sp, ch 3, (2 dc, ch 1, 3 dc) in same sp, ch 2, sk 2 dc, dc in next dc, ch 2, dc in 3rd ch of tch, ch 5, turn.

Row 4: Sk 1st dc, (dc in next dc, ch 2) 2 times, sk next 2 dc, (3 dc, ch 1, 3 dc) in ch-1 sp, ch 1, turn.

Row 5: Sk 1st dc, sl st in next 2 dc, sl st in ch-1 sp, ch 3, (2 dc, ch 1, 3 dc) in sm sp, ch 2, sk next 2 dc, dc in next dc, (ch 2, dc in next dc) 2 times, ch 3, dc in 3rd ch of tch, ch 5, turn.

Row 6: Sk 1st dc, (dc in next dc, ch 2) 4 times, sk next 2 dc, (3 dc, ch 1, 3 dc) in next ch-1 sp, ch 1, turn.

Row 7: Sk 1st dc, sl st in next 2 dc, sl st in ch-1 sp, ch 3, (2 dc, ch 1, 3 dc) in sm sp, ch 5, turn.

Rep Rows 2-7 for desired length.

Edging: Working along pointed edges, attach thread to 1st ch-2 sp, (sc, ch 3, 2 dc) in each ch-2 sp and dc post around, in each ch-5 sp (tip of pointed edge) work (sc, ch 3, 2 dc) 3 times.

11. Chain 12.

Row 1: (2 dc, ch 2, 2 dc) in 8th ch from hk (shell made), ch 2, sk 2 ch, dc in last 2 ch, ch 3, turn.
Row 2: Sk 1st dc, dc in next dc, ch 2, shell in ch-2 sp of shell, ch 3, 5 dc in tch, ch 4, turn.
Row 3: Sc in dc, hdc in next dc, 2 dc in each of next 3 dc, ch 3, dc in next ch-3 sp, ch 2, shell in shell, ch 2, dc in last dc, dc in tch, ch 3, turn.
Row 4: Sk 1st dc, dc in next dc, ch 2, shell in shell, ch 3, sk next ch-2 sp, 5 dc in next ch-3 sp, ch 4, turn.
Rep Rows 3-4 for desired length. End with Row 3.

12. Chain 21.

Row 1: Dc in 8th ch from hk, ch 2, sk 2 ch, dc in next 4 ch, ch 2, sk 2 ch, dc in next ch, ch 5, sl st in last ch, ch 2, turn.
Row 2: 7 dc in ch-5 lp, ch 4, sk next dc and ch-2 sp, dc in next dc, ch 2, sk 2 dc, dc in next dc, ch 2, dc in next dc, ch 2, sk 2 ch, dc in next ch, ch 5, turn.
Row 3: Sk 1st dc, dc in next dc, ch 2, dc in next dc, 2 dc in ch-2 sp, dc in next dc, ch 2, dc in next ch-4 sp, ch 1, (dc in next dc, ch 1) 6 times, dc in top of tch, ch 3, turn.
Row 4: (Sc in next ch-1 sp, ch 3) 6 times, sc in next ch-1 sp, sl st in top of next dc, ch 2, 2 dc in ch-2 sp, dc in next dc, ch 2, sk 2 dc, dc in next dc, 2 dc in ch-2 sp, dc in next dc, ch 2, sk 2 ch, dc in next ch, ch 5, turn.
Row 5: Sk 1st dc, dc in next dc, ch 2, sk 2 dc, dc in next dc, 2 dc in ch-2 sp, dc in next dc, ch 2, sk 2 dc, dc in top of ch 2, ch 5, sc in 1st ch-3 sp of scallop to left, ch 2, turn.
Rep Rows 2-5 for desired length. End with Row 4.

13. Multiples of 8 plus 6.

Row 1: Sc in 2nd ch from hk, * (ch 5, sk 3 ch, sc in next ch), rep from * across row, ch 2, turn.
Row 2: (Dc, ch 2, dc, ch 1, 3-ch picot, ch 1, dc, ch 2, dc) in next ch-5 sp (shell made), * ch 4, sk next ch-5 sp, shell in next ch-5 sp, rep from *, ending row with ch 2, join with sl st to last sc.

14. Chain 11.

Row 1: Dc in 4th ch from hk, dc in next ch, ch 5, sk 5 ch, (dc, ch 3 in last ch) 3 times, dc in same ch, ch 1, turn.
Row 2: (Sc, hdc, 3 dc, hdc, sc) in next ch-3 sp (shell made), shell in next 2 ch-3 sp, ch 5, dc in next 2 dc, dc in tch, ch 3, turn.
Row 3: Sk 1st dc, dc in next 2 dc, ch 5, (dc, ch 3 in 1st dc of 1st shell) 3 times, dc in same sp, ch 1, turn.
Rep Rows 2-3 for desired length.

15. Chain 14.

Row 1: (3 dc, ch 2, dc) in 8th ch from hk, * sk 2 ch, (3 dc, ch 2, dc) in next ch, rep from * 1 time, ch 6, turn.
Row 2: * (3 dc, ch 2, dc) in next ch-2 sp, rep from * 2 times, ch 6, turn.
Rep Row 2 for desired length, ch 5, turn to work along edge.
Finishing: * Sc in next ch-6 sp (turning ch of prev Row), ch 5, rep from * across.

16. Chain 7, join with sl st to form ring.

Rnd 1: Ch 6, dc in ring, (ch 3, dc in ring) 6 times, ch 3, join to 3rd ch of beg ch 6. (8 ch-3 lp)

Rnd 2: Ch 1, (sc, 3 dc, sc) in each ch-3 lp around, do not join.

Rnd 3: (Ch 8, sl st around back of next dc post of Rnd 1) 8 times, do not join.

Rnd 4: (Sc, hdc, 5 dc, hdc, sc) in each ch-8 lp around.

Make a 2nd rose through Rnd 3, join to 1st rose as follows: (Sc, hdc, 3 dc) in next ch-8 lp, sl st to center st of any petal of 1st rose, (2 dc, hdc, sc) in same ch-8 lp of uncompleted rose, (sc, hdc, 3 dc) in next ch-8 lp, join to center st of next petal on 1st rose, (2 dc, hdc, sc) in same ch-8 lp, (sc, hdc, 5 dc, hdc, sc) in each rem ch-8 lp of uncompleted rose. Continue to make roses for desired length, join as above.

17. Chain 5.

Row 1: (Dc, ch 2, 2 dc) in 5th ch from hk, ch 5, turn.

Row 2: (2 dc, ch 2, 2 dc) in ch-2 sp (shell made), ch 5, turn.

Rep Row 2 for desired length, end with odd number of ch-5 sp.

Edging: Ch 5, turn to work along side, * yo twice, insert hk in next ch-5 sp, yo, pull through, (yo, pull through 2 lp on hk) 2 times, [yo twice, insert hk in same ch-5 sp, yo, pull through, (yo, pull through 2 lp on hk)] 2 times, yo, pull through last 3 lp on hk (cl st made), ch 3, sl st in 3rd ch from hk (picot made)(ch 3, cl st, picot in same ch-5 sp) 2 times, ch 3, sc in next ch-5 sp, ch 3, rep from *, ending row with ch 5, sl st at base of beg shell, working on opposite side (ch 7, sc in next ch-5 sp), rep ( ) across row, **F.O.**

18. Multiples of 5 plus 3.

Row 1: (2 dc, ch 2, 2 dc) in 6th ch from hk, * ch 2, sk 4 ch, (2 dc, ch 2, 2 dc) in next ch, rep from * across, ending row with sk 1 ch, dc in last ch, ch 3, turn.
Row 2: * (2 dc, ch 2, 2 dc) in next ch-2 sp, ch 2, sk next ch-2 sp, rep from * across, ending row with (2 dc, ch 2, 2 dc) in last ch-2 sp, dc in tch, ch 3, turn.
Row 3: Rep Row 2 for width desired.

19. Multiples of 10 plus 6.

Row 1: Sc in 2nd ch from hk, sc in next 4 ch, * ch 2, sk 2 ch (dc, ch 2 in next ch) 3 times, sk 2 ch, sc in next 4 ch, rep from * across, ending row with sc in last 5 ch.

20. Multiples of 12 plus 2.

Row 1: Sc in the 2nd ch from hk and in each ch across row, ch 6, turn.
Row 2: 3 dc in 1st sc, * sk 5 sc, (3 dc, ch 3, 3 dc) in next sc, rep from *, ending row with (3 dc, ch 3, dc) in last sc.

21. Multiples of 16 plus 2.

Row 1: Sc in 2nd ch from hk, * ch 4, sk 3 ch, (sc, ch 3, 2 dc) in next ch, rep from *, ending row with ch 4, sk 3 ch, sc in last ch, ch 5, turn.
Row 2: Sc in 1st ch-4 sp, * ch 4, (sc, ch 3, 2 dc) in next ch-4 sp, rep from *, ending row with ch 4, sc in last ch-4 sp, ch 2, dc in last sc, ch 1, turn.
Row 3: Sc in 1st dc, * ch 4, (sc, ch 3, 2 dc) in next ch-4 sp, rep from *, ending row with ch 4, sc in 3rd tch, ch 5, turn.
Rep Rows 2-3 for desired width.

22. Multiples of 13 plus 13.

Row 1: Dc in 10th ch from hk, ch 3, sk 2 ch, dc in next ch, * ch 2, sk 2 ch, 2 dc in next ch, ch 1, 2 dc in next ch, ch 2, sk 2 ch, dc in next ch, (ch 3, sk 2 ch, dc in next ch) 2 times, rep from * across row, ch 1, turn.
Row 2: Sc in 1st dc, ch 3, sk next ch-3 sp, sc in next ch-3 sp, * ch 2, sk next dc, dc in next dc, 2 dc in next dc, ch 2, 2 dc in next dc, dc in next dc, ch 2, sc in next ch-3 sp, ch 3, sc in next ch-3 sp, rep from *, ending row with sc in 4th tch, ch 6, turn.
Row 3: Sc in next ch-3 sp, ch 3, * dc in next dc, 2 dc in next dc, dc in next dc, ch 3, dc in next dc, 2 dc in next dc, dc in next dc, ch 3, sc in next ch-3 sp, ch 3, rep from *, ending row with ch 3, sc in last ch-3 sp, ch 3, dc in last sc, ch 1, turn.
Row 4: Sc in 1st dc, ch 3, * dc in next 2 dc, 2 dc in next dc, dc in next dc, ch 4, dc in next dc, 2 dc in next dc, dc in next 2 dc, ch 3, rep from *, ending row with ch 3, sc in 4th tch, ch 6, turn.
Row 5: * Dc in next 2 dc, 2 dc in next dc, dc in next 2 dc, ch 5, dc in next 2 dc, 2 dc in next dc, dc in next 2 dc, ch 1, rep from *, ending row with ch 3, dc in last sc.

23. Chain 28.

Row 1: Dtr in 16th ch from hk, ch 2, sk 2 ch, dtr in next ch, ch 2, sk 2 ch, tr in next ch, ch 2, sk 2 ch, dc in next ch, ch 2, sk 2 ch, sc in last ch, ch 1, turn.
Row 2: * Sc in next st, ch 2, sk ch-2 sp, rep from * 3 times, ending row with sc in last st, ch 1, turn.
Row 3: Sc in 1st sc, ch 2, dc in next sc, ch 2, tr in next sc, (ch 2, dtr in next sc) 2 times, ch 1, turn.
Row 4: Rep Row 2, ch 15, turn.
Row 5: Dtr in 1st sc, ch 2, dtr in next sc, ch 2, tr in next sc, ch 2, dc in next sc, ch 2, sc in last sc, ch 1, turn.
Rep Rows 2-5 for desired length, ch 1, turn.
Finish: Sc evenly across side, 15 sc in each 15-ch sp, working across other side, sc evenly across base of row, **F.O.**

24. Chain 16.

Row 1: 2 dc in 16th ch from hk, ch 2, (yo, insert hk in same ch, yo, pull through, yo, pull through 2 lp on hk) 2 times, yo, pull through last 3 lp on hk (2-lp cl st made), ch 7, turn.
Row 2: (Cl st, ch 2, cl st) in next ch-2 sp, ch 15, turn.
Row 3: (Cl st, ch 2, cl st) in next ch-2 sp, ch 7, turn.
Rep Rows 2-3 for desired length, end with Row 3, ch 3, turn work to side.
Finishing
Row 1: 7 dc in each ch-7 sp, ch 3, join to base of 1st cl st, ch 5, turn.
Row 2: * 7 dc in next ch-15 sp, ch 3, sc in 3rd ch from hk (picot made), 7 dc in same ch-15 sp, rep from *, ending row with ch 5, join with sl st to ch-2 sp of last cl st group.

25. Multiples of 6 plus 5.

Row 1: Sc in 2nd ch from hk, * ch 2, dc in same ch, sk 2 ch, sc in next ch, ch 5, sk 2 ch, sc in next ch, rep from *, ending row with ch 2, dc in same ch, sk 2 ch, sc in last ch, ch 6, turn.
Row 2: * (Sc, ch 3, sc) in center of next ch-5 lp, ch 6, rep from *, ending row with sc in last sc.

26. Multiples of 21 plus 11.

Row 1: Sc in 2nd ch from hk and in each ch across row, ch 5, turn.

Row 2: Sk 1st 3 sc, dc in next sc, * ch 2, sk 2 sc, dc in next sc, rep from * across row, ch 1, turn.

Row 3: Sc in each dc and ch across row, 3 sc in tch, ch 5, turn.

Row 4: Sk 1st 3 sc, tr in next sc, * (ch 2, sk 2 sc, tr in next sc) 2 times, sk 2 sc, tr in next sc, (ch 4, 5 tr around post of tr just made, sk 2 sc, tr in next sc) 3 times, ch 2, sk next 2 sc, tr in next sc, rep from *, ending row with ch 2, tr in last sc, ch 1, turn.

Row 5: Sc in each tr and ch across row, ch 4 at end of each 5-tr group, continue to sc across row, ch 6, turn.

Row 6: Sk 1st 3 sc, tr in next sc, (ch 2, sk 2 sc, tr in next sc) 2 times, * (tr in top of next ch-4 sp, ch 4, 5 tr around tr just made) 3 times, sk 5 sc, tr in next sc, (ch 2, sk 2 sc, tr in next sc) 3 times, rep from *, ending row with ch 2, tr in last sc, ch 1, turn.

Row 7: Rep Row 5, except (sc, ch 3, sc) in each tr for picot.

27. Chain multiples of 10 plus 4.

Row 1: Dc in 6th ch from hk, * sk 2 ch, 5 dc in next ch, sk 2 ch, dc in next ch, (ch 1, sk 1 ch, dc in next ch) 2 times, rep from *, ending row with ch 1, sk 1 ch, dc in last ch, ch 4, turn.

Row 2: Sk 1st dc, * dc in next 7 dc, ch 1, dc in next dc, ch 1, rep from *, ending row with dc in next 7 dc, ch 1, dc in 2nd ch of tch, ch 5, turn.

Row 3: Sk 1st 2 dc, dc in next dc, * dc in next 4 dc, (ch 2, sk next dc, dc in next dc) 2 times, rep from *, ending row with dc in next 4 dc, ch 2, sk last dc, dc in 2nd ch of tch, ch 6, turn.

Row 4: Sk 1st 2 dc, * dc in next 3 dc, ch 3, sk next dc, dc in next dc, ch 3, sk next dc, rep from *, ending row with dc in next 3 dc, ch 3, sk last dc, dc in 3rd ch of tch, ch 7, turn.

Row 5: Sk 1st 2 dc, * dc in next dc, ch 4, sk next dc, dc in next dc, ch 4, sk next dc, rep from *, ending row with ch 4, sk last dc, dc in 4th ch of tch.

28. Chain 12.

Row 1: Dc in 4th ch from hk, dc in next ch, (dc, ch 2, dc) in next ch, ch 2, sk 2 ch, dc in last 4 ch, ch 3, turn.

Row 2: Sk 1st dc, dc in next 3 dc, (dc, ch 2, dc) in next dc, ch 2, sk next dc, dc in next 2 dc, dc in top of tch, ch 3, turn.

Row 3: Sk 1st dc, dc in next 2 dc, ch 2, (dc, ch 2, dc) in next 2 dc, dc in next 3 dc, dc in top of tch, ch 3, turn.

Row 4: Sk 1st dc, dc in each dc and ch across row, dc in top of tch, ch 3, turn.

Row 5: Sk 1st dc, dc in next 2 dc, (dc, ch 2, dc) in next dc, ch 2, sk 4 dc, dc in next 4 dc, ch 3, turn.

Rep Rows 2-5 of pattern for length desired, end with Row 4.

29. Multiples of 19 plus 19.

Row 1: Dc in 4th ch from hk, dc in each ch across row, ch 3, turn.

Row 2: Sk 1st dc, dc in next 3 dc, * ch 3, sk 3 dc, dc in next 3 dc, ch 3, sk 3 dc, dc in next 10 dc, rep from *, ending row with dc in last 3 dc, dc in tch, ch 3, turn.

Row 3: Sk 1st dc, dc in next dc, * ch 3, sk (2 dc, ch-3 sp), 3 dc in next dc, ch 1, sk next dc, 3 dc in next dc, ch 3, sk (ch-3 sp, 2 dc), dc in next 6 dc, rep from *, ending row with dc in last dc, dc in tch, ch 6, turn.

Row 4: Sk 1st 2 dc, * dc in next 3 dc, ch 3, 3 dc in ch-1 sp, ch 3, dc in next 3 dc, * ch 3, sk (ch-3 sp, 2 dc), dc in next 2 dc, ch 3, sk (2 dc, ch-3 sp), rep from *, ending row with ch 3, sk (ch-3 sp, dc), dc in tch.

30. Chain 17.

Row 1: (2 dc, ch 2, 3 dc) in 4th ch from hk, ch 9, sk next 12 ch, (3 dc, ch 2, 3 dc) in last ch (shell made), ch 2, turn.

Row 2: Shell in 1st ch-2 sp, ch 11, shell in next ch-2 sp, ch 2, turn.

Row 3: Shell in 1st ch-2 sp, ch 7, insert hk bet 2 shells under ch sp of last 3 rows, sc tog, ch 1, turn, sc in next 7 ch, * (ch 1, turn, sc in next 7 sc) 3 times (square made), ch 2, shell in next ch-2 sp, ch 2, turn.

Row 4: Rep Row 2.

Row 5: Shell in 1st ch-2 sp, ch 9, shell in next ch-2 sp, ch 2, turn.

Row 6: Rep Row 2.

Row 7: Shell in 1st ch-2 sp, ch 7, sc in top corner of last square made (working tog ch sp of last 3 rows), rep from * of Row 3.

Rep Rows 4-7 for desired length, end with Row 6. Complete pattern as follows: Shell in 1st ch-2 sp, ch 5, sc in top corner of last square made (working tog ch sp of last 3 rows), ch 5, shell in next ch-2 sp.

31. Multiples of 6 plus 8.

Row 1: Dc in 8th ch from hk, * ch 2, sk 2 ch, dc in next ch, rep from * across row, ch 6, turn.

Row 2: Sk 1st dc, * tr in next dc, 2 tr in next ch-2 sp, tr in next dc, ch 2, sk next ch-2 sp, rep from *, ending row with ch 2, tr in 3rd ch of tch, ch 1, turn.

Row 3: Sc in 1st tr, * ch 3, sk 2 ch, sc in next tr, ch 3, sk next 2 tr, sc in next tr, rep from *, ending row with ch 3, sk 2 ch, sc in next ch of tch, ch 1, turn.

Row 4: 5 sc in each ch-3 sp.

32. Multiples of 6 plus 6.

Row 1: Tr in 9th ch from hk, * ch 2, sk next 2 ch, tr in next ch, rep from * across row, ch 1, turn.
Row 2: Sc in 1st tr, * ch 10, sk next tr, sc in next tr, rep from * across row, ch 4, turn.
Row 3: *(3 tr, 3-ch picot in next ch-10 lp) 3 times, 3 tr in same ch-10 lp, rep from *, ending row with tr in last sc.

33. Chain 12, join with sl st to form ring.

Rnd 1: * 10 sc in ring, turn, ch 6 (counts as tr, ch 2), sk 1st sc, tr in next sc, (ch 2, tr in next sc) 8 times, ch 1, turn. (Fan made)
Rnd 2: Sc in each tr, 2 sc in each ch-2 sp, ch 12, turn.
Rnd 3: Sk 1st 2 sc of completed fan, sl st in next sc, rep from * of Rnd 1, ch 1, join with sl st to 7th sc of completed fan, ch 1, turn.
Rnd 4: Rep Rnd 2.
Rep Rnds 3-4 for desired length.

34. Chain 15, join with sl st to form ring.

Rnd 1: Ch 1, 25 sc in ring.
Rnd 2: Ch 6, (sk next sc, tr in next sc, ch 2) 5 times, sk next sc, (tr, ch 3, tr) in next sc (tip of scallop), (ch 2, sk next sc, tr in next sc) 6 times, ch 1, turn.

Rnd 3: Sc in each tr, 2 sc in each ch-2 sp, (3 sc in ch-3 sp at tip of scallop), ch 1, turn.
Rnd 4: Sk 1st sc, sc in each sc to center sc at tip of scallop, 3 sc in center sc, sc in each rem sc, ch 1, turn.
Rnds 5-7: Rep Rnd 4.
Rnd 8: Rep Rnd 4, except sc in first sc.
Rnd 9: Sl st in 1st sc, ch 4, tr in same sc, ch 3, sk 2 sc, * [2 tr in next sc, (hold 1 lp on hk for each tr, yo, pull through 3 lps on hk) (tr cl made), ch 3, sk 1 sc], rep from * 8 times until tip of scallop is reached, work (tr cl, ch 3, tr cl) in center sc, (tr cl in next sc, ch 3, sk 1 sc) 7 times, tr cl in last sc, ch 1, turn.
Rnd 10: (Sc, 3 dc, sc) in each ch-3 sp around.

35. Multiples of 9 plus 5.

Row 1: Sc in 2nd ch from hk, sc in next 3 ch, * ch 7, sk 5 ch, sc in next 4 ch, rep from * across row, ch 1, turn.
Row 2: Sc in 1st sc, * ch 2, (3-lp cl st, ch 2 in next ch-7 lp) 4 times, sk next 2 sc, sc in next 2 sc, rep from *, ending row with sk 3 sc, sc in last sc, ch 1, turn.
Row 3: Sc in 1st sc, * ch 3, sc in next cl st, rep from *, ending row with ch 3, sc in last sc.

36. Multiples of 17 plus 4.

Row 1: Dc in the 4th ch from hk, * ch 3, sk 3 ch, 4-dc pc st in next ch, (ch 1, sk next ch, pc st in next ch) 4 times, ch 3, sk 3 ch, dc in next 2 ch, rep from * across row, ch 3, turn.
Row 2: Sk 1st dc, dc in next dc, * dc in next ch, ch 3, pc st in next ch-1 sp, (ch 1, pc st in next ch-1 sp) 3 times, ch 3, sk 2 ch, dc in next ch, dc in next 2 dc, rep from *, ending row with sk 2 ch, dc in next ch, dc in next dc, dc in tch, ch 3, turn.
Row 3: Sk 1st dc, dc in next 2 dc, * dc in next ch, ch 3, pc st in next ch-1 sp, (ch 1, pc st in next ch-1 sp) 2

times, ch 3, sk 2 ch, dc in next ch, dc in next 4 dc, rep from *, ending row with sk 2 ch, dc in next ch, dc in last 2 dc, dc in tch, ch 3, turn.

Row 4: Dc in next 4 dc, * dc in next ch, ch 3, pc st in next ch-1 sp, ch 1, pc st in next ch-1 sp, ch 3, sk 2 ch, dc in next ch, dc in next 6 dc, rep from *, ending row with sk 2 ch, dc in next ch, dc in last 3 dc, dc in tch, ch 3, turn.

Row 5: Sk 1st dc, dc in next 4 dc, * dc in next ch, ch 3, pc st in next ch-1 sp, ch 3, sk 2 ch, dc in next ch, dc in next 8 dc, rep from *, ending row with sk 2 ch, dc in next ch, dc in last 4 dc, dc in tch.

37. Multiples 6 plus 2.

Row 1: Sc in 2nd ch from hk, * ch 3, sk 2 ch, 5-dc pc st in next ch, ch 3, sk 2 ch, sc in next ch, rep from *, ending row with sc in last ch, ch 7, turn.

Row 2: Sl st in 4th ch from hk (counts as dc, picot), dc in 1st sc, * sc in top of next pc st, (dc, 3-ch picot in next sc) 4 times, rep from *, ending row with (dc, picot, dc) in last sc.

38. Multiples of 6 plus 2.

Row 1: Sc in 2nd ch from hk, sc in next ch, * ch 6, turn, sc in 2nd ch from hk, hdc in next ch, dc in next 3 ch, sk next 3 ch of foundation row, sc in next 3 ch, rep from *, ending row with sc in last 2 ch, ch 7, turn.

Row 2: * Sc in top of next ch-6 group, ch 2, dtr in center sc of 3-sc group, ch 2, rep from *, ending row with dtr in last sc, ch 3, turn.

Row 3: (Dc, 3-ch picot, ch 3, 3-lp puff st) in 1st dtr, * sc in next sc, (3-lp puff st, ch 3, 3-lp puff st, 3-ch picot, ch 3, 3-lp puff st) in next dtr, rep from *, ending row with sc in last sc, (3-lp puff st, 3-lp puff st, 3-ch picot) in 3rd ch of tch.

39. Chain multiples of 14 plus 2.

Row 1: Dc in 6th ch from hk, * ch 1, sk 1 ch, dc in next ch, rep from * across row, ch 1, turn.

Row 2: Sc in 1st dc, (ch 3, sc in next ch-1 sp) 2 times, * ch 7, sk next 2 ch-1 sp, sc in next ch-1 sp, (ch 3, sc in next ch-1 sp) 4 times, rep from *, ending row with ch 7, sk next 2 ch-1 sp, sc in next ch-1 sp (ch 3, sc in tch) 2 times, ch 4, turn.

Row 3: Sc in next ch-3 sp, ch 3, sc in next ch-3 sp, * ch 3, (2-lp puff st, ch 3, 2-lp puff st) in next ch-7 arch, (ch 3, sc in next ch-3 sp) 4 times, rep from *, ending row with ch 3, sc in next ch-3 sp, ch 3, sc in last ch-3 sp, ch 1, dc in last sc, ch 1, turn.

Row 4: Sc in 1st dc, ch 3, sc in next ch-3 sp, * ch 4, sk next ch-3 sp, (2-lp puff st, ch 4, 2-lp puff st) in next ch-3 sp, ch 4, sk next ch-3 sp, sc in next ch-3 sp, (ch 3, sc in next ch-3 sp) 2 times, rep from *, ending row with sc in last ch-3 sp, ch 3, sc in 2nd ch of tch, ch 4, turn.

Row 5: Sc in 1st ch-3 sp, * ch 5, sk next ch-4 sp, (2-lp puff st, 3-ch picot, ch 3 in next ch-4 sp) 3 times, 3-ch picot, 2-lp puff st in same ch-4 sp, ch 5, sc in next ch-3 sp, ch 3, sc in next ch-3 sp, rep from *, ending row with ch 5, sc in last ch-3 sp, ch 1, dc in last sc.

40. Chain multiples of 8 plus 3.

Row 1: Dc in 4th ch from hk and in each ch across row, ch 1, turn.

Row 2: Sc in 1st dc, * ch 3, sk 3 dc, (3-lp puff st, ch 3, 3-lp puff st) in next dc, ch 3, sk 3 dc, sc in next dc, rep from *, ending row with sc in last ch, ch 3, turn.

Row 3: Dc in 1st ch-3 sp, * ch 3, (3-lp puff st, ch 1, 3-ch picot, ch 1, 3-lp puff st) in next ch-3 sp, ch 3, dc in next ch-3 sp (leave 2 lp on hk), dc in next ch-3 sp, yo, pull through 3 lp on hk (2 dc tog made), rep from *, ending row with 2 dc tog in last ch-3 sp and sc.

41. Chain multiples of 3 plus 5.

Row 1: Sc in 2nd ch from hk and in each ch across row, ch 4, turn.
Row 2: 3-lp puff st in 1st sc (leave 1 lp on hk), * sk 2 sc, 3-lp puff st in next sc, pull through 2-lp on hk (2 puff st tog), ch 1, 3-ch picot, ch 1, 3-lp puff st in sc just worked (leave 1 lp on hk), rep from *, ending row with puff st tog completed in last sc, ch 1, dc in same sp.

42. Multiples of 12 plus 8.

Row 1: Dc in 8th ch from hk, * ch 2, sk 2 ch, dc in next ch, rep from * across row.
Row 2: Ch 5, sc in 1st ch-2 sp, * ch 3, sk next ch-2 sp, (dc, ch 4, dc) in next ch-2 sp, ch 3, sk next ch-2 sp, sc in next ch-2 sp, rep from *, ending row with ch 2, dc in 3rd ch of tch, ch 1, turn.
Row 3: Sc in 1st dc, * ch 3, (3 dc, ch 2, 3 dc, ch 2, 3 dc) in next ch-4 sp, ch 3, sc in next sc, rep from *, ending row with sc in 3rd ch of tch, ch 1, turn.
Row 4: Sc in 1st sc, * ch 3, sk next dc, 5-dc pc st in next dc, ch 3, (pc st in next ch-2 sp, ch 3, sk next dc, pc st in next dc, ch 3) 2 times, sc in next sc, rep from * across row, ch 1, turn.
Row 5: Sc in 1st sc, * 3 sc in ch-3 sp, (sc in pc st, 3-ch picot, 2 sc in ch-2 sp) 4 times, sc in next pc st, 3-ch picot, 3 sc in next ch-3 sp, rep from *, ending row with sc in last ch-3 sp, sc in last sc.

43. Multiples of 2 plus 6.

Row 1: Sc in 8th ch from hk, * ch 4, sk next ch, sc in next ch, rep from * across row, ch 5, turn.
Row 2: * Sc in next ch-4 sp, ch 4, rep from *, ending row with ch 2, dc in 5th ch of tch.

44. Chain 7.

Row 1: Dc in 4th ch from hk, dc in next 3 ch, ch 3, turn.
Rows 2-5: Sk 1st dc, dc in next 3 dc, dc in tch, ch 3, turn.
Rep Rows 2-5 for desired length.
Edge: Ch 2, turn work, sk next row, * dc in side of next row, (ch 2, dc) 4 times in same sp, ch 2, sk next row, join with sl st to side of next row, ch 2, sk next row, rep from *, end with ch 2, join with sl st to last row, ch 1, turn, (sc, ch 3, sc) in each ch-2 sp across edge.

45. Chain 4.

Row 1: 3 dc in 4th ch from hk, (ch 2, 2 dc) in same ch, ch 5, turn.
Row 2: (2 dc, ch 2, 4 dc) in ch-2 sp, ch 3, turn.
Row 3: (4 dc, ch 2, 2 dc) in ch-2 sp, ch 5, turn.
Rep Rows 2-3 for desired length.
Edging: After last row is completed, ch 8, turn, * sc in next ch-5 sp, ch 5, rep from * across row, dc in base of tch, ch 1, turn, sc in dc, sc in each sc and ch across, end with sc in 1st 6 ch of tch.

46. Chain 4.

Row 1: Dc in 4th ch from hk, ch 6, turn.
Row 2: Dc in 1st dc, dc in tch, ch 3, turn.
Row 3: Sk 1st dc, dc in next dc, ch 6, turn.
Rep Rows 2-3 for desired length, end with Row 3, ch 3, turn work to side, (dc, ch 3, dc, 3-ch picot, ch 3, dc) in each ch-6 lp across edge, ch 3, join with sl st to base of beg dc.

47. Multiples of 14 plus 9.

Row 1: 5 dc in 6th ch from hk, * sk 2 ch, dc in next ch, ch 7, sk 7 ch, dc in next ch, sk 2 ch, 5 dc in next ch, rep from *, ending row with sk 2 ch, dc in last ch, ch 3, turn.
Row 2: Sk 1st 3 dc, * 5 dc in next dc, sk 2 dc, dc in next dc, ch 7, dc in next dc, sk next 2 dc, rep from *, ending row with 5 dc in next dc, sk 2 dc, dc in tch, ch 3, turn.
Row 3: Sk 1st 3 dc, * 5 dc in next dc, sk next 2 dc, dc in next dc, ch 3, insert hk under ch-7 sp of 3 prev rows, sc tog, ch 3, dc in next dc, sk next 2 dc, rep from *, ending row with 5 dc in next dc, sk next 2 dc, dc in tch.

48. Multiples of 16 plus 2.

Row 1: Sc in 2nd ch from hk, * ch 5, sk 3 ch, sc in next ch, rep from * across row, ch 5, turn.
Row 2: * Sc around center of next ch-5 sp, ch 5, rep from *, ending row with ch 2, dc in last sc, ch 1, turn.

Row 3: Sc in 1st dc, * ch 5, sc around center of next ch-5 sp, ch 3, 3 dc in center of next ch-5 sp, ch 3, sc around center of next ch-5 sp, ch 5, sc around center of next ch-5 sp, rep from *, ending row with sc in 3rd ch of tch, ch 6, turn.

Row 4: * Sc in center of next ch-5 sp, ch 3, 2 dc in next dc, dc in next dc, 2 dc in next dc, ch 3, sc in center of next ch-5 sp, ch 5, rep from *, ending row with ch 3, dc in last sc, ch 1, turn.

Row 5: Sc in 1st dc, * ch 3, 2 dc in next dc, dc in next 3 dc, 2 dc in next dc, ch 3, sc in center of next ch-5 sp, rep from *, ending row with 2 dc in next dc, dc in next 3 dc, 2 dc in next dc, ch 3, sc in 4th ch of tch, ch 1, turn.

Row 6: Sc in 1st sc, * ch 3, (dc in next dc, 3-ch picot, dc in next dc) 3 times, dc in next dc, 3-ch picot, ch 3, sc in next sc, rep from *, ending row with rep ( ), ch 3, sc in last sc.

49. Multiples of 28 plus 3.

Row 1: Dc in 4th ch from hk and in each ch across row, ch 5, turn.

Row 2: Sk 1st 3 dc, dc in next dc, (ch 2, sk 2 dc, dc in next dc) 2 times, * ch 5, sk 4 dc, tr in next dc, ch 5, sk 4 dc, dc in next dc, (ch 2, sk 2 dc, dc in next dc) 6 times, rep from *, ending row with (ch 2, sk 2 dc, dc in next dc) 2 times, ch 2, sk 2 dc, dc in tch, ch 4, turn.

Row 3: (Dc in next ch-2 sp, ch 2) 2 times, dc in next ch-2 sp, * ch 5, sk 4 ch, sc in next ch, sc in tr, sc in next ch, ch 5, dc in next ch-2 sp, (ch 2, dc in next ch-2 sp) 5 times, rep from *, ending row with ch 1, dc in 3rd ch of tch, ch 5, turn.

Row 4: Dc in next ch-2 sp, ch 2, dc in next ch-2 sp, ch 5, sk 4 ch, sc in next ch, sc in next 3 sc, sc in next ch, ch 5, dc in next ch-2 sp, (ch 2, dc in next ch-2 sp) 4 times, rep from *, ending row with ch 2, dc in 2nd ch of tch, ch 4, turn.

Row 5: Dc in next ch-2 sp, ch 2, dc in next ch-2 sp, ch 6, sk next 4 ch, sc in next ch, sc in next 5 sc, sc in next ch, ch 6, dc in next ch-2 sp, (ch 2, dc in next ch-2 sp) 3 times, rep from *, ending row with ch 2, sc in 3rd ch of tch, ch 5, turn.

Row 6: Dc in next ch-2 sp, * ch 6, sk 5 ch, sc in next ch, ch 7, sk next 7 sc, sc in next ch, ch 6, dc in next ch-2 sp, (ch 2, dc in next ch-2 sp) 2 times, rep from *, ending row with ch 2, dc in 2nd ch of tch, ch 4, turn.

Row 7: Dc in next ch-2 sp, * ch 2, 2 dtr in next ch-7 sp, (ch 1, 2 dtr in same ch-7 sp) 5 times, (ch 2, dc in next ch-2 sp) 2 times, rep from *, ending row with dc in 2nd ch of tch, ch 1, dc in next tch.

50. Multiples of 14 plus 3.

Row 1: Dc in 5th ch from hk, 2 dc in same ch, * ch 2, sk 2 ch, sc in next ch, (ch 3, sk 1 ch, sc in next ch) 3 times, ch 2, sk 3 ch, (2 dc, ch 2, 2 dc) in next ch, rep from *, ending row with ch 2, sk 2 ch, (2 dc, ch 1, dc) in last ch, ch 4, turn.

Row 2: 2 dc in ch-1 sp, ch 2, * sc in next ch-3 sp, (ch 3, sc in next ch-3 sp) 2 times, ch 2, sk next ch-2 sp, (2 dc, ch 2 in next ch-2 sp) 3 times, rep from *, ending row with ch 2, (2 dc, ch 1, dc) in tch, ch 3, turn.

Row 3: (2 dc, ch 2, 2 dc) in next ch-1 sp, * ch 2, sc in next ch-3 sp, ch 3, sc in next ch-3 sp, ch 2, sk next ch-2 sp, (2 dc, ch 2, 2 dc) in next ch-2 sp, ch 1, (2 dc, ch 2, 2 dc) in next ch-2 sp, rep from *, ending row with ch 2, (2 dc, ch 2, 3 dc) in tch, ch 4, turn.

Row 4: (2 dc, ch 2, 2 dc) in next ch-2 sp, * ch 2, sc in next ch-3 sp, ch 2, (2 dc, ch 2, 2 dc) in next ch-2 sp, ch 2, sc in ch-1 sp, ch 2, (2 dc, ch 2, 2 dc) in next ch-2 sp, rep from *, ending row with (2 dc, ch 2, 2 dc) in last ch-2 sp, ch 1, dc in tch.

51. Multiples of 16 plus 3.

Row 1: Dc in 4th ch from hk, dc in next 6 ch, * ch 1, sk next ch, dc in next 8 ch, rep from *, ending row with dc in last 8 ch, ch 1, turn.

Row 2: Sc in 1st dc, * ch 5, sk next 3 dc, sc in next dc, ch 3, 5 dc in ch-1 sp, ch 3, sk 3 dc, sc in next dc, ch 5, sk 3 dc, sc in next dc, rep from *, ending row with sc in tch, ch 5, turn.

Row 3: * Sc in next ch-5 sp, ch 3, dc in next dc, (ch 1, dc in next dc) 2 times, ch 1, dc in same dc, (ch 1, dc in next dc) 2 times, ch 3, sc in next ch-5 sp, ch 5, rep from *, ending row with ch 2, dc in last sc, ch 1, turn.

Row 4: Sc in 1st dc, * ch 3, dc in next ch-3 sp, (ch 1, dc in next dc) 6 times, ch 1, dc in next ch-3 sp, ch 3, sc in next ch-5 sp, rep from *, ending row with ch 3, sc in 3rd ch of tch, ch 4, turn.

Row 5: * 2 tr in next ch-3 sp, 3-ch picot, (2 tr in next ch-1 sp, 3-ch picot) 7 times, 2 tr in next ch-3 sp, 3-ch picot, rep from *, ending row with ch 1, dc in last sc.

52. Multiples of 10 plus 8.

Row 1: Dc in 4th ch from hk and in each ch across row, ch 1, turn.
Row 2: Sc in 1st dc, * ch 5, sk next 4 dc, dc in next 6 dc, rep from *, ending row with ch 5, sk next 4 dc, sc in tch, ch 6, turn.
Row 3: * Sc in next ch-5 sp, ch 10, rep from *, ending row with sc in last ch-5 sp, ch 3, dc in last sc, ch 1, turn.
Row 4: Sc in 1st dc, ch 2, * dc in next ch-10 arch, (ch 1, dc in same ch-10 arch) 7 times, rep from *, ending row with ch 2, sc in 4th ch of tch, ch 1, turn.
Row 5: Sc in 1st sc, sc in each ch and dc across.

53. Muliples of 8 plus 4.

Row 1: Dc in 6th ch from hk, * ch 1, sk 1 ch, dc in next ch, rep from * across row, ch 5, turn.
Row 2: Sk 1st dc, * sc in next dc, ch 5, sk next dc, rep from *, ending row with sc in last dc, ch 2, dc in 2nd ch of tch, ch 1, turn.
Row 3: Sc in 1st dc, * ch 3, dc in next ch-5 sp, ch 3, 3-ch picot, 3 dc around post of last dc worked, ch 3, sc in next ch-5 sp, rep from *, ending row with sc in 3rd ch of tch.

54. Multiples of 6 plus 6.

Row 1: Dc in 6th ch from hk, * ch 1, sk 1 ch, dc in next ch, rep from * across row, ch 4, turn.
Row 2: Sk 1st dc, sc in next dc, * (sc in next ch-1 sp, sc in next dc) 2 times, ch 3, sc in next dc, rep from *,

ending row with (sc in next ch-1 sp, sc in next dc) 2 times, ch 1, hdc in tch, ch 1, turn.

Row 3: Sc in hdc, ch 3, * dc in same sp, ch 3, 4 dc around post of dc just worked, sc in next ch-3 sp, ch 3, rep from *, ending row with sc in tch.

55. Multiples of 8 plus 3.

Row 1: Dc in 4th ch from hk, dc in next ch, * ch 2, sk 1 ch, sc in next ch, ch 2, sk 1 ch, dc in next 5 ch, rep from *, ending row with ch 2, sk 1 ch, sc in next ch, ch 2, sk 1 ch, dc in last 3 ch, ch 1, turn.

Row 2: Sc in 1st dc, * ch 1, (dc, ch 3, dc) in next sc, ch 1, sc in 3rd dc of 5-dc group, rep from *, ending row with ch 1, sc in tch, ch 3, turn.

Row 3: * 3 dc in beg of next ch-3 sp, 3-ch picot, 3 dc in center of same ch-3 sp, 3-ch picot, 3 dc in same ch-3 sp, rep from *, ending row with dc in last sc.

56. Multiples of 10 plus 2.

Row 1: Sc in 2nd ch from hk, * ch 1, sk 4 ch, dc in next ch, (ch 1, dc in same ch) 6 times, rep from *, ending row with ch 1, sk 4 ch, sc in last ch, ch 4, turn.

Row 2: Dc in sc, (ch 1, dc in same sp) 2 times, * ch 1, sc in 4th dc of 7-dc group, (ch 1, dc in next sc, ch 1, dc in same sc) 6 times, rep from *, ending row with ch 1, sc in 4th dc of 7-dc group, ch 1, dc in last sc, (ch 1, dc in same sc) 3 times.

57. Multiples of 8 plus 3.

Row 1: Dc in 4th ch from hk and in each ch across row, ch 1, turn.

Row 2: Sc in 1st dc, * ch 3, 2 dc in sc just worked, sk 3 dc, sc in next dc, rep from *, ending row with sc in tch, ch 4, turn.

Row 3: Dc in 1st sc, ch 6, * sk next ch-3 sp, dc in next ch-3 sp, (dc, ch 3, dc) in next sc, sc in next ch-3 sp, ch 6, rep from *, ending row with (dc, ch 1, dc) in last sc, ch 1, turn.

Row 4: Sc in 1st dc, (5 dc, 3-ch picot, 5 dc) in next ch-6 sp, * sc in center of next ch-3 sp, rep from *, ending row with (5 dc, ch-3 picot, 5 dc) in last ch-6 sp, sc in last ch.

58. Multiples of 2 plus 8.

Row 1: Dc in 6th ch from hk, * ch 1, sk 1 ch, dc in next ch, rep from * across row, ch 1, turn.

Row 2: Sc in 1st dc, * ch 6, sk next ch-1 sp, sc in next ch-1 sp, rep from *, ending row with ch 6, sk last ch-1 sp, sc in 2nd ch of tch, ch 3, turn.

Row 3: 4 dc in 1st ch-6 sp, * ch 1, 4 dc in next ch-6 sp, rep from *, end with dc in last sc.

Patterns Using Edgings and Trims

Ruffles & Bows Infant Set

This beautiful infant set includes a baby afghan and a baby hat. The ribbon in accent colors can dress it up or down according to your preference.

Baby Afghan

Multiples of 8 plus 5.

Materials needed: Worsted weight yarn: 10 ounces white, 1-1/2 ounces multi-colored; Size H aluminum crochet hook; 4 yards of 3/8" satin ribbon in each color: yellow, pink, and blue.

Gauge: 1 set of multiple 8 = 1/2" x 3"

Finished size: 27" x 27"

This quick and easy to make afghan can be easily enlarged by increasing your foundation row in multiples of eight.

Using white yarn, ch 101.

Row 1: Dc in 6th ch from hook, * ch 1, sk 1 ch, dc in next ch, rep from * across row, ch 4, turn.

Row 2: Sk 1st dc, dc in next dc, * ch 1, dc in next dc, rep from * ending with dc in 2nd ch of tch, ch 4, turn.

Row 3: Sk 1st dc, dc in next dc, ch 1, * (dc in next dc, dc in ch-1 sp) 2 times, dc in next dc, ch 1, dc in next dc, ch 1, rep from * across row, ending with dc in 2nd ch of tch, ch 4, turn.

Row 4: Sk 1st dc, dc in next dc, ch 1, * (dc in next dc) 5 times, ch 1, dc in next dc, ch 1, rep from * across, ending with dc in 2nd ch of tch, ch 4, turn.

Rows 5-44: Rep Row 4.

Row 45: Sk 1st dc, dc in next dc, * ch 1, dc in next dc, (ch 1, sk 1 dc, dc in next dc) 2 times, ch 1, dc in

next dc, rep from * across.

Row 46: Rep Row 2, **F.O.**

Edging

Row 1: Using multicolored yarn, join with sl st to any dc in Row 46, * ch 6, sk 1 dc, sc in next dc, rep from * around edge of afghan. (When working sides) ch 6, sk 1 row, sc in last st of next row, join with sl st to beg of 1st ch-6 lp.

Row 2: 4 dc in 1st ch-6 lp, * ch 1, 4 dc in next ch-6 lp, rep from * around, ending with ch 1, join with sl st to 1st dc in beg dc group, turn.

Row 3: * Ch 6, sc in next ch-1 sp, rep from * around, join with sl st to beg ch-6 lp, **F.O.**

Finishing: Cut ribbons into four equal lengths. Weave ribbon through last two spaces of each side of afghan, and in 1st ch-6 sp in edging. Tie ribbons into bows at each corner of afghan. Treat ribbon ends with a no-fray product.

Ruffles & Bows Infant Hat

Materials needed: Worsted weight yarn: small amount white, small amount multi-colored; Size H aluminum crochet hook; 1 yard of 3/8" ribbon in each color: yellow, pink, and blue.

Gauge: 1 set of multiple 8 = 1/2" x 3"

Finished size: 6" x 6"

Using white yarn, ch 61.

Row 1-4: Rep Rows 1-4 of afghan.

Rows 5-13: Rep Row 4.

Row 14: Sk 1st dc, dc in next dc, * ch 1, dc in next dc, (ch 1, sk 1 dc, dc in next dc) 2 times, ch 1, dc in next dc, rep from *, ending with dc in 2nd ch of tch, **F.O.** Fold work in half and sew Row 14 tog.

Scalloped Collar

Materials Needed: Approx. 250 yards #30 white cotton thread; #11 steel crochet hook.

Finished Size: 18" around inner neck edge.

Gauge: 1 Motif = 2 1/2"

Motif (Make 7)

Chain 15, join with sl st to form ring.

Rnd 1: Ch 1, 25 sc in ring.

Rnd 2: Ch 6, (sk next sc, tr in next sc, ch 2) 5 times, sk next sc, (tr, ch 3, tr) in next sc (tip of scallop), (ch 2, sk next sc, tr in next sc) 6 times, ch 1, turn.

Rnd 3: Sc in each tr, 2 sc in each ch-2 sp, (3 sc in ch-3 sp at tip of scallop), ch 1, turn.

Rnd 4: Sk 1st sc, sc in each sc to center sc at tip of scallop, 3 sc in center sc, sc in each rem sc, ch 1, turn.

Rnds 5-7: Rep Rnd 4. (45 sc at end of Row 7)

Rnd 8: Rep Rnd 4, except sc in first sc. (47 sc)

Rnd 9: Sl st in 1st sc, ch 4, tr in same sc, ch 3, sk 2 sc, * [2 tr in next sc, (hold 1 lp on hk for each tr, yo, pull through 3 lps on hk) (tr cl made), ch 3, sk 1 sc], rep from * 8 times until tip of scallop is reached, (tr cl, ch 3, tr cl) in center sc, (tr cl in next sc, ch 3, sk 1 sc) 7 times, tr cl in last sc, ch 1, turn.

Rnd 10: (Sc, 3 dc, sc) in each ch-3 sp around.

Finishing: Using same crochet thread, sew 1st scallops (sc, 3 dc, sc) of 2 pieces together using an overcast stitch, rep until all but 2 end scallops are joined tog.

Inner neck edge:

Row 1: Ch 11, * join with sl st to top edge of Rnd 8, sl st in top of each rnd (across top of motif), ending with Rnd 3 (5 sl sts made), ch 5, join with sl st to top of Rnd 3 (on next side of motif), sl st in top of each rnd through Rnd 8, ch 15, rep from *, in each rem

Edging

Row 1: Using multicolored yarn, join with sl st to 1st dc in Row 1, * ch 6, sk 1 dc, sc in next dc, rep from * across row, continue working around in last sts of Rows 2-14 (both sides), join with sl st to 1st dc.

Row 2: Working only in ch-6 sp of Row 1 of hat, * 4 dc in ch-6 sp, ch 1, rep from * across, turn.

Row 3: * Ch 6, sc in next ch-1 sp, rep from * across, ending with sl st in last dc, **F.O.**

Finishing: Weave ribbon through spaces of Rows 1 and 2 and in spaces of first ch-6 sp in edging.

Leave enough ribbon on ends to tie secure.

With any extra ribbon, tie bow to top of hat by inserting through an opening in Row 14.

Treat ribbon with a no-fray product.

motif, end with ch 11 after last sl st, ch 1, turn.

Row 2: Sc in each ch or sl st across, ch 1, turn.

Row 3: Sc in 1st sc, * sk next sc, 3 dc in next sc, sk next sc, sc in next 2 sc, rep from * across, ending with sc in last sc, ch 1, turn.

Row 4: Sc in 1st sc, * 3 dc in 2nd dc, sc in each of next 2 sc, rep from * across, end with sc in last sc, **F.O.**

Joining Scallop:

Row 1: Join with sl st to sc bet 3rd and 4th scallop of motif side, ch 11, join with sl st to next motif bet 3rd and 4th scallop, ch 1, turn.

Row 2: Sc in each ch, across, ch 1, turn.

Row 3: Sc in 1st sc, * sk next sc, 3 dc in next sc, sk next sc, sc in next 2 sc, rep from * across, ending with sc in last sc, **F.O.** Rep on all remaining motifs, leaving two end motifs unattached.

Optional: Sew hook and eye set to edges of neck edging.

Lightly starch if desired.